# THE
# WING-FOOTED
# WANDERER

# THE
# WING-FOOTED
# WANDERER

## CONSCIENCE AND TRANSCENDENCE

### DONALD E. MILLER

ABINGDON • NASHVILLE

*Library of Congress Cataloging in Publication Data*

MILLER, DONALD EUGENE. 1929-
  The wing-footed wanderer.
  Includes index.
  1. Conscience. 2. Moral education.
I. Title.
BJ1471.M54          171'.6          77-1503

*ISBN 0-687-45690-8*

MANUFACTURED BY THE PARTHENON PRESS AT
NASHVILLE, TENNESSEE, UNITED STATES OF AMERICA

*To*
*Eliza Coning Miller*
*and*
*Daniel L. Miller,*
*my beloved parents*

# Acknowledgments

The ideas expressed in this book have been many years developing. In classes taken with the Committee on Human Development at the University of Chicago in the early fifties with such teachers as Robert Havighurst and Bruno Bettelheim I was first introduced to the works of Sigmund Freud, Erik Erikson, and Jean Piaget. A decade later in courses on Christian ethics at Harvard University with such teachers as James Luther Adams, Paul Lehman, Paul Tillich, and Robert Bellah I sharpened my interest in the development of conscience.

A dozen years in the classroom instructing seminarians about moral development, ethical choice, and Christian education have shaped my views. Perhaps some of my faculty colleagues as well as my students will recognize ideas to which they have contributed in classroom and hallway discussions. A sabbatical leave granted for the academic year 1968-1969 by Bethany Theological Seminary and sponsored by the Association of Theological Schools permitted me to spend an academic year at Yale University, where I was in conversation with James Gustafson and Randolph Crump Miller. A second sabbatical leave seven years later allowed me to be affiliated with Westminster and Cheshunt Colleges at Cambridge University, Cambridge, England. There I received counsel from R. Bambrough of Cambridge University and R. S. Peters of the University of London. To all these persons I owe a debt of gratitude, though of course mine is the sole responsibility for what is written here.

Some of the materials of this book were first presented to the Association for Professors and Researchers in Religious Education and the American Theological Society, the Midwest chapter, both of which gave vigorous responses. Several different persons have typed the manuscript, but most recently Kathy Nicholson.

# CONTENTS

# INTRODUCTION:
## In Search of a Definition

*Our quest, like every such exploration, is a moral quest, for we are seeking the bases on which a morality for a new age can be founded. Every sensitive person finds himself in Stephen Dedalus' position: "I go forth . . . to forge in the smithy of my soul the uncreated conscience of my race."*   —Rollo May

The contours of conscience must be described anew in our day, which is the purpose we have set for ourselves in what follows. Several tendencies of modern life have conspired to bring about the need for such a reinterpretation. We have inherited from the cultural tradition of the Western world the idea that conscience is the voice of heaven within the person, the deputy of God within the human breast, or the sense of the universal moral law directing all who will pause to listen. However, the findings of modern psychology suggest that the sense of obligation may be evidence of illness rather than righteousness. Sociology and anthropology teach us that the dictates of conscience simply reflect the customs and traditions of the society within which we live. Philosophy has challenged the idea of a universal moral law. The result is that an appeal to conscience often lacks moral authority or, indeed, persuasiveness of any kind. Yet we do continue to appeal to conscience as a justification for what we do. Either the meaning of conscience must be rediscovered or we must finally drop such appeals. Let us look at this anomaly more carefully.

The idea of conscience seems to have been born in ancient Greece. The first known use of the term appears in a moving passage written by Democritus (460-361 B.C.) some twenty-four hundred years ago: "Some men, not knowing the dissolution of mortal nature, suffer wretchedly throughout their lifetime from distress and fear because of their consciousness of the evildoing in their lives, making false speculations about the time after death."[1] The themes of self-criticism, judgment, and fear of death are frequently picked up in discussions of conscience since Democritus' day. The Greeks for the most part considered conscience to be a faculty planted in the awareness of every person that judges a deed either by anticipation or reflection to be good or bad. This fits together nicely with the idea that everyone knows implicitly what is good or bad, and therefore conscience makes its judgments according to the universal moral law. Like a witness brought before a court of law to testify for or against a defendant, the conscience is the witness of oneself for or against oneself. As such it can bring great pain to us when we have violated it.

One unusual and highly interesting first-century A.D. reference to conscience occurs in a source somewhat dubiously ascribed to Epictetus: "When we were children our parents handed us over to a nursery slave who would watch over us everywhere lest harm befall us. But when we were grown up, God hands us over to the conscience *(suneidesei)* implanted in us, to protect us."[2] The reference is interesting because it places the emphasis upon the protection of conscience rather than its judgment, although the latter is not wholly absent. Conscience has the weakness of a nursery slave who can approve or criticize, but who has no authority to give more than mild punishment. Like the nursery slave, the conscience is a judge without the authority to enforce its judgments. The passage is also interesting because it relates conscience to the manner in which we are reared as children, anticipatory of themes in contemporary developmental psychology.

The notion of conscience that the modern Western world has inherited is one that was formulated by the Greeks and reinterpreted by Christian teaching. The apostle Paul regularly referred to the approval of his conscience as a justification for what he was doing. In the same way, the church fathers supported and used the idea of conscience. According to Origen, "Conscience is that spirit which, the Apostle says, is found in the soul as tutor, companion, and guide. Its function is to advise one about the best course of action, and to rebuke and chastise one for sin."[3] John of Damascus appealed to the law of the mind: "God's law enters our mind and draws it to itself by stirring up conscience, which itself is called the law of our mind."[4]

Thomas Aquinas' very influential interpretation drew upon the church fathers before him, but with a significant difference. Aquinas separated the conscience into two parts. One part understands the universal moral laws and is to be called *synderesis,* while the other part applies moral truths to individual circumstances and is to be called *conscientia.* When we perform particular acts or deeds that do not conform to the moral law, then the second activity of conscience (i.e., the *conscientia)* is the source of our feelings of remorse.

Perhaps the most influential interpretation of conscience since Aquinas is that of Immanuel Kant, who also taught that each person is able to intuit directly the precepts of the moral law. In particular circumstances, a person will know what ought to be done because of the leading of conscience. We may test our acts by asking ourselves whether the reasons we give ourselves for our acts are worthy to be legislated as moral laws. If not, then our consciences will be offended at the suggestion. When tempted to lie, steal, or commit any other questionable act, we may ask ourselves whether we could conscientiously will that everyone act by the same principles by which we are acting. In this way Kant supported the idea that conscience is the voice of the moral law within each soul.

The reader will hardly need to be reminded just how much these traditional views are in question today. Nearly everyone is aware of the psychological attack upon the sense of obligation, which Kant held to be almost divine. Sigmund Freud put it this way:

> The philosopher Kant once declared that nothing proved to him the greatness of God more convincingly than the starry heavens and the moral conscience within us. The stars are unquestionably superb, but where conscience is concerned God has been guilty of an uneven and careless piece of work, for a great many men have only a limited share of it or scarcely enough to be worth mentioning.[5]

Freud was thinking of how some of his patients suffered acute pains of conscience over the most trivial things on one day, and yet on another day they were quite willing to do those same things. He was also aware how the conscience seems to reflect the commands given to a person as a child, even when those commands run counter to the normal sense of morality. He concluded that conscience is often a sign more of sickness than of health, of neurosis rather than of ego strength.

Recent anthropological and sociological studies have supported the relativity introduced by Freud. Murder is not the same thing for an aboriginal head-hunting tribe as for the inhabitants of a modern European city. A good Moslem man may conscientiously have three or four wives, while a devout Christian could never have more than one. Some people's conscience tells them to defend their native land, and others' conscience forbids them from fighting at all. Some consciences prompt absolute allegiance to parents, and others urge separation from parents. Considerations such as these led Emil Durkheim to the conclusion that nothing is found in the conscience that was not put there by the society in which a person lives. In the words of Montaigne, "The laws of conscience, which we pretend to be derived from nature, proceed from custom."[6] Therefore the conscience will vary as much from one place to another as do the ways of life of various peoples.

Philosophy has given its support to these views. Many contemporary philosophers question whether we can know universals of any kind. What is considered to be true in one generation becomes obvious error in another generation. One generation's certainty is the next generation's absurdity. The postmortem dissection of human bodies was the height of moral wrong in an earlier day but is the cornerstone of medical science in our day. The moral authority of government was once considered to be by the divine right of the monarch, but is now understood to be by the consent of the governed. Truth seems to be limited by the perspective of a given generation and subject to historical change.

The result of such psychological, social, philosophical, and historical studies is to undermine the moral authority of conscience. It seems indeed to be a "shoddy and uneven piece of work." Yet we do continue to appeal to conscience. Should we consider such appeals to be outmoded vestiges of a heritage that has not quite died, but inevitably shall do so, or should we look again at the meaning and function of conscience to see whether in any sense it continues to be an expression of human strength and virtue?

Before going further let us offer a preliminary definition of what I mean by conscience. From what has already been said it can be seen that the idea includes such phenomena as the following: feelings of approval and disapproval about deeds already done or being contemplated; judgments about what is right or wrong, good or bad; beliefs and moral principles held with conviction; the sense of wholeness, coherence, and integrity; commitment to the ethos of one's various communities of loyalty. Any adequate account must somehow allow for such phenomena. Let me therefore propose that conscience is a dispositional unity of knowing, doing, and feeling wherein a person is joined together with other persons in a community or moral purpose and direction. Conscience is a dispositional expression of human agency that develops as a mixture of human virtue and weakness within various communities of loyalty.

In what follows we are proposing a reinterpretation of conscience that draws upon the various views that have made its authority questionable. Our proposal is that while conscience does at times express the immaturity of a childhood disposition, at other times it reflects the virtue of a mature disposition. If it reflects the changing stages in the life story of every individual person, it also expresses certain qualities that are characteristic of all human agency. If it reflects the relativity of a community's way of life, it also embodies the ways in which that community makes universally human responses to its situation. Our proposal draws heavily upon the understanding of human agency supplied by psychoanalysis, particularly that of the ego psychologists (chapters 1 and 2). We explore the stages of moral development that have resulted from the studies of human maturation (chapters 3 and 4) and the relativities of custom given by the sociologist (chapter 5). Finally, we consider the relationship of conscience to transcendence in order to comprehend what meaning there is in the belief that conscience is the voice of God (chapter 6).

# Chapter I

# A THOUSAND SEVERAL TONGUES:
## *The Accusing Conscience*

*My conscience hath a thousand several tongues,*
*And every tongue brings in a several tale,*
*And every tale condemns me for a villain.*
                              *—Shakespeare*

Perhaps no person has made a more concerted effort to describe the accusing conscience in modern times than Sigmund Freud. His work not only has affected the modern practice of psychiatry, but has greatly shaped the literary and popular imagination of the twentieth century. At the same time, he as much as anyone has seriously challenged the long-acknowledged authority of conscience. Freud has taught us that conscience is a manifestation of neurosis rather than of emotional maturity.

Freud also has given as good a description of the process of moral formation in infancy and early childhood as can be found. Few child psychologists would refuse to acknowledge their indebtedness to him. In his work we have the coincidence of Democritus' and Shakespeare's accusing conscience and of a keen description of moral development in early childhood. Freud's attack on conscience therefore serves as a pivotal case study in our reinterpretation of conscience. Our reinterpretation must take into account what he said.

### Accusation Versus Guidance

It will become more evident as we proceed that Freud's account of conscience is more one of accusation than of guidance. He focuses upon release from guilt rather than creativity, isolation rather than mutuality, passivity rather than activity, reducing emotional pain rather than expressing emotional strength, the freedom of inner awareness rather than the freedom of person related to person. In a word, he is more concerned about release from the bondage of the past than about hope for the future.

Not that we may easily gainsay what Freud described. One cannot read his works without being impressed by the tremendously creative power of his intelligence, the carefulness of his observations, and the courage of his conclusions. His account ought not to be considered wrong so much as limited in its point of view. Elaborating the pathological, looking behind human inhibitions, unearthing a cultural epoch—in all this he was vastly more right than wrong. Yet his followers have found certain weaknesses and certain inadequacies. In what follows we are especially concerned about his treatment of matters related to freedom, agency, virtue, character, and justice.

Let us take the clue for our analysis from Freud himself, from the assumption that all psychological symptoms must be considered in terms of their origin, as well as their structure and conflicting functions. His terms were etiology, topography, and dynamics. When one compares the earlier and later writings of Freud, it becomes clear that several kinds of observations and ideas contributed to his theory of conscience. His earlier interests were in hysteria and compulsive behavior; later he turned to psychoses such as paranoia and schizophrenia. The theory of superego came late in his career, and with it he tried to account for a diverse group of behaviors, such as the distortions that occur in dreams, the taboos of religion, and the despair of the melancholiac—to mention only a few. It is to these behaviors and Freud's interpretation of them that we now turn in order to understand what he meant by conscience.

## The Represser

Since Freud tended to personify functions within personality, perhaps we may be forgiven for personifying the various elements of his theory. We do this with some justification since his theory moves toward just such an idiom. His early writings refer to "the censorship" of dreams, but later this becomes "the censor." His earliest views may without too much distortion be assembled under the heading "the represser." The theory of repression was an attempt to explain the symptoms of hysteria.

As a young doctor whose interests were turning from neurology to emotional disorders, Freud began to experiment with ways of getting patients to discuss their problems. He found hypnosis to be severely limited because so many people resist its use. Therefore he turned to the method of free association. The procedure, as is now well known, was to encourage the patient to speak freely about whatever came to mind, without thought for logic, morality, or any other restrictions.

Freud was much impressed by the experience of his colleague Dr. Joseph Breuer, who had treated a young woman with an hysterical paralysis of the right arm and leg.

> She had a severe paralysis of both right extremities with anaesthesia, and at times the same affection of the members of the left side of the body; disturbance of eye-movements, and much impairment of vision; difficulty in maintaining the position of the head, and intense *Tussis nervosa*, nausea when she attempted to take nourishment, and at one time for several weeks a loss of the power to drink, in spite of tormenting thirst. Her power of speech was also diminished, and this progressed so far that she could neither speak nor understand her mother tongue; and, finally, she was subject to states of 'absence,' of confusion, delirium, alteration of her whole personality. . . . The illness first appeared while the patient was caring for her father, whom she tenderly loved, during the severe illness which led to his death, a task which she was compelled to abandon because she herself fell ill.[1]

She could be relieved for short periods by discussing a symptom, but the debilitating condition always returned within several days. Under hypnosis she began to speak about her father, "whom she loved dearly." After some time, and with considerable hesitation, she began to express feelings of anger and hostility toward him. When she had spoken in this way the paralysis subsided, and she began to regain normal use of her bodily functions.

Freud rejected the explanation of Janet, the famous Parisian specialist in nervous disorders, namely, that hysteria is due to a constitutional deficit in the psychic capacity to synthesize experience. Rather, Freud hypothesized an incompatability between certain deeply held ideas and certain other memories. He considered the consciousness of an hysterical patient to be split in two, with the accompanying emotion "held back because it cannot be reconciled with an accumulation of ethical, aesthetic and personal pretensions."[2] The emotional "affect" that accompanies the "forgotten" wish may be turned into bodily malfunction like blindness or anesthesia. It may be turned into anxiety, or finally and more constructively, it may begin to undergird and reinforce a more acceptable wish.

By this account, repression is the consequence of certain conscious intentions and ideals that a person holds for fear of breaking relationship with some significant person.[3] The initial resistance of his patients to speak about certain feelings as well as their recovery when they had so spoken led Freud to posit "repression" as a designation for the process of blocking and holding back, and to posit "the unconscious" as the realm of those memories that are blocked off and held back. If a person cannot remember what pains him, it must be somehow walled off, that is, repressed, and the memories so affected must somehow remain present though unconscious. The two concepts, repression and the unconscious, are absolutely fundamental to all of Freud's later ideas about conscience.

He next turned his attention to the nature of these unconscious memories, which he began to study through the dream life of his patients. Only later did he give his full attention to those moral and aesthetic ideas that were causing repression.[4] His interests turned from the symptom to the unconscious to the instincts and finally to the ego, although throughout this development he had not forgotten the "resisting, repelling, repressing agency."[5]

## *The Censor*

As Freud's investigations turned from the fact of repression to the question of what is being repressed, he was driven inexorably to the conclusion that the "forgotten" memories were sexual in nature. Furthermore, those memories did not lie dormant and inactive in their separated state. They pushed for conscious recognition, and failing that, they found some other course of expression, albeit unrecognized by the person himself. Freud's patients were most reluctant to recall sexual experiences, even though many of their inhibitions seemed to reflect a sexual basis. He began to listen to his patients' dreams as a way of approaching their unconscious urges and memories.

As an example, there is the instance of a fifty-year-old woman whose son was serving in the army. The mother dreamed that she had gone to the military hospital to speak to the Chief Medical Officer about offering her "services" there. She explained her intentions to the guard at the gate by saying that, since the boys were having to risk their lives, she and other women were willing to . . . (at this point the words "turned into a mumble")[6] for the troops. She could see that the officers present were embarrassed, but also that they were grinning slyly at one another. Feeling only that she was doing her duty, she walked up an interminable staircase to find the Chief Medical Officer. Upon awakening she was highly disgusted at herself for dreaming "stuff like this."

Though I have considerably condensed the account, the reader will immediately see that the woman dreamed she was offering herself to fulfill the erotic needs of soldiers, a thought that could hardly be unrelated to the fact that her own son was a soldier. However, when the sexual image came very close to actual expression, the words were lost even to the dreamer herself.

Freud attributed such omissions and distortions to the operation of a "dream censorship."

Instances like this convinced Freud that "forgotten" memories behave more like active forces, sexual drives surging for expression. His term was *libido*. Against these sexual urges is a counterforce, repressing and censoring. Only in sleep—and occasionally in jokes or slips of the tongue—can the forbidden wish be expressed, and only then in the disguise of dream symbolism. The woman mentioned above could dream about a sexual urge disguised as a service and a duty, but when the wish became more explicit, the dream censor also became more active.

To criticisms lodged against his theory of dreams Freud was willing to make one minor concession, though it in no way changes the basic idea. While many dreams can be traced back to "immoral, incestuous, and perverse impulses, or . . . murderous and sadistic lusts," some dreams are of a different kind. There is the "punishment dream" in which the dreamer finds himself chastised and tormented in some way. Here again a basic urge is involved, but in this case, the urge for punishment. Punishment dreams express the wishes of the "critical, censuring, and punishing function of the mind,"[7] but leave unexpressed the underlying urge against which the censor reacts. This very device betrays what it hides, for the guilt itself is evidence of the unexpressed and unacceptable urge.

There are then three basic types of dreams. In the first, the sexual wish has been so altered that it goes unrecognized by the dream censor and thus preserves sleep by releasing tension. Second is the anxiety dream, in which the underlying urge is recognized by the dream censor only sufficiently to arouse anxiety. The dreamer may awaken full of anxiety or disgust, though without knowing why. Finally, there is the punishment dream wherein the hidden urge remains suppressed and only the activity of the dream censor is given symbolic expression.

Both repression and censorship were later to be taken into the theory of the superego,[8] but we have a number of other observations and concepts to consider before taking up that topic.

## The Taboo

Increasingly, Freud became interested in compulsive behavior as well as hysteria and dreams. A compulsion is an act or thought that a person feels to be forced upon him from within and against his own immediate sense of voluntary effort. An example comes from the life of another of Freud's patients.

Upon one occasion a young man came to Freud because of fears that he might cut his own throat with a razor or that something dreadful might happen to two of the persons he loved most. He could not banish the dread thought that both his girl friend and his father would each be tortured by being bound with buttocks over a potful of vicious rats. One particular summer this young man decided that he ought to lose weight. He began a program of running, forcing himself to the top of a mountain as fast as he could manage. The suicidal character of this exercise became evident when at the top of the mountain he felt the urge to fling himself over a cliff. In the course of therapy it occurred to the patient that he was intensely jealous of a man whom his girl friend found to be quite attractive. His feelings of anger and outrage were so great that, he had to admit, for an instant the thought of killing the other passed through his mind. This occurred at just the time when he had decided upon the program of exercise.

Freud considered both the obsessive impulse and the suicidal command to be reactions "to a tremendous feeling of rage, which was inaccessible to the patient's consciousness and was directed against someone who had cropped up as an interference with the course of his love."[9] Further analysis suggested that the real object of rage was the father of this young man, who had disciplined him as an infant with cruel physical punishment. The compulsive commands are therefore to be interpreted as an effort by the ego to counteract and control feelings of hatred originally directed toward his father.

Compulsive thoughts and acts occur when both love and hate are present, are split apart, and love must act compellingly to resist the strength of the hate.[10] A person then "doubts" the genuineness of his own love, but this only strengthens the ego's efforts to resist all doubt. Nevertheless, the doubt remains, and the compulsive thoughts are extended into many areas of life in an unsuccessful effort to bring the doubts under control.

Freud was of the opinion that many religious ceremonies and social taboos are an expression of compulsiveness: they serve to restrain basically undesirable urges. The totemism of primitive peoples is a network of ritual taboos whose unrecognized purpose is to restrain incestuous sexual interest of a boy for his mother and to command respect for the father in the face of powerful feelings of rage. Paradoxically, the ceremonies of totemism conjure up enough of the forbidden experience, albeit in a negative way, that the underlying urge is in part satisfied. The taboos and the accompanying rituals serve directly to restrain the forbidden impulses, but, indirectly, to give them some satisfaction.

With Freud's theory of compulsive behavior we have his first explicit explanation of conscience.

> Conscience is the inner perception of objections to definite wish impulses that exist in us; but the emphasis is put upon the fact that this rejection does not have to depend on anything else, that it is sure of itself. This becomes even plainer in the case of the guilty conscience, where we become aware of the inner condemnation of such acts which realized some of our definite wish impulses. . . . Taboo is a command of conscience, the violation of which causes a terrible sense of guilt which is as self-evident as its origin is unknown.[12]

Repressed urges are felt internally as temptation, while the ego's efforts at restraint produce anxiety. When anxiety is generated in this way, it tends to destroy hope in the future in the form of "expectant anxiety." With customary acuteness, Freud has pointed out that conscience is related to a person's sense of time.

## Beginnings

By this time, Freud was thoroughly convinced that sexual impulse is the repressed urge at the root of many emotional disturbances, certainly of hysteria and compulsive neurosis. Furthermore, the free associations of his patients led to a series of traumas, personal crises of severe fright, ridicule, or punishment. Each trauma seemed to be preceded by a still earlier trauma, leading back to the earliest experiences of childhood. Emotional disturbance apparently develops through a series of personal crises, but in reverse order to that in which they are remembered.

What then caused the earlier crises? Freud's first hunch was to look to early, but "forgotten," sexual experience. However, when his patients' accounts of their early sexual life often turned out to be fantasy rather than reality, Freud was forced to look for another explanation. He decided that while sexual impulses of various kinds are present in the life of the infant from birth, they are constantly inhibited by a series of crises. Memories of their actual expression are mixed with the fantasy life of the child. Eventually the urges as well as the memories and fantasies associated with them are repressed.

Far from occurring all at once, repression comes by a number of steps or stages conditioned primarily by the developing sensitivity of the body and its increasing capacity for satisfaction. The earliest form of human relationship is that between a mother and her child. The infant "identifies" with the mother, that is, imitates her, feels that she is part of himself, takes her into himself.[13] Indeed he literally takes the mother into himself when he nurses at her breast. The infant explores his world with his mouth, inserting and sucking anything within reach. Identification is the most fundamental relationship between persons and is central to the establishment of an internal sentinel capable of repression, censorship, and self-reproach. This earliest period of bodily enjoyment he called the oral stage.

The developing body of the infant allows control and

25

sensitivity to move from the mouth to other parts of the body. Especially important is the satisfaction gained from the eliminative processes. The infant's increasing capacity for control is accompanied by increasing demands from the parents, which serve to restrict the child's enjoyment of his own body. He must learn to use the potty; he must not soil himself. The double fear of losing the love of his parents and of being punished causes the child to hold back the urges he feels. Frustration brings on strong feelings of rage, and these too must be held back. Those situations in which the child's urges are countered by the overwhelming control of the parents become decisive for the child's development. Parental restriction becomes converted to internalized compulsive demands. Because of the focus around elimination, the second period is called the anal stage.

Sometime between the third and fifth years of a child's life the enjoyment of his growing body centers increasingly in his genitals. Now he develops a specifically sexual interest in his mother over and above his earlier identification with her. He gains new pleasure from being held and fondled. However, several decisive circumstances deprive the child of these basic satisfactions; the very smallness and immaturity of his body, the decreasing amount of interest and attention he can gain from his mother, the father's unchallenged sexual and affectional prerogatives with the mother, and the father's threats to punish force the child to modify his fundamental urges. Caught in a mixture of urges clustered about both the mother and the father, the young boy turns away from the mother and identifies strongly with the father.

Identifying with the father satisfies the child's real affection for the father, but, more importantly, it is an indirect and vicarious way of satisfying sexual interest through the father's actual access to the mother. Feelings of rage and grief for the mother are expressed by turning away from her, while hostile feelings toward the father are now blotted out for the sake of the new identification. The demands of the parents became a permanent part of the child's personality. The pain of the situation that gave rise to these processes is so great that the memory of them is further blotted out, repressed. Condemnation, guilt, and repression act automatically for the rest of the person's life, largely without his conscious knowledge. Because of the direct sexual interest involved, Freud called this the genital period, and the cluster of conflicting emotions were named the Oedipal complex, a reference to the famous drama by Sophocles.

Following the sixth or seventh year of life, the child increasingly turns his attention away from the parents and toward teachers, pastors, relatives, and other acquaintances. New emotional attachments become established and suppressed according to the Oedipal pattern laid down in the genital period. Every new identification leaves its own stamp upon the personality. The authority of the parents is extended to a wide number of other persons, eventually to the whole society. The term for this period is the latency stage, a reference to the child's seeming loss of sexual interest.

The theory of infantile sexuality and of identification serve as an explanation for the way the conscience comes to be established in the personality. Each stage has its own importance, but the genital period with all its attendant conflicts seems to be most decisive. What happens then becomes a prototype for relationships with all other persons. Repression, guilt, and condemnation come to be automatic.

### The Observer

As Freud's theory developed, more and more his interests turned away from the unconscious sexual urges and toward the conscious ego processes, from the "victims" of repression to the agent of repression. He hoped to extend the method by which he had analyzed hysteria and compulsiveness to the more intransigent conditions of paranoia, schizophrenia, and melancholia. These latter observations are decisive for his theory of the superego.

27

Paranoia in particular is a condition in which a person feels that he is being observed, threatened, and persecuted. He may elaborate an extensive explanation to account for his observers and persecutors. Perhaps a brief account of a person with only mild symptoms will serve our purposes of illustration.

Our example comes from the life of an attractive young woman of thirty who was brought to Freud by her lawyer. Unmarried, without brothers or sisters, and deprived of a father who had died many years before, she had lived alone with her mother for many years. Unexpectedly she became involved in an affair with a gentleman employed in the office where she also worked. At his insistence she accepted an invitation to come to his home.

It was during a second visit to his home that a critical event occurred. They were fondling one another when she heard a click, like that of a camera. At first she thought nothing of it, but later when she left the apartment she saw two men carrying a small item down the stairway. The next day she noticed that her gentleman friend was confiding in a motherly woman who acted as her superior. Was he not telling their secret? And had this man not arranged to have a picture taken of them embracing each other?

This instance, as Freud noted, has the characteristic paranoiac illusion of being observed and persecuted. Freud suggested that the illusion was the consequence of a conflict between the erotic needs of the young woman and her abnormally close attachment to her mother. She projected her mother's feelings—rather, her perception of her mother's feelings—upon the "mother" supervisor, and then suspected herself to be observed and criticized. The illusions of paranoia expose the human ego's capacity to observe itself and to attribute that observation to another. Freud concluded that the capacity for self-observation may be built into every personality. Perhaps every ego can be split, can observe itself as an object, and can even criticize itself from that stance. "The lament of the paranoiac shows that at bottom the self-criticism of conscience is identical with and based upon self-observation.''[14]

Surely Freud here was pointing to a fundamental human capacity—that of being able to imagine other times and circumstances, to view present events from the vantage point of another person or another occasion. Human freedom, the ability to purpose and to act, come in part from the capacity to imagine circumstances and perspectives other than those in which one presently stands. The illusions of paranoia are the distortion of a process basic to human freedom.

### The Ideal

Several kinds of observations led Freud to include self-esteem in his theory of conscience. In 1899 Paul Naecke had used the term *narcissism* to denote "the attitude of a person who treats his own body in the same way in which the body of a sexual object (that is, a loved person) is ordinarily treated." Such a person may look at his body, stroke it, and fondle it until "he obtains complete satisfaction through these activities."[15]

Another pertinent observation is that persons with schizophrenia seem to withdraw all emotional interest from the outside world, to turn all attention inward, and to regard themselves with exaggerated importance. It is as though the ego could return all of its energies into itself. Or consider the fact that primitive people and children characteristically overestimate the power of their own thoughts. A person believes that one can punish an enemy simply by thinking the thought. A child feels that he has injured his parent simply because the thought has crossed his mind.

Still other observations: People who are physically ill lose interest in the outside world and become highly satisfied or dissatisfied with the functions of their own bodies. Hypochondriasis is a malady in which this concern for the body takes the form of exaggerated though unfounded suspicions about the body's malfunction.

Consider the fact that people who are in love show an interest not only in the one who is loved, but also in the lover's regard for them. A lover's self-esteem seems to be tied to being loved by the other person. One might say that he loves himself through his lover. Freud observed that women are more likely to love in this manner. A man directs his primary interest toward the woman, but she loves herself in his regard for her. Whether or not Freud was right in his analysis of feminine self-love, he was almost surely right in his observations about human self-esteem.

All of these observations suggested to Freud that the basic life urges may be directed outwardly to other persons or inwardly to the personality itself. Freud's way of putting it was that libido is of two types: object-libido and ego-libido. From the time of birth the ego seems increasingly able to appropriate for itself an expanding reservoir of energy which is subject to the purposes of the ego. As the child grows, his thinking, intending, choosing, and acting increase in satisfaction and spontaneity. Barring a mishap, he tends to become an emotionally involved, reality-oriented, deliberative, choosing agent.

Emotional urges directed to the ego itself were called narcissistic by Freud, a reference to the Greek hero who loved to view his own reflection. A person may gain self-esteem, that is, narcissistic satisfaction, from what he now is, what he has been, or what he would like to be. His esteem may also be tied to his children, who are an extension of his own body.

The earliest life impulses of the infant are directed not only toward the mother in identification, but also toward the ego in its satisfaction with itself. Increasing parental demands not only force identification to shift from mother to father, but change the direction of self-esteem to loving himself for what he can be rather than what he is. During the genital period the child projects before himself an ideal, the ideal of his parents, which controls the lost self-esteem of his infancy. Taken in by identification with the father and the mother, ideals are elevated above the remainder of the ego and enforce repression of undesirable urges from that stance. The ego ideal captures the ego's self-esteem and dispenses it according to whether motives and behavior match the ideal. Since libidinal urges never fully match the ideal, the ego is always caught in a sense of guilt. The ideals and ethical requirements of persons originate from childhood experiences that are as abhorrent as they are attractive.

The theory of idealization supplements identification as the process by which the conscience comes into being. Identification accounts for the repression and taboo of sexual interest, and idealization accounts for the loss of self-esteem. The ideal is also a link with the wider society, since an ideal is always more or less widely shared by other persons. What was originally a fear of loss of love has become a general sense of guilt.

### The Tormentor

The idea that the ego may become its own tormentor is only a small extension of what we have already said. The basic data comes from the lives of persons who are mourning the death of a loved one or the "loss of an abstraction" such as country or liberty.[16] More exaggerated are the feelings of the melancholic patient who constantly berates himself.

> The distinguishing mental features of melancholia are a profoundly painful dejection, cessation of interest in the outside world, loss of the capacity to love, inhibition of all activity, and a lowering of the self-regarding feelings to a degree that finds utterances in self-reproaches and self-revilings, and culminates in a delusional expectation of punishment.[17]

In mourning, the loss is conscious and known; in melancholia, the loss is unconscious and unknown. The mourner's whole world is empty, while the melancholiac's ego is impoverished "on a grand scale."[18] Further, melancholic dissatisfaction with the ego seems to be primarily on moral grounds.[19] The mourner searches through various memories, apparently to reorient himself to the loss of a loved one and to withdraw emotional attachment from all those experiences in which the other was involved. The melancholiac seems to withdraw all emotion into the ego rather than to direct interest to another person.

What happens to the emotional energy withdrawn by the melancholiac from the outer world? Freud suggested that part of the ego comes to be identified with the lost loved one, while the other part of the ego is idealized and acts as tormentor and critic. The intrapsychic conflict exhausts the melancholiac as long as the attack lasts. "In this way an object-loss was translated into an ego-loss and the conflict between the ego and the loved person into a cleavage between the critical agency of the ego and the ego as directed by identification."[20]

In summary, the loss of a loved one, when that loss is mixed with strong feelings of rage and even hatred, leads to a kind of self-torment wherein the ego rages against itself. Even so, this kind of self-punishment may have its own enjoyment, for it usually causes those loved ones near at hand a kind of pain to which they cannot respond directly. Unacknowledged hostility finds an indirect expression, even though at the cost of considerable mental anguish. The pain of conscience is a kind of internal torment within the ego itself.

### The Death Wish

We have now enumerated the elements that go into the superego with possibly one exception. We must look at Freud's reformulation of his theory of life urges to include the death instinct. This will lead us to the superego itself. We must then see how people are bound into civilized groups, which in turn leads to the concept of the cultural superego.

Probably the experience of World War I left an indelible impression upon Freud. During those years one finds him rather frequently writing on the subjects of war, transience, and death. He finally moved to the position that human destructiveness is much too massive to attribute to the adaptive behavior of the life instincts. There must be a more fundamental explanation. Human urges must include an instinct directed toward destructiveness and ultimate quiescence along with and beside the life instincts. The struggle for life is not only against necessity, hunger, and decay, but also against the impulses for destruction and death to be found in the instinctual roots of every person.[21]

The life urges protect life by turning destructive impulses inward against themselves. So conceived, the conscience is the intrapsychic battle of the death instinct against itself. We have already seen how repressed rage and hatred played an important part in Freud's early theory of conscience. At that time, he had considered hate and sadism to be libidinal reactions to the restrictive forces of the environment. Do not life impulses turn to rage when they are frustrated or deprived? Thus Freud suggested that aggressive behavior has a more fundamental instinctual basis. External necessity is only another face of the internal reality of death itself. The death instinct is hidden beneath—but also expressed—in the self-berating, guilt, and moral anxiety of conscience.

The existence of a death instinct has been vigorously debated, but not very widely accepted by students of Freud. It places the concept of self-preserving (ego) and species-preserving (libido) instincts, with their attendant capacity for rage and aggression, within a much different framework. Ego and libido become expressions of the life-sustaining instincts, while aggression and rage may serve the life-denying instincts. It is not our task here to try to defend the idea of a death urge. Rather we want to point out that within this formulation the conscience becomes a vehicle for the death wish. The idea of the conscience as repressive rather than guiding is thus extended still further.

### The Superego

The superego is the final formulation in Freud's various efforts to understand the place of the conscience within the structure of personality. The superego brings together the source of repression, the dream censor, the observer, the tormentor, and the ego ideal into one single but complex mental activity.[22]

It may function to enforce a compulsive taboo, a paranoid sense of guilt, a rewarding ideal, or a tormenting melancholic persecution. Characteristically, these emotions are variations in the human capacity for self-awareness and self-criticism as they are molded by decisive expectations of other people.

The character and severity of the superego depends partly upon the behavior of the parents who rear a child and of significant other persons outside the family. But guilt is also a function of the child's internal emotional processes, the strength of his creative and destructive instincts, and perhaps the indefinable uniqueness of his personhood.

In the latter years of his career Freud altered his views about anxiety. You may remember that he had early considered anxiety to be a poison, a toxin, that is often released as a consequence of repression. Later he suggested that anxiety is a signal within the ego itself, a signal by which the ego is warned of the presence of any threat. Anxiety is to the ego what pain is to the body. The ego may experience various kinds of anxiety. Reality anxiety is the signal of an external danger such as the punishment of an angry parent. Neurotic anxiety results from an overly strong sexual urge; and moral anxiety, from the threat of the superego. The anxiety signal is a part of the character of the ego and is present from the time of birth until the time of death.[23]

The traumas by which the conscience is formed are no longer understood to be the internal experience of an "overabundance of stimuli," a concept that is overly mechanical. The developing ego responds to genuine external threats by being anxious. The restrictions of parents, the destructive urges of other persons near at hand, are realities for which the ego may legitimately be anxious. Whereas parents seldom destroy their children (although some have in various times and places), the overwhelming power of parents over their children is a reality. Moral anxiety is always an internalization of what was once reality anxiety.[24]

The superego is largely unconscious, so that a person is hardly aware of all his moral impulses and ideals.[25] Freud observed that the superego has a more direct access to the impulses of the id than to the ego. A person can more easily fall under a compulsion of unreasoning moral indignation than he can reasonably and realistically assess the circumstances of a situation. By Freud's analysis no one is fully aware of the guilt that lies within oneself.[26] Health can come only as people begin to acknowledge the guilt they actually feel.

The superego not only observes, restricts, criticizes, and directs the ego; it also affects the ego's ability to test reality. What people perceive in the world around them is already distorted by their ideals, many of which have been taken over from their parents. People tend to perceive not simply "what is there" by any impartial report, but what their own values and ideals dictate must be there. More generally stated, the conscience often distorts the perception of events in time and space.

### Civilization

The theory of idealization was the link that allowed Freud to relate his findings about conscience to the wider society. His early studies, as we have emphasized, were concerned about the life instincts behind dreams, fantasy, and hysteria. Gradually, as his attention turned to the ego and the real environment within which any person exists, it was perhaps inevitable that he should become more curious about the world of other people. Freud's final writings concerned the problems of sociology, politics, and history.

A group may be defined as an association of persons who are dedicated to a common ideal.[27] They have identified with the same father figure and have idealized the same moral directives in order to resolve the dilemma of conflicting feelings of love and rage that they all share in common. It may then easily be understood that groups assemble to strengthen and heighten a group ideal. Not only was this done in the totemistic religion of primitive peoples, but it may also be observed in the consuming ethical interests of many groups today, especially the church.

Why then do crowds often act in the most immoral ways, destroying, pillaging, and raping as an individual never would? Freud's answer is that a crowd gives each individual a sense of strength that may reduce his fear of the superego. When this happens, basic impulses, ordinarily inhibited, will be expressed. Freud had long maintained that the conscience is a "fear of society," originally a displaced fear of the father.[28] An individual's fear of a group along with a need for approval may reverse the superego's ordinary requirements. However, such behavior is an exception to the way the power of the ideal ordinarily binds people together.

At this point we should make clear something that was passed over in our description of the beginnings of conscience. Children do not idealize their parents' actual behavior. Rather they idealize those values by which their parents are governed, and in this manner the ideal is passed from one generation to the next.[29] Esthetic and ethical values become a cohesive, albeit repressive, force binding men together in social existence.

We have already noted that idealization implies a corresponding repression. Freud had suggested that human beings universally repress incestual urges as well as the rage they feel toward those who enforce early repressions. If this be so, people are bound together by a common resistance to incestual feelings as well as to the authority by which those resistances are enforced. These taboos are recorded in the unconscious emotions of all people, and they correspond generally to the conscious content of ethical ideals and values. The history of the race is thereby imbedded in the forbidden impulses of every person.[30]

The existence of common ideals and repressions leads inevitably to what might be called a cultural superego. The ideals of people have been shaped by the lives of great leading personalities who have left their high standards with their followers. The outstanding example that Freud chose to study was Moses' effect upon Israel. The cultural superego has something of an objective existence in the ethical codes and writings of any civilization. By way of confirmation, Freud suggested that psychoanalysis will uncover those same values in the life of any person, even though deeply hidden and repressed.

Freud seemed to believe fatalistically that repression is both inevitable and necessary for the existence of society, perhaps more to restrain violence than sexuality. The cultural superego joins persons together in society in order to preserve them from the destructive impulses of one another. Hence, repression is the cost of civilization, and the freedom of emotional expression is directly at odds with the requirements of social existence. Society must erect "every possible reinforcement" against the aggressive instincts of people.[31]

Social justice, in Freud's view, is an ideal that is very closely related to the repressions by which civilization lives. "Social justice means that we deny ourselves many things so that others may have to do without them as well, or what is the same thing, may not be able to ask for them. This demand for equality is the root of social conscience and the sense of duty."[32]

The hope of humanity does not lie in the path of increasing ethical aspiration, nor in the direction of heightening the conscience, for this way involves deeply self-destructive urges. The way lies rather in acknowledging and recognizing basic impulses so that they may be handled by whatever strength and resources the ego has at hand. Reasoning, deliberative, reality-oriented, conscious activity offers greater satisfaction than does the self-destructive torment of conscience. The aim of life is not morality but maturity.

## Agency

There are hints of another approach to conscience in Freud's writings, and while they never become so pronounced as his analysis of the repressive conscience, they must nevertheless not be ignored. Our thesis is that conscience may become a guiding activity of human agency, transforming the restrictive, inhibitive conscience during the course of our life pilgrimage. Conscience as a guiding activity is not to be seen as isolated within the solitary self, but as an internal reflection of the dialogue that takes place within communities of common concern and affection. Life is lived between the inhibiting and the guiding conscience, always with the hope that the powers of strong agency may be more fully expressed in the guiding conscience.

Freud's powerful, elaborate description of the restrictive conscience makes it likely that no adequate account of the maturation of conscience can be given without full attention to what he has described. Yet there are other suggestions in his work that may be taken as the basis for conscience as a guiding activity of human agency. For example, Freud was not willing for superego to be equated with conscience; he insisted repeatedly that the two are not identical. Although, so far as I have discovered, he never made clear the reasons for this reservation, he may have sensed that the common everyday meaning of the word *conscience* includes more than what he intended to include under the term *superego*. Whether this is so or not, we may find a basis in his work for the guiding conscience.

Consider Freud's claim that one of the functions of therapy is to integrate the superego within the ego so far as is possible. He listed the various functions of the ego as consciousness, perception, reality testing, anxiety, self-observation, anticipation and action. Behind all these functions is "ego strength," the capacity to maintain some kind of integrity in the midst of pressures from within and without, to synthesize a variety of perceptions, impulses, and images. To the extent that the superego is integrated into the ego, inhibition, taboos, and self-observation may be accepted with deeper understanding into underlying motives. In other words, one may freely choose and accept ideals and restrictions in view of the limitation of a real world and the actual feelings and impulses that one has. When ideals and restrictions are freely chosen, then bondage to inhibitions is transformed into the freedom of self-direction.

Clearly, therapy is designed to bring about this change, and indeed it may be the most important therapeutic change, since the superego enforces the repressions that cause so much emotional pain and illness.

Our account of the change that takes place in therapy suggests that when behavioral norms and values are integrated into the ego, that is, when they are freely chosen and accepted, the ego's capacity to guide itself becomes stronger. Along with this enlarged strength of self-guidance, consider Freud's observation that the ideals of the superego are those shared with parents and with the wider community. In the formation of the superego, community ideals are taken in at an unconscious level, involving deep emotional attachments, but without the deliberative powers of the ego. The integration of the ideals of the superego into the ego will necessarily involve thinking through, reconsidering, discussing, debating, and deciding about those values to which the strong emotions of the superego have been attached. The underlying hidden emotions will be recovered, and the values will be judged by the ego according to its capacity to discuss and decide about what is genuine. Thus, when the ideals of the superego are integrated into the ego, they become the basis for guidance and self-direction. Freud's conception of therapy thereby offers the possibility of a guiding conscience alongside the restrictive conscience.

What we have said so far indicates that in therapy the superego may be transformed by deeper awareness, intentionality, and coherence. Our proposal is that human agency includes these three characteristics along with a fourth, that is, mutuality. Does Freud offer suggestions about the possibility of a wider mutuality for the superego? One answer has been given. Values integrated into the ego will necessarily involve deliberation, discussion, and decision. Such activities almost always include both private reflection and public discussion.

However, there is another answer in Freud's work that must not be overlooked. While his formulations about the superego and the ego are entirely about processes within the psyche, and therefore without explicit mutuality, his ideas about therapy always involve at least two persons. Therapy goes on between the patient and the therapist, and it is the therapist's task to notice when the patient's responses are inappropriate. When does the patient make assumptions about the therapist for which there is no basis in fact? Perhaps the patient considers the therapist cruel, or perhaps timid. Freud's term for such inappropriate responses was *transference*. The therapist uses these clues to help the patient understand how he or she falsely reads the situation. They explore the feelings behind the transference together. In this way the distortions that the superego imposes on the ego are traced back to their emotional roots so that they may be reassessed by the ego.

We have already described how the ideals of the superego may be integrated within the ego. Our point here is that such a transformation occurs within an interpersonal situation of mutuality between patient and therapist. The therapist teaches the patient how to look deeper into his or her own feelings, how to recover deeper intentions, and how to facilitate the integration of the impulses of the superego. In other words, the therapist gives a model for self-understanding. The therapist gives the patient new respect for honesty, self-regard, and self-expression. In the mutuality of the relationship between patient and therapist, the guiding conscience as an expression of agency is strengthened, and the inhibiting conscience as the weakness of agency is overcome; therefore, the mutuality that Freud describes in the therapeutic relationship serves as a basis for describing the guiding conscience.

This leads me to suggest that there are implicit norms and values within Freud's very therapeutic method. Philip Rieff has written about Freud's underlying egoism coupled with his ethic of honesty. Freud was quite clearly working for a greater strength of ego functions, that is, intelligence, critical judgment, deliberation, and scientific discussion. He said of himself, "I believe that in a sense of justice and consideration for others, in disliking making others suffer or taking advantage of them I can measure myself with the best people I know."[33] Surely he considered such values as more than a defense against underlying resentment. They were freely chosen with a penetrating self-understanding and an empathetic awareness of the pain that other persons suffer. Yet his work never gave a firm theoretical basis for these values. They represent the depths of his own guiding conscience, but his final concepts give a very narrow basis for them.

Freud's work left the need for a description of health that is more than the absence of illness. What is needed is a description of moral judgment as a manifestation of the strength of human agency. We may build upon the clues he offered in this direction. While norms are often repressive and self-destructive, there must also be norms and values that grow out of freely chosen direction and purposes. Such norms do not cause illness; rather, they give guidance to the healthy expression of agency. The ego that Freud too often described in isolation must be seen to exist within a set of social relationships. Then immediately the conscience is seen to be a social agency, an expression that occurs in discussion and mutual agreement between persons. Deeply personal on one hand, it is deeply social on the other. What is needed is a better description of how the restrictive conscience is transformed into the guiding conscience.

In passing, let me say that Freud's critique of religion as neurosis also leaves much to be desired. He occasionally seemed to sense the inevitability of religious understanding with regard to the wider reaches of human experience. He even spoke of the instincts as his own "mythology." His work did, however, make one very important contribution to religious understanding. He as much as anyone has shown that religious ideas can be held in a defensive or neurotic way. No matter how much courage a religious idea may give to one person, it may serve to rationalize a neurosis for someone else. His works suggest that religious persons ought to be aware of the ways that faith may be emotionally distorted to become faithless. Of this we will say more in a later chapter.

We want now to turn our attention to the development of the strength or virtue of human agency. Such strength always will be limited by the power of the repressive superego. To understand the basis of human virtue we must keep Freud's account in mind. Erik Erikson has greatly extended Freud's conception of the restrictive conscience in the direction of the guiding conscience. To some extent Erikson's work is complemented by that of Jean Piaget, who was especially interested in the development of moral judgment and intelligence. We therefore lean upon Erikson and Piaget as we turn to describing the development of conscience as an expression of the strength of human agency.

# Chapter II

## A TALE OF MANY POSSIBILITIES:
### *The Sponsoring Conscience*

*Sponsor: One who binds himself to answer for another's default; . . . one who assumes responsibility for some other person or thing.* —*Webster's New World Dictionary of the American Language*, 1961

### *Fate and Hope*

Our discussion of Freud led us to conclude that he viewed the human conscience largely as restrictive, repressive, self-destructive, and infantile, though at the same time the necessary "price" of civilization. He had less to say about human hope and integrity. He did, however, have some very significant things to say in this regard, something that has been dramatically called to our attention by Erik Erikson and others.[1] Erikson's more positive interpretation of conscience is also, in our view, consonant with the basic ideas of Jean Piaget.

Our procedure will be to emphasize certain principles by which Erikson has complemented or extended Freud's theory. Only occasionally does he deliberately contradict his mentor. For the most part, Erikson builds upon and reformulates traditional psychoanalytic theory. Yet the result is so altered in emphasis that a significantly different type of moral theory results. If Freud wanted to uncover the fateful emotional contradictions that destroy health, Erikson wants to describe the hopeful emotional strength that brings health.

Our method is then to underline the principles by which Erikson proposes to extend and alter the theory of the accusing conscience. For each principle we shall draw illustrations from one of the successive stages in the development of mature moral judgment, beginning with infancy and proceeding to adulthood. Having done this, we shall more carefully and critically examine his use of normative ethical language. We will concern ourselves especially with questions about freedom, virtue, character, volition, and justice.

At this point a diagram may help the reader to understand what Erikson has to say.

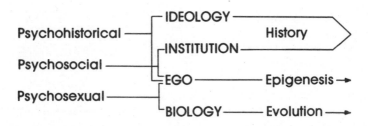

The diagram can be clarified by a brief explanation. The ego is bounded by biological processes on the one hand and institutional/ideological processes on the other hand. The term *institution* refers to the social environment as a whole, including especially interpersonal relationships. *Ideology* refers to the whole complex of meanings that make up a culture and includes the fundamental orientation of a person or community. The relationship between the ego and the biological processes is the realm of the psychosexual. Similarly, the relationship of the ego and the social world is the psychosocial. The relationship of ego and culture is the realm of the psychohistorical. The development of the ego from infancy to adulthood is called epigenesis.

Biological development is called evolution, while the long-range change of institution/ideology is called history.

The diagram should make clear that the ego is related to, shaping, and being shaped by various forces, that is, biological, institutional, and ideological. Furthermore, the ego passes through various stages of development, a process that may be called epigenesis. The growth of the ego is interdependent on one hand with biological evolution and on the other with historical and institutional change. Let us begin by considering the origin of ego strength within its biological, institutional, and ideological setting.

### Premoral Ego Strength

Much of Freud's work was taken up with unearthing the hidden instinctual motives of human behavior. This task led him to conclude that primary emotional pleasure moves from the mouth to the anus and finally to the genitals as a person matures. The instinctual energy (libido) in each instance meets a particular crisis at some time during childhood. Those crises are brought on by weaning, cleanliness training, and restriction of interest in the genitals, respectively. Such crises are determinative in the formation of neurotic symptoms as well as morality.

Erikson proposes that Freud's model be expanded to include the mutual activation and control that parents and children exert upon one another. The focus then shifts to the psychosocial relationship between the child and the significant persons who care for her. The quality of the relationship is mutual and reciprocal in that it is reflected in the attitudes of both child and adult. Furthermore, those attitudes, as they develop in the personality of a child, become more or less characteristic of her ego throughout her lifetime.

For example, in the nursing situation, the infant's oral needs are satisfied by taking in the mother's milk. Her whole attitude at that time is one of taking in, or possibly of spitting out. Everything in her limited world goes to her mouth. Through her mouth she learns to trust the one who cares for her as well as the world about her.

The mother, on the other hand, has her own maternal needs satisfied by giving the infant milk. These needs are more complicated in that they include not only the bodily satisfaction (or dissatisfaction) of having her breasts stimulated, but also the mother's self-esteem as shaped by her own personal life experience, by those who love and protect her, by the cultural ideal of motherhood, and by present historical events. Any of these elements can severely limit the mother's capacity to communicate trust to the child for whom she is responsible.

Trust in one another is confirmed by both the infant and the mother. Mother and child are related in a process of mutual verification and recognition. Out of this psychosocial relationship the infant develops a deep sense that life is more or less trustworthy. When such trust is absent, or perhaps severely restricted, then the child may fall into pathological despair, withdrawing from all contact with other persons. Babies without hope may die, even when their physical needs are being thoroughly cared for.

The crisis of trust is brought on by a combination of psychological and social factors. The baby's physical growth and increasing skill in handling her own body mean not only that she will be weaned, but that in every respect she will receive less attention from her mother. The increasing separation between mother and infant brings on a crisis, which is then resolved only as the infant ego establishes some balance of trust over mistrust.

Erikson speaks of hope as the particular ego strength that results from the crisis of trust. "Hope is the enduring belief in the attainability of fervent wishes, in spite of the dark urges and rages which mark the beginning of existence."[2] Presumbably, basic mistrust of other persons is accompanied by inward despair. Once hope is established, it becomes a basis upon which further growth of ego strength may take place. Future experiences may well modify hope, but various developmental changes turn the ego in other directions and toward other crises.

Will is the quality of ego strength that follows immediately upon hope in the epigenesis of the ego. According to the epigenetic principle, developmental stages take place in a given sequence such that one stage must be more or less successfully completed before the following stage can proceed. Furthermore, a stage may be hampered by missing its proper time for development. The concept is borrowed from the physiological growth of the fetus in the mother's uterus. Should the heart or the nervous system fail to develop in the proper sequence or at the proper time, then the organs that normally evolve thereafter will be seriously impaired. Applied psychologically, this means that should the infant fail to gain a sufficiently strong sense of Hope, the further development of Will, Purpose, Competence, Fidelity, Love, Care, and Integrity will be hampered.

Erikson's concept of mutual activation goes considerably beyond what Freud meant by reality. Though it could impose itself upon the individual by threat or deprivation of instinct, reality for Freud always remained outside and external to the individual. The person was related to the world of persons and things primarily by the formation of images to which emotional drives were attached (cathected). Whereas various energy transformations take place within the individual, one remains within a Cartesian wall of self-awareness.

Erikson's concept of actuality denotes that a person may be actively engaged with the environment, especially that part of the environment constituted by other persons.[3] The ego may do more than achieve insight into its own insatiable needs in relation to the limitations of a restrictive reality. The ego may be engaged with other egos such that the strengthening of one also strengthens the other. The power of hope may literally and directly move from one ego to another in interpersonal encounter. For that matter, the hope that one generation invests in institutional practices and ideals, or that a people invest in historical events, may also strengthen (or weaken) the hope of persons for whom such ideals and events are an immediate reality.

The development of will follows that of hope and parallels what Freud described as the crisis of cleanliness training. He showed that a child's pleasure in her own bowel movements is threatened by the disgust and demands of the parents. Erikson notices that the muscular control involved in bowel movements is that of holding and letting go. Furthermore, a two-year-old-child actively holds and lets go with mouth and hands as well as sphincter.

In the struggle over holding and letting go *of a child's sphincter muscles* parent and child are influencing the child's control of her own body. Nothing less than the child's autonomy is at stake. To the extent that parent and child develop a pattern of mutuality and control, the autonomy of each is strengthened. Should a parent under- or overcontrol the child, she in turn reacts with "willfulness." Out of a sense of shame and doubt about the freedom of her own bodily movement, the child, in what appears to be stubborn persistence, controls the parent. "Willfulness" is actually a weakness of will arising from the shame and doubt that both parent and child experience in the breakdown of a pattern of mutual control.

The parents of course have priority in the establishment of mutual control, but their autonomy is limited by their own childhood experiences, the quality of the regulated relationships about them at home, at work, and elsewhere, as well as by the more general ideals of lawfulness and regularity that they and others espouse. Out of the crisis of autonomy the child develops a certain genuine strength or weakness of will, an ego quality that is mutually activated by both parent and child.

As an example of the crisis of autonomy and will, consider Erikson's account of a four-year-old named Peter, who had held his bowel movement for a week.[4] Although his bowel and his abdomen were abnormally distended, he was in such a state of emotional conflict that he suffered the pain of the swelling material in his body rather than let go. Briefly, the emotional dynamics involved a nurse who had served as Peter's substitute mother. The nurse was dismissed when Peter's mother discovered the real affection he was developing for the employee. The nurse informed Peter that she was leaving home because she was to give birth to a child.

Peter himself had been born by Caesarean section when he had proved too large to be born in the normal manner. Taken together, these events developed in Peter's mind into an unconscious belief that he was pregnant. It is not surprising therefore, when he discovered that babies are born through the vagina rather than through the rectum, that he had an enormous bowel movement. It was only through a long process of therapy that Peter and his mother developed a more satisfactory mode of mutual control.

While hope and will are basic premoral virtures, they not only vary from person to person, but more systematically from culture to culture. The Sioux Indians, unlike other Americans about them, are little concerned to wean or toilet train their children at an early age.[5] The young child can nurse whenever she likes, as long as she likes, and from whomever is available to furnish her milk. The limitation to this generosity comes suddenly and painfully when teeth develop, when she can bite the mother's nipple. The mother will then sharply snap her on the head. At that point, the Sioux consider crying good for the lungs. Of a boy they say, "It will make a good hunter of him." [6] Bowel training is often left to the other children.

These practices seem to be interwoven with certain ego strengths and weaknesses. Sioux adults are very trusting of one another but may be brought to a furious and sadistic rage in hunting or battle. Women use their teeth a great deal in their handiwork, and they are often to be seen clicking and snapping their teeth. During the sun dance men will drive little sticks into their chest muscles and then rip them out so that blood flows down their bodies. In such a manner they seem to atone for evil and regain a sense of hope. Sioux are generous to a fault (by white standards), giving away property that a white man would hold and save.[7]

Hope and will are premoral virtues that develop out of the

earliest of relationships between infant and parent. Erikson's view has the advantage of tracing the roots of morality to the very beginning of social relationships from birth on. He thereby overcomes the implicit Cartesian isolation from which most theories of development attempt to establish a theory of morality.

### The Onset of Morality

Premoral ego strength, hope and will, gives way to morality proper as a child passes through the years from three to seven. At this point, it is important to note Erikson's distinction between the moral and the ethical sense. Morality differs from ethics, he proposes, because of their different psychological dynamics. The moral develops at an earlier age on a more immature level, while the ethical must wait until group ideals and personal identity have been established.

The distinction between the moral and the ethical is forcefully put in the following quotation.

> I would propose that we consider *moral* rules of conduct to be based on a fear of *threats* to be forestalled. These may be outer threats of abandonment, punishment and public exposure, or a threatening inner sense of guilt, of shame or of isolation. . . . In contrast, I would consider ethical rules to be based on ideals to be striven for with a high degree of rational assent and with ready consent to a formulated good, a definition of perfection, and some promise of self-realization.[8]

The above quotation makes it clear that Erikson uses the term *moral* with his own special definition. His use is just the opposite from what is often called the "moral point of view."[9] However, the distinction Erikson seeks to make is similar to that frequently made between heteronomous and autonomous moral judgments.[10] Heteronomous judgments are controlled by emotions or external requirements, while autonomous judgments are based upon the intrinsic appeal of reason. Erikson's statements about "a high degree of rational assent" and "a ready consent to a formulated good'' make it clear that his appeal to ethical rules is close to what may be called the intrinsic motivation of reason.

The onset of morality is described by Freud, and for that matter also by Piaget, as the internalization of alien requirements. The superego arises out the crisis of the Oedipal conflict that attends a young child's relationship with his parents. The withdrawal from the mother and the idealization of the father—in the case of the boy—satisfies both libidinal and aggressive instincts in the child. The result is a transformation in the ego such that a permanent tension is established, largely at an unconscious level, between ideal demands and actual performance. Henceforth the observant superego initiates repression and inhibition, which are accompanied by an eternal sense of guilt. Such is the price of civilization.

Erikson is quite willing to accept Freud's description of the onset of morality, but with a noticeable change in emphasis. The passing of developmental crises establishes not only certain neurotic tendencies but also new ego strength. The child's first year brings not only oral dependency but also some degree of trust and hope. The second and third years bring not only elements of shame and compulsiveness but also some degree of autonomy, will, and generosity. So, too, the Oedipal crisis brings not only guilt and self-condemnation but also some sense of initiative and purpose. The other side of the accusing superego is the sponsoring superego. An encouraging element is to be found in the superego, which need not always be cruel and derisive, even though it may always retain the capacity to become so.

Erikson builds upon several concepts that were muted in our description of Freud, and legitimately so, since Freud himself gave them little attention. I speak of the superego as the repository of self-esteem and the locus of the ego ideal. The superego dispenses self-esteem upon the ego when the latter acts in appropriate ways. Thereby the superego takes over the sense of comfort and protection that was once given by the parents, particularly the father. The superego is also the locus of group ideals that guide a person throughout life. As a person more or less succeeds in living according to those ideals, he experiences within himself a sense of worth and genuine self-love.

The important point is that the superego serves not only as a source of aggression and rage against the ego; it also preserves the sense of self-worth. A superego that is relatively free of pathological tendencies is a source of encouragement by which the deeply ambivalent motives accompanying all human behavior are overcome. With the resolution of the Oedipal conflict the child is more or less prepared to enter into a wide variety of social relationships and to act out of an internalized sense of self-worth that may be influenced by, but is not wholly dependent upon, the ideals of other persons and groups.[11]

These considerations prompt Erikson to say, "The 'Oedipal' stage thus eventually results not only in a moral sense constricting the horizon of the permissible; it also sets the direction toward the possible and the tangible which attaches infantile dreams to the varied goals of technology and culture."[12] Solidarity with group ideals may strengthen volition and integrity, extending "the horizon of the permissible," while an accusing superego diminishes self-worth, constricting volition and imagination. As in the case of hope and will, purpose is established as a mutual relationship between parent and child. "Something passes from the [father's] bodily presence into the child's budding self."[13]

We should emphasize, nevertheless, that whatever the ratio of self-punitive versus self-loving capacity that is established between parent and child, the superego remains an archaic, internalized, and largely unconscious proclivity to authority. Erikson seems to be uncertain whether the superego is a mental mechanism that has become irretrievably established by evolutional development, or whether the emotional excesses of the superego might be bypassed with proper understanding, though he seems to lean to the former view.

Whereas the superego may dispense a divine assurance of well-being, it is also equally capable of releasing great wells of infantile rage whenever ideals fail or obligations are not followed. Consider the rage of Adolf Hitler, which became such a potent force in Nazi Germany. Erikson believes Hitler's behavior exhibited a double ambivalence toward both his father and his mother. He despised the petty office that his father held. Until he died he refused to become a father, either in the sense of propagating children or in the sense of protecting Germany. He yearned for and detested the simple childlike virtues of women. This double attitude is reflected in his relationship to Eva Braun, whom he loved (illegitimately) and whom he shot to death. By him the mother-nation was highly exalted and almost totally destroyed. His drive for unity of will and purpose demanded repression, destruction, and total solutions, of which the most despicable was his policy of slaughtering the Jews.[14]

By way of contrast, compare Martin Luther, in whom Erikson finds a similarly severe Oedipal dilemma. Luther, however, was able to find unity of purpose and direction, a sense of identity, a new ego strength that was not overcome by infantile rage. Luther, who was probably cruelly punished by his father, long fought his father's wish for him to become a lawyer, and later fought the Pope's wishes on a grand historical scale. Yet Luther was fortunate enough to have a faithful and confident confessor in Staupitz, through whom he could regain a sense of purpose and resolution. In his reading of the Psalms and the Pauline Epistles, in the words "justification by faith," Luther found an identity that could contain his abysmal ambivalence. Significantly, his newly found ego strength permitted him to marry and to father children, while at the same time sponsoring the rebirth of the church.

The early years of childhood are the occasion for the establishment of moral impulses and values that, for the most part, dominate the ego throughout life. They can be either a source of strength or of weakness, but more mature ideals cannot be espoused without passing through the encouraging or demanding imperatives of infantile morality. The way that early (perhaps conflicting) imperatives will be generalized, altered, reconciled, and justified in a way of life remains for later development to disclose.

## Childhood Ideals

We have seen how the ego ideal can "sponsor" a person's initiative. We now want to lay special emphasis upon the way that ideals are modified and generalized during childhood. The ideal not only gives the ego a sense of worth, but it also has a social side, being held in common with family, class, or nation. After initial identification with the ideals of parents, the child turns to the ideals of teachers and other significant persons in his social world. So it is that parental ideals become generalized and modified to coincide with larger social groups.

Erikson lays special stress upon the distinction between the archaic superego and the more flexible, more nearly conscious ego ideal.

> The superego is conceived as a more archaic, more thoroughly internalized and more unconscious representative of man's inborn proclivity toward the development of a primitive, categorical conscience. Allied with early introjects, the superego thus remains a rigidly vindictive and punitive inner agency of "blind" morality. The ego ideal, however, seems to be more flexibly and consciously bound to the ideals of the particular historical era as absorbed in childhood. It is closer to the ego function of reality testing: ideals can change.[15]

This quotation indicates that the superego is more primitive, internalized, unconscious, authoritarian, punitive, and blind than the ego ideal, which is characteristically more flexible, conscious, reality-oriented, and related to history. The ego ideal represents "a set of to-be-striven-for but forever not-quite-attainable goals for the Self."[16]

From Erikson's brief remarks it is not entirely clear whether ideals belong primarily to the Oedipal period, to latency, or to adolescence. Since they are more mature than categorical *ego* *ideals*

commands, but less so than identity, it would seem that they fit into the period of latency, ages six to ten or twelve. Initiated by parental values and completed during the identity crisis of adolescence, ideals develop and expand as a child forms various significant relationships with persons and groups. Please notice that this is the time for which Piaget has documented the increasing ability of the child to make mature moral judgments —*to move* as she passes from an attitude of unilateral respect to mutual respect. The expansion of ideals fits together nicely with Piaget's observations about moral generalization during childhood. Ideals are interwoven with the child's proficiency in playing games, using language, relating to others her own age, and acquiring the various skills that are necessary for adult life.

The particular ego strength involved is that of competence. Should a child be plagued by a sense of guilt and self-restriction rather than self-confidence, she will have difficulty achieving a sense of competence. Unable to acquire the skills that others acquire, or to meet the ideals that she shares with those who are significant for her, both children and adults, she will be weakened by a sense of inferiority. From some mixture of the strength of competence and the weakness of inferiority, the child approaches the adolescent identity crisis. Otherwise stated, on the basis of values that are modified and extended, espoused or despised, the adolescent approaches the general orientation that will become her way of life.

There is, in Erikson's view, always an interweaving between ego needs and institutional structures. A child's needs for competence are met in technical societies by moral training in schools. The strengths or weaknesses of the schools are mutually reflected in the values that the child espouses. In less technical societies apprenticeship serves the same function. The survival of both society and the individual depends upon a mutual strengthening of institution and child. The early "tribal" conscience of the family is expanded and generalized to the "social" conscience of the wider society.

## The Sense of Identity

A unique characteristic of Erikson's theory is that it extends the pattern of epigenesis throughout the life-span. Whereas Freud considered morality to be exclusively a survival of infantilism, Erikson proposes that throughout the course of life there occur significant crises, the resolution of which is determinative for morality in its more mature forms. This is especially evident in his description of adolescence.

In classical psychoanalytic thought adolescence is a renewal of the Oedipal dilemma after a long period of relative quiet, during which the body grows in strength and general capability. Adolescence is the time when a person attains some degree of mature genitality. Such maturity involves (1) the unifying of sexual orgasm and sexual needs from other parts of the body, (2) the unifying of love and sexuality, and (3) the unifying of sexual, procreative, and work productive patterns.[17]

In the Erikson proposal the psychosocial modality that corresponds to mature genitality is the formation of a secure identity. The concept of identity, perhaps oversimplified, is the selective continuity of unique experience in its relationship to social roles, institutions, and ideals. The term admittedly has multiple connotations. At one time it refers to (1) a conscious sense of individual uniqueness, (2) an unconscious striving for continuity of experience, (3) a solidarity with group ideals. Identity includes both the synthesizing function of the ego and the integration of self and role images.[18] Whereas the ego ideal is never quite attainable, ego identity is the actually attained but forever to be revised sense of the reality of the self within social reality.

A remarkable expression of the meaning of identity is to be found in the following quotation from William James:

> Hitherto, when I have felt like taking a free initiative, like daring to act originally, without carefully waiting for contemplation of the external world to determine all for me, suicide seemed the most daring form to put my daring into; now, I will go a step

further with my will, not only act with it, but believe as well; believe in my individual reality and creative power. My belief, to be sure, can't be optimistic—but I will posit life (the real, the good) in *the self-governing resistance of the ego to the world.* Life shall [be built in] doing and suffering and creating.[19]

Identity involves not only putting all childhood identifications and ideals into a pattern that is uniquely one's own, but implies mutual recognition and confirmation. For instance, Henry James, Sr.'s report of his son's "great and liberating thought experience" includes the following comment: "He has been shaking off his respect for men of mere science as such, and is even more universal and impartial in his mental judgments than I have known him."[20] The liberating experience and its recognition by another significant person are mutually related.

Adolescence is a period of social role play, during which various available roles are tried on for size. A person may take a moratorium, rejecting normal social roles for a period of one or several years. A negative identity can border on the pathological, as in the case of William James, who moved from art school to medical school, from New England to South America to Europe. He spent his late twenties as a "neurotic invalid" in his father's home. It was not until he was thirty that he accepted a teaching position in anatomy at Harvard, and thence, in his own words, "drifted into psychology and from a sort of fatality."[21]

The environment of personal identity is not only persons and institutions, but history itself. Psychohistorical actuality is "the sum of historical facts and forces which are of immediate relevance to the adaptive anticipations and maladaptive apprehensions in the individuals involved."[22] History shapes individuals, who in turn shape history. William James's resolution of his own identity crisis resulted in his own philosophy of pragmatism, which in turn has become a major force in the wider American identity. Luther's "Here I stand. I can do no other" not only expressed a resolution of his own identity crisis; it became a powerful force reshaping the modern world. Tragically, Hitler's "final solution" to the Jewish problem became a demonic negative identity for the modern world.

What is the peculiarly ethical quality of adolescence? Youth must work out an ideology which they can call their own, which they share with significant other persons, and into which they can pour an array of powerful and conflicting impulses. They must work out some justification for the values and ideals to which they are to commit their lives. Youth gain the capacities by which they can consider the universal principles of human good. "The adolescent learns to grasp the flux of time, to anticipate the future in a coherent way, to perceive ideas and to assent to ideals, to take—in short—an *ideological* position for which the younger child is not cognitively prepared." [23]

The importance of new cognitive capacity reminds us of Piaget's discovery that youth are able to conceptualize the general moral principles by which the rules or moral reasoning are judged, whereas the child is limited to the application of rules. Erikson, however, stresses something that Piaget ignores. Youth's new capacity for ethical reasoning is no guarantee of *actual* ethical reasoning. "In adolescence, then, an ethical view is approximated, but it remains susceptible to an alteration of impulsive judgment and odd rationalization." [24]

The excessive energies of youth, the quest for new experience as well as orientation, may take the form of prophetic idealism. The civil rights marches, the Peace Corps, and the campus demonstrations are examples of energetic rebellion against current injustice in the name of a new and more noble world order. However, elements of idealism may be combined with ever-present infantile rage in the form of destructive fanaticism. The Weathermen marches in Chicago in 1970 seemed to combine elements of the highest idealism with vicious and destructive impulses.

Paul Taylor's study of ethical language offers four levels of moral discourse: (1) moral prescriptions are justified in relation to (2) moral rules and values. Value is surely quite close to what we mean by ideals. Value in turn receives its validation by (3) the reasonable cannons of the "moral point of view." The latter is vindicated by a more total orientation called (4) "a way of life." [25] We might diagram the hierarchy of orientation as follows:

> Way of life
> Moral point of view
> Moral rules and values (ideals)
> Moral prescriptions

By the age of adolescence, youth have gained the rational capacity to take a moral point of view. However, youth may, and often do, act impulsively at the level of prescriptions and rules, which means that they often appeal to lower levels of moral discourse without regard to the higher. In Erikson's view it is normal for youth to "play" with various points of view before coming to that larger orientation which he calls identity and which certainly includes preference for a way of life.

With a more or less satisfactory resolution of the identity crisis, youth gain a peculiarly new ego strength which may be called fidelity. Fidelity is a sense of being enough at one with oneself, one's community, and one's historical epoch that he can give a lifetime of commitment and care to those concerns that are worthwhile. [26] The sponsoring conscience comes to include fidelity to what one is in his own group and in his own time.

### The True Ethical Sense

The resolution of the adolescent identity crisis prepares the way for adult responsibility. Freud had little to say about the peculiar crises of adult life, except for his concept of "mature genitality," which we have already mentioned. Simply stated, the mature person can learn to love and to work without either inhibiting the other.

To Freud's psychosexual description of mature genitality, Erikson adds the psychosocial element of intimacy. Adults must develop not only a satisfactory sexual exchange, but also a style of intimacy in all realms of social intercourse. Failure to do so will leave a deep sense of isolation that in turn limits adult creative potentiality. Every adult will develop some balance of intimacy and isolation in relationships with other adults, but especially in the relationship between husband and wife.

The peculiar ego strength of adulthood is the capacity to love. Freud was biting in his analysis of the repressive character of the love commandment. He thought it to be civilization's exaggerated effort to stay the destructive impulses of human nature. Erikson avoids that criticism by considering love to be an ego strength rather than a moral inhibition. Love is rooted in the ego's capacity to activate strength in another ego while exercising its own. Thus, nothing is so satisfying as the mutual recognition that two persons give one another, and nothing is so enraging as the withholding of such recognition.

The true ethical sense "encompasses and goes beyond moral restraint and ideal vision, while insisting on concrete commitments to those intimate relationships and work associations by which man can hope to share a lifetime of productivity and competence."[27] The immediate commitments of the true ethical sense also have their danger. They may lead to a kind of defensiveness of one's own group or territory or nation that gives expression to a deeper sense of isolation and despair.

The true ethical sense is the culmination of the direction set by the sponsoring conscience. Premoral hope leads to purpose, value, fidelity to a way of life; and that in turn leads to committed care for what is worthy in life. However, every ego has its own weakness, so that persons are tempted by despair, primitive tribal demands, inability to perform according to ideals, confusion about a way of life, and defensiveness about their own narrowly defined group. The true ethical sense (could we say the mature conscience?) has the qualities of spontaneity, rational assent, and mutuality, while the accusing conscience has the qualities of impulsiveness, arbitrariness, and loss of mutual control. All human life is lived with some mixture of these qualities.

## *The Meaning of Freedom*

We turn now from a rather schematic description of Erikson's view to a more critical comment about his use of ethical language. Crucial for our analysis will be an attempt to characterize his view of moral freedom. I use "moral" now as a reference to what is normative rather than to what is infantile. Let us begin again with a brief statement about what Freud meant by freedom.

Our clue is the method of "free association," according to which a patient expresses whatever spontaneously comes to mind, with absolutely no limitations imposed upon what is acceptable. Much of Freud's work was given over to discovering what inhibits free expression. He concluded that spontaneity of expression is modified according to the reality principle. Freedom is that degree of spontaneity consonant with the fullest awareness of inner and outer consequences. Freudian freedom remains exclusively internal, intrapsychic, and nonpolitical. "Freedom is no more than a metaphor, for Freud, when applied to any form of society; it can be properly said to exist only within the person, when there is a right balance among parts of the psyche."[28]

Contrast Piaget's concept of freedom as a fine balance of spontaneity, rationality, equality, and mutual consent. Mature moral judgments become possible as a youth comes to appreciate and exercise a combination of mature intelligence and mutual respect. Maturity of intelligence and mutuality can be fully realized only in a society of equals, all of whom recognize the reciprocal basis of moral judgment.

I believe that we may discover Erikson's understanding of human freedom by examining his view of "ego strength." Erikson has chosen to speak of strength rather than freedom, but it is important to grasp what kind of freedom is implied in ego strength if we are to appreciate his use of ethical language. Furthermore, ego strength is the central thrust of all of Erikson's

*writing*

writing, the thrust that gives his writing a much different ethical quality than that of Freud.

Many psychoanalysts have come to believe that the ego is not a late formation in the life of human instincts brought on by the press of external threat. Rather, the ego is already functioning in the infant at birth, established during the long course of human evolution as a precondition of all human experience. The characteristics of the ego are therefore constitutive for human freedom. The ego is free in its strength and bound in its weakness. This at least is our contention, and so we want now to look to ego strength for the characteristics of freedom. These may, I believe, be considered under four headings: (1) awareness, (2) volition, (3) coherence, and (4) mutuality. Let us see how Erikson's ideas support our notion of human agency.

Erikson is himself fond of speaking of this ego as an "agency." The following quotation will serve to illustrate.

> [The ego is] the domain of an inner "agency" safeguarding our coherent existence by screening and synthesizing, in any series of moments, all the impressions, emotions, memories, and impulses which try to enter our thought and demand our action, and which would tear us apart if unsorted and unmanaged by a slowly grown and reliably watchful screening system.[29]

(1) The first mark of the freedom of agency is awareness or insight. The ego is free to the extent that it is unfettered from debilitating defenses and emotional conflicts. An example of a person who lacks insight is one who is unable to act because of an extreme inner turmoil which is so painful that the person would rather not think about it. During his twenties, William James was just such a person. He was time and again on the verge of emotional collapse, unable to gain insight into his own emotional struggle. Rollo May writes about the modern sexual compulsiveness, which measures a person by overt sexual behavior but lacks insight into the feelings that are often blocked off from such behavior. All neurotic behavior is an

inability to be aware of deeper feelings, and thereby the loss of awareness limits the freedom of human agency.

(2) Occasionally Erikson uses the term *agens* to denote the volition, a second quality of ego strength. The term refers to "an inner state of being unbroken in initiative and of acting in the service of a cause which sanctions this initiative." The loss of volitional strength might be designated by *patiens,* "a state of being exposed from within or without to superior forces which cannot be overcome without prolonged patience or energetic and redeeming help." [30]

Volition, or *agens,* is not the same as overt activity, which is often controlled by unconscious impulses or inhibitions. Rather volition is an inner intentional state which may find expression in either activity or passivity. However, should the ego lose its tension with actuality, then it becomes exposed to the over-whelming power of instinctual impulses and inhibitions.

"The ego's over-all task is, in the simplest terms, to turn passive into active, that is, to screen the impositions of its counterplayers in such a way that they become volitions." [31] The "counterplayers" referred to above are basic impulses, the restrictive conscience, and the controlling power of other persons. Basic impulses, when touched by the ego, may become familiar and enjoyable motives. Conscience may become bearable and supportive of active expression. Interpersonal relationships may become mutually enhancing.

The volitional quality of ego is to be seen in its screening, selecting, and choosing. Screening goes on at a preconscious level in which memories and experiences are admitted to awareness. Thus *agens* is an unconscious as well as a conscious quality of ego, equally characteristic of infants and adults. Dreaming is a preconscious activity by which the ego regains its volitional powers. At a higher level of awareness, volition is expressed as conscious and deliberate choosing. The higher activity of volition allows people to be purposefully related to their environment. When in control of its own divergent impulses, the ego can anticipate, plan, choose, and act in relation to other actors and various conditions.

(3) A third characteristic of ego strength, and therefore of freedom, is coherence. The ego is the "guardian" of individuality, unity, and indivisibility, "a selective, integrating, coherent and persistent agency."[32] From an overwhelming variety of memories, emotions, and perceptions, the ego strives to establish and to maintain some degree of individuality, intelligence, and integrity. The ego grants continuity to the rich variety of experience with which it is constantly confronted, albeit a continuity that must be constantly revised in face of new experience. The ego establishes and maintains relative coherence by selecting from and integrating the discontinuous moments of experience.

The integrating activity of the ego moves simultaneously in several directions. It brings together what has already occurred with what is now and what is yet anticipated, thereby maintaining some sense of persistence and permanence through time. It brings together the wide range and variety of experiences, thereby maintaining a sense of integrity. It relates perception of itself with perceptions that other persons hold, thereby maintaining a more or less conscious sense of selfhood. It strives for some organization of experience, thereby maintaining some sense of orientation and meaning.

In a word, the ego gives centeredness to experience, the conscious and unconscious awareness of what is uniquely one's own. To the extent that such awareness is conscious, it is designated by the pronoun "I." The ego also differentiates itself from what is not "I," but is rather "you" or "he" or "it." The integrating capacity of the ego is then again seen in mutuality, the joining together and "interliving" of more than one person, designated by the pronoun "we." What the ego totally disowns may become an alien force, internal or external, against which it needs to preserve its coherence.

Rationality is a capacity of the ego. Perhaps we should consider rationality as a separate characteristic of ego strength rather than discussing it as a part of coherence. There is, however, no doubt that Erikson considers the use of intelligence to be a mark of ego strength. In any case, rationality involves selective awareness, deliberation, reality testing, establishing priority, and finding continuity in multiple experiences. Intelligence brings coherence between inner impulses and external reality. On the other hand, intelligence may be driven by unconscious chaotic impulses. To the extent that rationality is driven by such impulses, the ego has lost its strength, hence its freedom. Rationality is thus a mark of freedom.

(4) Finally, the ego, and therefore human freedom, is characterized by mutuality. The most important element in the ego's environment is another ego. Nor are egos accidentally related to one another. Every ego is related to other egos in a process of mutual activation and regulation. This fact is not disproved by the hermit, for he too was dependent in infancy, interprets his behavior in terms of a language he learned from others, and survives by skills he learned in a process of interaction with others. Parent and child, teacher and pupil, doctor and patient, friend and friend—the ego strength of each activates that of the other as they carry out their separate functions. We may also say that the freedom of each is enhanced by the freedom of the other.

Persons are so related that the inner world of one ego is organized to include the reality of another ego, and similarly the inner world of the latter is organized to include the former. Hence, a mutual confirmation serves to strengthen both ego and other. It is worth mentioning again that nothing is so satisfying as mutual recognition and confirmation between egos. On the other hand, nothing is so prone to release uncontrollable and destructive rage as the inward denial of one ego by another.

Our comments thus far might be interpreted to indicate that mutuality is restricted to the interpersonal realm. Such a conclusion is not true. Institutions and historical events both activate and weaken individual egos. We have already cited Martin Luther's identity crisis as an instance of mutuality between ego and historical event. The events of Martin Luther's life in turn activate hundreds of thousands of others. Witness the dramatic effect that the assassination of President John F. Kennedy had upon most Americans, or the powerful effect that the fasting of Mahatma Ghandi had upon his followers.

Before concluding our discussion of freedom, let us make a brief comment on the "illusion of freedom." Erikson is one with Freud in maintaining that persons entertain certain collective illusions and secret delusions in order to guard their individuality and integrity. Among these are the sense of freedom of choice. Freedom may be characterized as "the effort through which the inevitable comes to pass—or the will to choose what is necessary. Man is a creature who does well if he manages to restore or undo what he has upset and wrought in the tiny and dark corner that he, at best, can know."[33]

One is reminded of Kant's reference to the stars above and the conscience within as marks of human freedom. Both seem to have gone out in the "tiny and dark corner" that we can at best know. If persons tend to project their small measure of freedom upon omnipotent kings, priests, and gods, they also tend to project their doubts upon all being. In the above references, Erikson draws back from the implications of his own view of ego. Freud's ego was an epiphenomenon of the struggle between impulse and dark fate.[34] Erikson's ego has a limited autonomy with supports as well as threats.

The ego has an unconscious strength that is given even before awareness, even though threatened by multiple urges. The ego receives support in the "expectable environment" of human institutions and nature, even though beset by restriction, hunger, and death. Fate has a quality of charity as well as necessity. One need only recognize that the ego's freedom makes an experienceable difference in the course of human life, without denying that it is hemmed in on all sides within and without.[35] Surely Erikson would admit that Freud's discoveries have made a discernible difference in the course of the twentieth century, especially in America. The concepts of awareness, volition, coherence, and mutuality, taken together, move beyond inevitability, if only in the fact that other egos are the major environmental reality for every ego.

I suspect that, far from denying what he has affirmed about the ego, Erikson is attempting to quicken his reader's awareness of their own limited freedom. The danger is that our dizzy illusions about what humanity can do are serving sadistic and destructive impulses. Awakened from our isolated and compulsive attempts to storm the universe, aware of our drive to turn human reality into a machine, we may regain a freedom that is spontaneous, coherent, and mutually related to the freedom of all. If this interpretation is correct, the illusion of unlimited freedom is a culprit, unconsciously covering the limited but actual freedom we may enjoy.

We may summarize Erikson's view of human freedom under these points:

1) spontaneous expression not controlled by unconscious defenses, perceptual distortion, or ideology;
2) strong volition and intentionality;
3) conscious, rational deliberation and choice with constantly revised and renewed coherence of experience, meaning, purpose, and ideals;
4) mutuality between persons, institutions, and events such that each enhances all and all enhance each.

### Virtue and Character

The classical self-realization ethic of Aristotle defined virtue as a habit of deciding correctly. The good man decides and acts from such a habit, while the evil man decides and acts from the opposite habit of deciding incorrectly. Immanuel Kant was less concerned about virtue as a reasonable habit and more concerned about virtue as a volition that may be expressed in the maxims by which we act. Erikson's analysis has some affinities to both views.

Recall how Erikson sets virtue within an epigenetic

framework. This means that the ego is faced repeatedly with crises that threaten its freedom. The source of these threats may be either the maturation of the body and its various capacities or the changing requirements of persons, institutions, and history. The important point to be made, however, is that each crisis has the effect of limiting the freedom of the ego in every crisis that follows it. Relative success in the resolution of a crisis means strength and freedom, while relative failure means weakness and impulsiveness. A weak ego meets succeeding crises already vulnerable.

One may well ask whether a person's past is not irrelevant to whether this act should or should not be done. Are not normative judgments about ethics and therapeutic judgments about emotional health two different kinds of judgments? Consider how Sidney Carton in Dickens's *Tale of Two Cities,* wag though he was, made the supreme sacrifice of himself to the guillotine in order that his beloved might escape death. Would one judge this act by his emotional health? Or consider the work of Kierkegaard, Dostoevski, William James, and others who went through periods of severe emotional upset. Perhaps those very experiences contributed to rather than weakened their creative work.

To answer this question we need to be reminded that ego strength is characterized by awareness, volition, intelligence, deliberative choice, coherence, and mutuality. Whatever weakens the ego also limits its freedom as just described. Consequently, an act done from impulse rather than volition, from ideology rather than coherent and deliberative purpose, is right only in an external sense of the word. A genuinely right (or good) act must be done with maximum freedom. Those factors that limit freedom, among which one must include previously established and continuing impulses, are relevant to the consideration whether any act is right or good.

Erikson shies away from the use of the term "character." He finds it to be too static to describe the constant modification by which the ego maintains relative coherence; therefore, he speaks of identity. Negative identity and role confusion may mean that the ego must go through a long period of patient suffering and/or a redeeming encounter before a coherent identity can be established. The identity gained through such crises will and must include the experience of suffering in the newly found coherence. In this sense, suffering is always a contributing element in creativity.

The freedom of an act is not to be judged by some arbitrary reading of past events, as though the ego had been absorbed by fate. The past affects the present and the future in terms of the personal significance it has in addition to its determinative power. Whether or not virtue is habitual—and I suspect that it is only in a very limited sense—virtue implies that the freedom of the past in a very real way limits or expands the possibilities for free expression in the present and the future.

## The Golden Rule

We cannot avoid asking whether there is an intrinsic reasonableness in human affairs. The answer is a provisional yes, even though it be restricted, threatened, and distorted by powerful forces. The initial focus is upon *freedom* as a quality of lived experience. The good life refers to freedom's horizon of possibilities. "I would advocate a general orientation which has its center in whatever activity or activities gives man the feeling, as William James put it, of being 'most deeply and intensely active and alive.'"[36] We have already analyzed this "feeling" in the discussion of freedom above.

The ethic of human freedom is one of *mutuality,* by which Erikson intends to include both equality and reciprocity. Mutual threat is not a mark of freedom, but of weakness for both parties. Truly worthwhile acts promote a mutuality between the doer and the other—a mutuality that strengthens the doer even as it strengthens the other. Again let it be emphasized that the "other" may be an institution as well as a person. Only as persons and groups learn to express their own strength, that is, freedom, in behalf of the freedom of others, only then will the strength of both be enhanced.

The principle of mutuality must be interpreted through the principle of what Erikson likes to call *equity*. "This means that the doer is activated in whatever strength is *appropriate to his age, stage, and condition,* even as he activates in the other the strength appropriate to *his* age, stage, and condition."[37] Equity is more than the strong protecting the weak, which often is a form of dominating control. The freedom of the strong, for example, parent, teacher, doctor, civic leader, is enhanced as they strengthen the freedom of the weak on the way toward maturity. As the weak exercise their freedom, without controlling the strong by means of dependency relationships, they expand the freedom of the other. Each in an appropriate situation can strengthen the other by exercising his own strength.

Conscience in Erikson's description usually refers to the immature inhibitions of early childhood, but conscience in both everyday and historical use has a different meaning. It commonly means the integrity of personality, "the circle of self-being" (Heidegger). Conscience in the latter sense is a striving for coherence, a call of a spontaneity, unity, and mutuality that is as yet incomplete. It is the possibility of the coherence of the purpose and deed. But coherence entails the relationship of each to all and all to each. The silence and pliability of conscience in the latter sense is often overcome, though never completely contained, by infantile moralism.

In infancy, conscience is born of the possibility of reciprocal trust and goodwill between infant and parent. Later this becomes the possibility of reciprocal purpose with minimal guilt. In their turn come common ideals, identity, and commitment, with minimal shame, confusion, and arbitrariness. The struggle of conscience becomes a struggle between tribal loyalties and the possibilities of human freedom. Apparently, so long as people are born as infants and grow toward maturity among their own kind, they will never be able to avoid this struggle.

# Chapter III

## WHICHEVER COMES HANDIEST:
### *Conscience and Reason*

*They went off and I got aboard the raft, feeling bad and low,*
*because I knowed very well I had done wrong, and I see it warn't*
*no use for me to try to learn to do right; a body that don't get*
*started right when he's little, ain't got no show—when the pinch*
*comes there ain't nothing to back him up and keep him to his*
*work, and so he gets beat. Then I thought a minute, and says to*
*myself, hold on—s'pose you'd a done right and give Jim up;*
*would you felt better than what you do now? No, says I, I'd feel*
*bad—I'd feel just the same way I do now. Well, then, says I,*
*what's the use of learning to do right, when its troublesome to do*
*right and ain't no trouble to do wrong, and the wages is just the*
*same? I was stuck. I couldn't answer that. So I reckoned I*
*wouldn't bother no more about it, but after this always do*
*whichever come handiest at the time.* —Mark Twain

These ruminations of Huckleberry Finn occur just after he has
deceived two men trying to recapture the runaway slave whom
he has just helped to escape. Huck has always been taught to
look down upon black people and to keep them in their place; to
do otherwise goes against what his conscience tells him is right.
He is quite sure he will turn the slave, Jim, in, until he is faced
with the two men searching for him. They ask Huck to indicate
who is on the raft, to which Huck replies that a man is there.
They then ask whether he is black. Now Huck is brought face to
face with whether he will deliver Jim over to his tormentors,

*71*

something he had already resolved to do. There is a moment of hesitation. He cannot do it. After a fumbling silence the words come out, ''He is white.'' They insist in checking for themselves. Then with great ingenuity Huck makes up a story about his father being on the raft and needing help to tow the raft in. The two men suspect that the ''father'' has smallpox and quickly leave. At that point Huck has the above conversation about the ''wrong'' he has done in not turning Jim in. He concludes that since he will feel guilty whichever way he acts, he might as well do whatever comes handiest at the time.

The dilemma posed by Mark Twain in such a delightful way is a classic one. Immanuel Kant asked the question whether you should tell a murderer the truth about where to find his intended victim when you are hiding that person in your house. Kant's conclusion is that one must speak the truth since one cannot make a universal rule out of lying in order to avoid other evils. Were everyone to follow such a rule, truth would soon be impossibly disrupted, and the moral fabric of human relationships would be damaged. It is therefore essential to the character of morality to preserve truth-telling without exception, even at the expense of a human life.

Many people have been scandalized at Kant's position, as Mark Twain himself clearly is. Huck responds to the query of the two men out of respect for Jim as a person; he is not all that emotionally attached to Jim. Furthermore, as long as turning Jim in requires the additional effort of sneaking away and bringing someone back, Huck might be excused on the grounds that it requires too much effort. However, when the two men appear and are prepared to take Jim, so that all Huck needs to do is keep silent, then surely the easiest course would be simply to let them proceed. In spite of what Huck says, he takes the more difficult course in running the risk of deceiving the men, and he does it because his conscience would feel equally bad to do so as not to do so. In the terms in which we have been speaking Huck makes a decision out of the strength of agency rather than from the weakness of his primitive accusing conscience. Mark Twain is appealing to the reader's sense of common humanity which will in some instances tell a lie in order to keep another person from great suffering.

Dietrich Bonhoeffer was equally scandalized at the Kantian position.[1] Bonhoeffer asked whether one should reveal the hiding place of a Jew to a Nazi searching for Jews. Bonhoeffer concluded that even though we all stand under the obligation to tell the truth, as Kant had said, we must be willing to suffer the guilt of lying in order to act charitably to our neighbor. A Christian will follow Christ's example in taking guilt upon himself in order to serve the need of a neighbor. Bonhoeffer therefore approved of Huck's "wrongdoing."

A more recent commentator is Lawrence Kohlberg, who poses the same dilemma to children and youth in order to see how advanced they are in their moral development.[2] Kohlberg's conviction is that Kant does not clearly distinguish between the rule to tell the truth and the principle of justice, that is, "the right of every person to equal consideration of his claims in every situation" and the obligation to "treat each person as an end, not as a means." In Kohlberg's view, the principle of justice is supreme, for therein the inviolability of the freedom of every individual is recognized. Rules like truth-telling are ultimately for the sake of the freedom of the individual, so that if a conflict between truth-telling and justice arises, clearly the obligation stands on the side of justice. The murderer has as much claim as the intended victim to "equal consideration of his claims" and to being treated "as an end, and not as a means," but that in no way entails that he be given the truth about the whereabouts of his intended victim. Kant seems to presume that social order is a precondition to individual liberty, but Kohlberg argues, and I think rightly so, that social order presumes freedom of the individual. Ordinarily, social order enhances individual freedom, and admittedly the relationship between them is very close, but to violate the individual for the sake of order is finally to cut away the rationale for order. Therefore,

Huck chose the more profound obligation in lying for the sake of Jim's freedom.

The humor in Mark Twain's account seems to come from the contradiction between what Huck does and what he says. Huck acts as a person who has accepted the custom of oppressing a minority, but who wrestles his way to giving equal consideration to the claim of a minority person, and to treating him as an end, and not as a means. In other words, he acts as a person who is moving from conventional customary morality to a higher ethical stance. His reasons for his behavior do not, however, correspond to the deeds themselves. He speaks of the rightness of customary behavior: "I see it warn't no use for me to try to learn to do right." He also speaks of what a good person the slave owner is, and how he has no reason to injure her. Then he observes that he will feel bad in either case, and that usually doing the right is more difficult. Since one cannot avoid feeling guilty, he might as well do what comes handiest, that is, the easiest, a clear statement of hedonism.

As we have already observed, Huck has not done what comes handiest, else he would have simply given in to the two men who were seeking the runaway. Rather Huck acted with considerable courage and great ingenuity. But he seems unaware of this, and his statement about "whichever comes handiest" shows itself to be a lower-level rationalization for a higher-level decision. Just this contradiction between what Huck says and what he does certainly adds a note of humor. A possible undertone of the passage is that people usually do the reverse, giving higher-level reasons for lower-level behavior. Huck's "naïve" rationalization in the reverse direction is perhaps a humorous but biting chastisement of the human propensity to give high reasons for low behavior.

Twain's account of Huck and Jim raises a question about Kohlberg's investigations of the development of moral judgment. Kohlberg has argued that the most observable and verifiable consistency of moral behavior is the logical structure of the reasons we give for what we do.[3] Consideration of inconvenience to other persons is a higher-level argument than consideration only of one's own advantage (hedonism). Consideration of social order is a higher-level argument than that of inconvenience to other persons, and consideration of the rights of a minority person is a higher-level argument than that of social order alone. Huck's reasoning, though, does not match his behavior, as we have shown above. This raises a serious question about whether one can assess moral maturity in terms of the way one reasons about a moral dilemma. True enough, Kohlberg acknowledges that moral reasoning lags behind the growth of reason in any individual.[4] He may also follow Jean Piaget's dictum that moral reasoning tends to be elaborated only after moral behavior has been established. Even so, the problem still remains: how closely related is moral behavior to the structure of moral reasoning? In my judgment Kohlberg has not attended carefully enough to this question.

Kohlberg attempts to speak to this question when he cites experimental studies in which "principled" undergraduates were less likely to cheat than those who were "unprincipled."[5] The principled persons were separated from those who claimed to believe in a higher level of morality, but whose moral reasoning was at a lower level, that is, the rationalizers. As he reports them, the studies involve a meager number of subjects. Furthermore, they do not touch the Huck Finns, those whose behavior is better than their reasons. It is an important point that needs further consideration.

Aside from the question of the relationship of act and deed, perhaps Mark Twain is pointing up the inconsistencies of the common level of ethical thinking. Huck's concern for the inconvenience to the slave owner totally ignores the inconvenience to the slave. Therefore, a person who thinks purely in terms of convenience to himself, "whichever comes handiest," is at least as moral as the person who considers the claims of some other persons, while ignoring the claims of others. Twain put this not in the formal terminology we have just used, but in the lowest level of what feels best, a level that everyone can understand. It suggests that there may be some feeling for humanity in most of us, and that there may be some correspondence between feeling and the maturity of moral reason. This is something that Kohlberg rules out as unworthy of consideration.[6] It is, however, something that others, including myself, feel to be of considerable importance.[7] Let us consider how reason and the following of rules are related to the formation of conscience. Before we proceed, it may be helpful to look at some of our assumptions about the relationship between conscience and reason.

### Conscience and Reason

There is a long-standing debate between those who consider conscience to be an emotion and those who consider it to be a rational judgment. The first view is sometimes called emotivism, and the second may be called intuitionism. According to the emotivists, conscience is one or another of such emotions as fear, anxiety, pain, desire, satisfaction, security, or pleasure as these become associated with commands, rules, reasons, and policies. "I ought to speak the truth" may mean that I am afraid not to speak the truth or that I have been afraid at some time in the past not to speak the truth and at that time formed the habit of speaking the truth. It may also mean that I am commanded to speak the truth, that I receive great satisfaction, security, and pleasure from telling the truth, or that one of these has happened in the past.

In the emotivist view the same emotion can be quite as well associated with different commands, rules, reasons, and policies, given a different set of circumstances. Just as Huck Finn was taught that he ought to keep a slave in his place, Oliver Twist under Fagan's governance was taught, "You've got to pick a pocket or two." "I ought to lie" may mean that I am afraid to speak the truth, am being commanded to lie, get great satisfaction from lying, or that for me these emotions have been associated with my lying in the past. The emotion of conscience may be attached to many kinds of behavior, including some that are very bizarre. A person's conscience may require one to exercise to the point of physical exhaustion, or to care for an aging parent to the point of hysterical symptoms. An emotivist will ordinarily conclude that conscience is fundamentally irrational, and that it becomes associated with certain reasons or rules according to environmental circumstances. Yet many emotivists are not so unqualified in their hedonism as this account might suggest. An unlimited conflict of emotions would lead to an intolerable situation, but reason permits us to curb our emotions. In Hobbes's view we avoid the "war of all against all" by agreeing to live at peace with one another. By Mill's account, the survival of human life depends upon nurturing and strengthening the sentiment for humanity in one another.[8] According to Freud, human reason is born as the pleasure principle is altered by the reality principle. Since we gain considerable advantages from having and using a language system, we do agree to tell the truth, and we teach our children to do so. It becomes clear that reason may assist us in restraining and redirecting our emotions for the sake of greater satisfactions. The gains from cooperation may be much greater than those of taking what we can get, and deferred pleasures may be considerably greater than more immediate ones.

Reason is then, in the emotivist view, the best tool we have to secure the satisfaction we want. A reasonable people will work out procedures for reconciling the various conflicting moral opinions among themselves. Various moral convictions will be tolerated so long as they do not bring serious harm to other persons or violate the procedures for arbitration. Since in the emotivist view conscience is an emotion that has been associated with a rule, often from early childhood, the dictates of conscience must be judged by reason. If Oliver Twist is reasonable, as he matures he will consider whether the rule "You've got to pick a pocket or two" will gain for him and all others involved the greatest possible satisfaction. So the dictates of conscience may be modified by the considerations of reason. In the same way, Freud argued that therapy occurs when we give voice to what we want and to what is possible, for in that way our feelings are themselves altered. His way of putting it was to say that in therapy the id (and superego) is integrated with the ego.[9] The transactional analytic way of putting it is to say that we grow in satisfaction as we get our strokes from our "adult" rather than our "child" or our "parent."

The intuitionists raise serious questions about the emotivist view. According to the intuitionists, conscience is a part of the structure of rationality itself. Aquinas taught that conscience has a theoretical and a practical side, both essentially expressions of reason. The theoretical side of conscience *(synderesis)* is able intuitively to grasp the fundamental principles by which we direct our lives, for example, respect for persons, truth-telling, and promise-keeping. The practical side of conscience *(conscientia)* is expressed as an intention to act according to the appropriate principle in any given situation. Huck Finn's intuitive respect for another human being *(synderesis)* was expressed as the act of saving Jim from being captured *(conscientia)*.

The intuitionist will ask the emotivist how we know that some pleasures are more desirable than other pleasures. How do we know that the principle of respect for all persons is morally superior to the satisfaction many gain from oppressing a minority? The answer of Kant and those who follow him is that respect for personality is equivalent to respect for reason. Reasonable beings intuitively respect the exercise of reason, which entails a respect for all persons.[10]

Perhaps we can put the matter this way. Any rule such as truth-telling yields a considerable gain for everybody involved, but to accept the rule also presumes the acceptance of the free consent of everyone involved. One cannot participate in truth-telling without tacitly assuming the prior free consent of everyone in the community of discourse, which finally extends to all of humanity. Truth-telling is like all other rules from which we gain social benefit in presuming this tacit foreknowledge of the free consent of persons.

In the intuitivist view, conscience is the instinctive call of reason, which all of us have to some degree. Kant suggested that we can maximize the use of our reason if we suppose that the reasons we give ourselves for acting in a certain way were to apply to all persons in similar circumstances. Otherwise put, every person deserves equal consideration of his or her claims in comparable circumstances. No person may be used simply as a means to our own satisfaction. Are we willing to live by those rules by which we could will that all others live? This is what R. M. Hare calls the criterion of universalizability, and what Piaget and Kohlberg call reversibility.[11]

I suggest that the relationship of reason and conscience can be resolved if we consider conscience to be an expression of human agency. Conscience is first of all a dispositional intention regarding who we are, to whom we belong, and what we shall do. It is therefore an emotion, for emotions connect what we perceive, experience, remember, and anticipate to what we intend, even when the relationship is deeply hidden to ourselves. The immediate connection between a more or less tacit assessment of what we experience and the experience itself is felt as emotion. To set the emotions against the will establishes an artificial division that may lead to a kind of emotionless stoicism.[12] Rather we may say that every intention has its attendant emotion, and every emotion an implicit intentionality. It is the work of therapy to uncover the hidden intentionality in emotion.[13]

Conscience is also an expression that is in some degree coherent, for there is no intention without some degree of coherence. This means that conscience always includes some degree of rationality, some rule, or some schema. Here it is important to distinguish between a mathematical or logical conception of reason and a poetic conception. The first presumes a set of concepts with the rules for their interrelationships strictly and univocally specified. It is the kind of reason that an engineer uses in building a bridge or that an airline pilot uses in charting the course of a flight. This is the reason in which the rules of behavior are clearly specified.

The second kind of reason is that used by the artist to create a painting, by a poet to write a poem, or by a therapist to reach the emotions of another person. The difference is what Paul Tillich called technical reason and the depth of reason. Of course the engineer uses basic artistic understanding in designing the bridge, and the artist uses technical understanding in creating a painting. The two kinds of reason therefore belong to each other and cannot finally be separated. Yet it is important to realize that conscience may be expressed in the strictness of technical reason or in the more analogical relationships of poetic reason.

Conscience is also mutual in that our intentions are formed in interaction with those whom we trust and in a community of common discourse. Conscience carries on the continuing dialogue with the moral community within oneself. It is not simply a daydreaming reflection about some behavior, but rather it is an active and dispositional intention that therefore judges what is already done or what is being contemplated. As a dispositional intention, it continues to carry on the conversations by which the disposition was shaped. It anticipates the responses of the moral community. While persons of conscience may be more or less alone with regard to the opinions of any present group, they are mutually related to the moral community who consider them of worth. It is with the community of mutual loyalty that the conversation goes on, even when that community is not immediately present. This means that the family and other childhood communities are decisive in the shaping of the early levels of conscience, but it also means that the conscience is reshaped by the communities of loyalty throughout life. This reshaping of conscience involves the more mature ranges of human reason.

We conclude that conscience is an intention that includes both emotion and judgment in relation to some form of coherence and reason. It may involve rules in the strict sense, something that is usually considered a mark of conscience. At the same time, it may involve stories and interpretations of our situation that are not quickly and easily reduced to rules. By the time that rules have been specified, the situation may have changed. In this sense conscience may function as an orientation to life that could lead to a variety of rules. In any case, conscience may reflect the differences between the concrete reason of childhood and the formal reason of adulthood, and between the strictness of technical reason and the analogies of poetic reason. With this account of the relation of reason and conscience, we want now to look more carefully at the developmental processes. Before proceeding, let us consider one example of a current attempt to resolve the emotivist-intuitionist controversy.

## The Piaget-Kohlberg Thesis

Jean Piaget and Lawrence Kohlberg, following in Piaget's footsteps, have attempted to avoid the rift between emotivists and intuitionists by conceiving a behavior as a structure that is invented by each person in an effort to resolve the conflicts within experience. Changes of the structure follow certain stages that are universal. Each stage in the development of moral judgment has a logical organization that is different from the preceding stage and will be different from the next stage. Every person passes through these same stages during the course of maturation. Although maturation is not inevitable, the sequence is invariant and cannot be altered by experience. Different experiences or different cultural settings may slow down or speed up the rate of maturation, but will not change the sequence in which the stages appear. The later stages of moral thought are increasingly universal and increasingly able to handle the conflicts within experience. In this way the formalism of the intuitionists is combined with the experientialism of the emotivists, although formalism finally wins out in the last analysis. Let us illustrate these ideas with a brief description of the stages proposed by Piaget and Kohlberg, and then we shall consider the advantages and problems of their thesis.

The relation of conscience and reason as Piaget pictures it can be seen in the following table:

| Stage | Conscience | Moral Reasoning | Age |
|---|---|---|---|
| 0 | Nonrespect | Moral innocence | 0-2 |
| 1 | Unilateral respect | Moral realism | 3-6 |
| 2 | Mixed respect | Concrete reciprocity | 7-10 |
| 3 | Mutual respect | Moral autonomy | 11 plus |

During the stage 0 the child has no attitude toward rules and is not able to reason by using rules. In stage 1 the child considers rules to be eternally true and inviolable, while moral reason is oriented to punishment and reward. During stage 2 there is a growing awareness that rules are established by mutual agreement, and the child begins to reason on the basis of what is fair. However, fairness means strict reciprocity ("an eye for an eye"), usually without regard to motives. Stage 3 permits the child to understand more fully that rules gain their legitimacy by mutual agreement, and that justice includes consideration of both motives and consequences.

By working with teen-aged young people Lawrence Kohlberg has modified and extended Piaget's stages. The relationship of Kohlberg's stages to those of Piaget may be diagramed in this way:[15]

| | *Piaget's stages* | | *Kohlberg's Stages* |
|---|---|---|---|
| 0 | Moral innocence | 0 | Naïve egoism |
| 1 | Moral realism | 1 | Punishment-obedience |
| 2 | Concrete reciprocity | 2 | Concrete reciprocity |
| 3 | Moral autonomy | 3 | Interpersonal mutuality |
| | | 4 | Social order |
| | | 5 | Social contract |
| | | 6 | Universal principle |

Stages 0 through 3 fairly well follow Piaget's description, but stages 4 to 6 go beyond it. In stage 4 a person understands that interpersonal relationships must be regulated by social order within which one lives. Stage 5 allows for changes in the social order by means of mutual consent. Stage 6 subsumes all social regulations under the universal principles of justice, "the right of every person to equal consideration of his claim in every situation."

Even from such a brief account one can see that there are obvious advantages to the Piaget-Kohlberg thesis. It has been unusually helpful in posing research questions and in helping to clarify issues. The work of both men has produced empirical findings that must be accounted for by anyone who wants to be well informed about moral development. They are able to give a coherent account of a subject that has been notoriously resistant to coherence. They bring together both philosophical and empirical methods and find important parallels between them. Their account allows for variety and change, but reaches beyond cultural relativism. They do not shy away from such controversial topics as human rights and civil disobedience. They are in touch with the long ethical tradition from Plato in the ancient Greek world to Martin Luther King in the modern world. Furthermore, one finds a loose correspondence between their stages and psychoanalytic observations. Unlike some theories, theirs gives actual guidance to teachers in specifying the aims, objectives, and procedures of education. In many ways it is a very useful thesis.

In spite of the obvious strengths of the Piaget-Kohlberg thesis there are a number of objections we can bring against it. Kohlberg keeps redefining his stages in the face of criticism, but it is not at all clear that the earlier formulation from which he did his research is the same one he is now defending. For example, he earlier spoke of stage 3 as the "good boy" period when a child is interested in being considered a good child from a conventional point of view. Now he defines the same stage in terms of the ability to understand multiple points of view in a situation. It is not at all clear that these definitions are describing the same thing.[16] At least Kohlberg owes us a fuller explanation.

A more serious charge is that the theory sacrifices ethical content to ethical form. The form of ethical reason becomes more important than what is decided. Should education move in this way, it may become less and less interested in what people are deciding, while retaining interest only in what kind of reasons are being given. It would be unfortunate indeed if logical analysis were to replace interest in the actual issues that face children and young persons.

Closely related is the objection that the moral dilemmas posed by Piaget and Kohlberg are designed to provoke certain decisions, but they are not the actual decisions that young people are making. This suggests that considerably more effort ought to be made to see that the issues being discussed are real for the discussants. Other approaches make a great effort to collect actual dilemmas that children face.[17] Surely it is important that educational methods relating to moral development be related to the moral issues that people actually face. Another way of putting this objection is to say that the analysis of the form of moral thinking has been separated from the moral context in life.

Still another objection is that, in spite of the effort to carry out his research in different cultures, Kohlberg has not given attention to the cultural factors that shape moral decision. He is rightly interested in trying to show that the structure of moral development is not affected by culture, but surely the interplay of various ways of life on moral development needs to be considered. Whether moral stages can so quickly and easily be separated from their cultural context is not yet satisfactorily demonstrated and must be investigated further. Of this we shall say more in a later chapter.

One may also question whether the utilitarian and idealistic orientations behind the thesis may not themselves be culturally relative. Kohlberg criticizes Piaget for suggesting that democracy is inevitably the highest stage of moral development. He calls Piaget's tendency toward democracy a "socio-emotive" factor and claims that it cannot be empirically verified.[18] However, the utilitarianism of stage 5 and the Kantianism of stage 6 run an equal risk of being part of the "socio-emotive" factor. It seems odd that moral development inevitably runs through a utilitarian stage at the upper levels.

Perhaps a way of putting this is to say that the proposed picture of the good is one of detached, unemotional, cognitive decision making. While there is a very strong tradition of depicting the good in these terms, it nevertheless has a strongly arbitrary element. Such an ideal is certainly preferable to impulsive egoism, but that is not the only other option. Our account of agency presumes coherence and volition, and therefore shares with Kohlberg a concern about both reason and decision making. Yet agency is also a mode of awareness and of mutuality, which means that within agency the socio-emotive factors are bound together with the cognitive factors.

Another way of saying this is that the technical mode of reason is separated from the poetic in Piaget's and Kohlberg's accounts. Both of these forms of reason are valid, and when one of them is repressed, a distortion occurs. Our civilization is threatened today by an overabundance of technology and a paucity of poetic vision. Clearly, technology can destroy everything, and we do not expect that a technology of morality can finally resolve the moral dilemma. The technical and legal mode of thought does not exhaust the deeper meanings of morality, even though it is equally true that morality without technical reasons is fumbling and ineffective. Perhaps children and youth need additional moral guidance from reading poetry and stories in which the technical dilemmas are not so prominent as the human images and relationships being represented.

Moral reason must finally not be separated from the sympathy for humanity.[19] Sympathy and feeling for other human beings are surely as important as right thinking in the development of conscience, although the reverse is also true. Sympathy for other persons is not something that comes automatically; it must be nourished, and it often gets derailed in sympathy for "my own group" and hatred for everyone else. Kohlberg's account of right thinking must be supplemented, perhaps modified, by an account of right feeling such as Erikson's. In fact, the strength of agency is the unity of right feeling and right thinking.

Much philosophical thought has gone into the effort to characterize the ongoing continuities of life without returning to the eternal structures of Platonism. Some accounts speak of ever-expanding structures and others suggest the analysis of the use of everyday language. Both of these approaches would seem closer to the special content of the ethical issues of life than the classical formal analysis. Both suggest paying more attention to the language that children actually use rather than to the language they ought to use.

The better guidance to teachers and parents will be concerned about the actual use of language, the stories they like to recite together, the poetry and drama they share together, as well as the reasons they give for moral choice. We need a better account of interrelationship of emotions, will, and reason as they are shaped into communities that can cope with modern problems. We need the researches of Piaget and Kohlberg, but they must be complemented by "sympathy for humanity," without which moral reason has no substance. In the account that follows we are attempting to balance some of the factors we find missing in the Piaget-Kohlberg thesis.

## The Beginning of Moral Understanding

One must look to the earliest months of infancy to view the beginning of the relationship between conscience and reason. We have seen how the dispositions to trust and to will originate during the first two years of childhood, but now we want to relate the development of understanding to these dispositions. There is a tendency to consider the roots of conscience in infancy to be only irrational, but this is due to the fact that the development of understanding in infancy is itself so little understood. The earliest commands of parents may be established in the conscience with great emotion, and in some cases that emotion may subvert the maturation of reason, but this in no way demonstrates that conscience is only emotive.

Jean Piaget has discovered certain constancies of behavior in the early months of infancy that are basic to the later development of intelligence.[20] By four months after birth most babies have gained hand-mouth coordination, evidenced by thumbsucking. By eight months there is usually hand-eye-mouth coordination, so that the infant can reach for a rattle or a bottle and bring it to her mouth. By eight months also infants ordinarily have a sense of the permanence of objects. Given a bottle with the nipple pointed away from her mouth, an infant will turn the bottle around and begin to suck. When the bottle is presented to a younger infant, she will cry until someone turns the bottle around. Apparently the younger child has no sense of the bottle as a permanent object that can be moved in space. When she can turn the bottle around, then she has begun to act as though she is making things happen, as though she is causing changes in the environment.

By eighteen months children usually have become aware that objects are related to one another so that one object can be used to push another object. The self seems now to be understood as the object of actions by other persons. The child can solve simple problems such as getting around the barrier, which shows that situations are kept in mind and alternatives are tried out. With the ability to retain mental images comes also the beginning of language. By age twenty-four months most children can speak about, draw, and pretend to be objects that are no longer present. The effects of acting a certain way can be inferred before the action is taken.

The disposition to trust and to will are closely related to these early events in the development of understanding. The sense of constancy and otherness is the basis for the sense of selfhood. In other words, the awareness of selfhood is mediated through the sense of otherness. Hand-eye-mouth coordination precedes object permanency; object permanency precedes the sense of the continuity of a caring person; and the continuity of a caring person precedes the continuity of selfhood. The self is a construct built of the interacting mutuality with other persons.

Not only is self-awareness born in the interaction between parent and child, but also the intention to be of worth to the one who is caring is established. This intention is inevitably mixed with frustration and resentment, which may become a malevolent intention to remain isolated from other persons.

Perhaps the relationship between understanding and trust can be illustrated by considering the instance of a high school age youth who stuttered badly. He related to me how, after many efforts to find a way to stop the stuttering, he consulted a doctor who suggested that hand-eye coordination may not have been well established during the early months of his infancy. For a year this young man worked day by day to draw images presented to him with a pair of goggles that were designed to prevent his being able to see what he was drawing. Gradually his hands learned to draw what his eyes were seeing, and as had been predicted, gradually the stutter disappeared.

Since psychoanalytic studies suggest that basic trust is impaired by the absence of "the mother factor" for long periods during the first year of infancy, I asked him whether in fact his mother had been absent. He replied that she had been gone for six months, and during this time he had been cared for by his elder brother! His experience illustrates dramatically the interplay of the disposition to trust and the development of reason. It suggests that the absence of the mother impeded the maturation of hand-eye coordination, and it seems likely that object constancy was also impaired. The preconceptual skills of coordination are closely related to the mutuality of basic trust.

Coordination, object constancy, and the recognition of other persons and objects become the basis for later concept formation. They are the protocognitive skills that belong to the protomoral disposition to trust or to mistrust. Later maturation of thought occurs by what Piaget has termed decentration, conservation, and reversibility.[21] Decentration is the ability to view things from a larger perspective, to avoid being locked into the immediate experience at hand. The infant begins to decenter when she can recognize things and persons rather than sensing only momentary feelings. Conservation is the ability to sense the deeper continuity in the endless change of experience. The infant begins to conserve experience when she can respond to the constancy of objects and persons. Reversibility is the ability to act in relation to differing states of something simultaneously. Coordination of hand, eye, and mouth is basic for later logical reversibilities. Coordination enables a child to push an item away or to pull it toward herself, and these earliest acts are basic to the logic of inclusion and exclusion.[22]

The self is constructed in an interactive situation in which other persons are recognized and responded to. The child will refer to herself first of all in the third person before coming to the more complicated construct of saying, "I." "Susan eat" is an early form of thoughts such as "I want to eat" or perhaps "I am eating."

The importance of constancy as a precondition to moral reasoning becomes evident in forms of brainwashing designed to disrupt all the constancies of normal living. Prisoners may be moved without notice, fed at erratic times, interrupted at any time of the day or night, kept in darkness where the regularity of day and night disappear, tortured or reprieved without any indication of what will come next, and so on. Such treatment destroys a person's ability to make decisions and finally the very sense of selfhood. It sets one back to total dependence upon whatever happens next. The effects of brainwashing illustrate again the importance of the constancies of objects and persons for establishing initial trust and reason.

Perhaps the greatest aid to the development of moral reasoning is the consistency and dependability of the caring community, coupled with nonpunitive acceptance.[23] Parents and groups that live by certain moral constancies without punishing children for violations seem best able to promote the development of moral reason. Even customary rules like saying "excuse me" upon leaving the table or always hanging up one's coat upon returning to the schoolroom, when consistently expected without punishment for violations, are likely more conducive to moral reasoning than concerns about justice accompanied with punishment. True enough, many children mature in the exercise of moral reason in spite of punishment, apparently because punishment may be handed out with fairness and also because punishment can reflect the continuing care and concern of the parent or the school. Nevertheless, a nonpunitive consistency seems better able to promote moral maturity than any form of punishment. We are not speaking of a compulsive consistency for detail, but rather of a consistency of care, will, and purpose that promotes and strengthens the protomoral dispositions in children.

Just as there is a close relationship between moral reasoning and trust, so there is also a close relationship between moral reasoning and will. We have already seen how will develops as a disposition in the interaction between parent and child during the second and third years of childhood. Child and parent put mutual limitations upon each other, and the circle of mutual agreement about expression and limitation becomes the arena where will develops and is confirmed. The limitations of being clean, not being noisy, learning the language, and a thousand other such particulars are the locus of struggle between parent and child. The child's developing abilities clash with the parental expectation, custom, and culture. To the extent that expression within limitation can be agreed upon in trustful mutuality, will develops as a disposition.

Reason matures during the second year in several ways. The conservation of selfhood develops as a child perceives herself to be the object of the actions of others. The beginnings of *reversibility* can be seen in a two-year-old child's delight in imitating other persons. Not only is there awareness of the other and of the self, but an ability consciously to act out the activities of others. A child can imitate only as she begins to keep in mind what she is doing and at the same time what other persons are doing. This double awareness prepares the way to associate activities with words, symbols that mean the same thing to other persons and to herself. Projecting a mental image of different possible actions of herself and others is basic to the development of language and shows the child's growing ability to be *decentered* from immediate experience. The constancy of self in interaction with others, the deliberate imitation of other persons, and the ability to hold mental images and to solve problems at a preverbal level are the protoconceptual skills that accompany the development of will as a disposition.

Jean Piaget speaks of the regularity of protoconceptual behavior as "motor rules," because they give shape to muscular (or "motor") behavior. He describes a three-year-old girl playing with marbles in this way:

> Jacqueline has the marbles in her hands and looks at them with curiosity (it is the first time she has seen any); then she lets them drop on the carpet. After this she puts them into the hollow of an armchair. . . . She puts them back on the carpet and lets them drop from a certain height. She sits on the carpet with her legs apart and throws the marbles a few inches in front of her. She picks them up and puts them on the armchair and in the same holes as before. . . . [She] puts them into her little saucepan to cook dinner.[24]

Jacqueline's play with the marbles has both spontaniety and regularity of detail. The same episode is repeated again and again. There is intentionality, but of a limited kind. The episode is not a part of a larger activity, but rather the oft repeated ritual will be dropped when something else catches Jacqueline's attention. The marbles are used to portray an imaginative imitation of the mother cooking. The symbolism of cooking is added to the skill of handling the marbles. A limitation upon Jacqueline is that her mother must do the cooking instead of giving constant attention to her. The play at cooking is a way for Jacqueline and her mother to accept mutual expression within limitation. In such play, protoconceptual skills mingle with the disposition to will.

In my judgment it is false to suppose that a child is either solely innocent or solely rebellious by predisposition. Children are "agentic" (meaning, having and expressing directly the qualities of agency), and agency shows itself in dispositions to trust and to will, mixed with mistrust and willfulness. Parental mistrust and willfulness foster similar responses in the child, but not in a way that allows one to predict what the dispositions of a child will be. Who can regularly predict what dispositions a child will display? Who can predict that one child will be a St. Francis and another a Hitler? Nevertheless, parents and schools can and certainly do foster certain dispositions. Perhaps we should consider children innocent while acknowledging that they do to some extent inevitably develop some degree of malevolent separation, mistrust, and rebelliousness. Part of the struggle of conscience is to act in ways that will enlarge the dispositions to trust and to will.

### Purpose and Moral Understanding

Just as will becomes possible when the awareness of the interaction of self and other is joined to the disposition to trust, so also purpose becomes possible when the capacities for imagination and language are joined to the disposition to will. The child between the ages of three and six gains new capacities for understanding that are closely related to the formation of conscience. Many accounts have featured trauma, punishment, and pleasure, which result in the formation of a primitive, repressive conscience that continues to control our behavior for the remainder of our lives. I want to try to elucidate the growth of common purpose and loyalty as the basic reality of conscience within which the repressive conscience inevitably develops. It is wrong to consider that rationality and common purpose are added to our lives sometime after a childhood that was dominated by a divided self. When the division in the self becomes too severe during early childhood, the condition called autism results.[25] In autism the child turns away from reality and lives only in her own fantasies. Normal development may include some severe traumata and repression, but in most cases these are set within a developing sense of purpose. While all persons struggle with hidden restraint, shame, and guilt, most persons are able to integrate these feelings into the ideals and common purposes by which their lives are guided. It is important that we understand the origins of purpose as well as of guilt.

Once a child of perhaps two years of age is able to entertain mental pictures of experience, and therefore in a very rudimentary way is able to imagine various consequences before they occur, language becomes possible. The child imitates the environment, principally those persons who care for her. She is able to imagine the action of other persons upon her, and she reduplicates that action, making it a part of her own self-awareness. Everyone has seen a child pretending to cook a meal while the mother cooks, or carefully wheeling a doll carriage behind her mother who is wheeling a younger child in a pram. Many children go through a period of repeating all the words spoken to them. This capacity to imagine and reduplicate what is happening opens the possibility for symbols, that is, sign-acts that can be commonly understood, because both parties know what is intended. In other words, imagination opens the possibility for language, and, with language, the whole cultural understanding.

Certain abilities mature that give the peculiar character to the behavior of children between the ages of two and six. While they are increasingly able to *conserve* the world of objects, they remain very much tied to images as they appear. Things far away are thought to be small because they look small, and things close at hand are considered to be large because they look large. The sun moves across the sky, as does the moon, and both are just out of reach. Distant objects go with you when you move. When two glasses of water of the same shape and volume are poured into two separate cylindrical containers, one tall and narrow and the other short and wide, the child will judge that the volume of water has changed in the pouring. Because the tall narrow cylinder appears to be larger, from the child's point of

*93*

view it does in fact contain more water. Children think that the hands of a clock move quickly when time seems to pass quickly, and slowly when time passes slowly. A child can conserve the world of objects, but she is tied to immediate sense perceptions. Only after many years will she learn to perceive the world in the way that her society considers to be real.

Two to six, as we have already suggested, is a golden age for the learning of language. The use of words allows the child to be *decentered* from experience, that is, to picture various experiences before acting. Behavior becomes less a matter of reflex and instinct than during the first two years. Language allows the child to remember certain experiences as well as to anticipate others. What is sometimes called childhood amnesia, our inability to remember our earliest years, coincides with the time when we were unable to symbolize our experience in words.

We have seen that preschool children are tied to immediate perceptions. Another way of putting this is to say that they are unable to be decentered from immediate perceptual imagery. Language allows children to decenter enough to give the world some coherence, but it does not allow them to be decentered from the perceptual appearance of the world. Children's use of language itself shows the same characteristic inability to decenter. With the constancy of interaction, language becomes possible, yet the child speaks from the immediate impact of words and meanings. Only gradually do children gain a sense of the constancy of meanings. Every child will use words in what adults consider to be an unusual manner. The child from age two to six is learning to become decentered from the immediate and accidental associations of the context in which a word was first learned. She learns that "mommy" refers only to her own mommy rather than all women and "doggy" refers only to canine animals rather than to all animals.

The child has a growing capacity for *reversibility*, but also within certain limitations. She can put together symbols and activities with increasing ingenuity. Play is a matter of allowing the skills of running, manipulating objects, and exploring to take on symbolic meanings. Pushing a block of wood on the floor is "driving the car," and lifting the piece of wood up becomes "flying a plane." The limitation of reversibility is that children cannot keep two such activities in mind at the same time, and therefore such activities lack the larger coherence of a game or a task. They can only play at tasks and games that older children perform, but this "playing at" represents a growing disposition to purpose.

We may summarize the growing intellectual capacities of children ages two through six by saying that they can conserve the constancy of the world as perceived, but that notions such as time, space, number, and volume, vary according to the impact of perceptual distortion. Language allows children to be decentered from experience, but the meanings of words and phrases vary according to accidental associations and circumstances. The child can reverse language and activity in symbolic play, but play episodes cannot be put together with coherent rules. There are growing abilities to conserve, decenter, and reverse experience, but within certain clear limitations. The child lives in a story world in which beings come and go at will; rules can be talked about but have no real constancy, and there is often confusion (from an adult point of view) between what the child imagines and what is actually happening.

The relation of reason and conscience is one of the child's taking on the more immediate purposes that are mutually meaningful to child and adult, but without the adult's sense of regularity and meaning in these purposes. When a child is compelled by an adult, something that cannot always be avoided, then trauma and repression do sometimes take place, and such repression is the common lot of all children. More fundamental, however, is the mutuality of purpose between child and adult, which allows the child (and the adult) to engage in activities that are satisfying to both. Caring parents inevitably put restraints upon their children, but they do this only within an awareness shared between them of the purposefulness of the child's symbolic activities. The impatient parent races ahead of the child, compelling activities that the child is unable to imagine or perform. Such a parent also continues to struggle against a dispositional willfulness that has been previously formed and that now expresses itself in purposelessness or perhaps deviousness. Faced with this problem, parents must search to expand those activities in which common purpose is growing, or perhaps consult someone who is able to help them confirm their child's sense of purpose.

Let us illustrate the relation of reason and purpose with the child's understanding of rules. As the three- to six-year-old child becomes aware that older children and adults are working and playing according to regular rules, she also tries to act according to these rules. Consider this description of Mar trying to play marbles:

> Mar (six years of age) seizes hold of the marbles we offer him, and without bothering to make a square he heaps them up together and begins to hit the pile. He removes the marbles he has displaced and puts them aside or replaces them again without any method. "Do you always play like that? — *In the street you make a square*. —Well, you do the same as they do in the street—*I'm making a square, I am.*" (He draws the square, places the marbles inside it and begins to play again. I play with him, imitating each of his movements.) "Who has won?—*We've both won.*—But who has won most?" . . . (Mar does not understand).[26]

Mar is aware that the children in the street make a square and place the marbles within it. However, he has no sense of how much practices relate to each other or how several children contend with one another. For the time being his attention is focused upon the individual ritual, which is the only way he can understand the rule. He follows the rule according to his own imaginary construction. Several children may play together in this manner, each improvising upon the ritual rule, but otherwise seemingly unrelated in what they are doing. Such play is called parallel play. What should be emphasized is not the absence of cooperation in parallel play, but just the reverse. The child's sense of purpose is confirmed in the purposive activities of those round about. As purpose becomes dispositional, cooperative games like marbles become possible.

Piaget has suggested that the conscience of the preschool child is characterized by a certain kind of respect for what is imposed from outside, that is, for what is given by a stronger person to a weaker. He goes on to suggest that such respect goes principally in one direction, from the child to the adult, and is to be called unilateral respect. It is to be distinguished from respect between equals, which moves simultaneously in both directions, arising by consent and cooperation. The latter type is to be called mutual respect.

To get at children's respect for rules, Piaget asked many of them where rules for the game of marbles came from and when they may be broken. Here are the responses of a five-and-a-half-year-old boy:

> We asked Leh quite simply if everyone played from the coche, or whether one could not (as is actually done) put the older ones at the coche and let the little ones play closer up. "No," answered Leh. *"That wouldn't be fair.—*Why not?*—Because God would make the little boy's shot not reach the marbles and the big boy's shot would reach them."* In other words, the divine justice is opposed to any change in the rules of marbles, and if one player, even a very young one were favored in any way, God himself would prevent him from reaching the square.[27]

Piaget concludes from interviews of this type that the child considers rules to be sacred, obligatory, unalterable, and eternal, even though the child may be very erratic in practicing them. For young children all rules are given together, have always existed, and shall always continue to exist. Piaget wants then to show us how this attitude, which he calls moral realism, changes radically as the child grows older.

A problem with Piaget's interpretation is that he seems to explain the child's answers to these questions from a literal point of view. "Always, unalterable, and eternal" cannot have the same meaning to a young child as to an adult simply because the child has no conservation for such concepts. The child thinks mythically and in story language. Beings come and go; symbolic play may change from one moment to the next. It is therefore inappropriate to impose adult categories of eternity upon a child, even when the child may use that language. Possibly the child senses a larger purpose beyond her own immediate purposes confirming and challenging them. Obviously parents and other children are acting over against the child, but the child seems dimly aware that they also stand within rules and limitation. That the child uses religious language to express this awareness is to be expected, especially if she is from a religious family. However it is certainly wrong to consider that children intend by the use of such language something Piaget's studies have shown that children of that age cannot intend.

Reference to God in this case is more likely a story-like reference to mutual purpose within a community of interacting persons. Since story is the symbolic mode of preschool thought, the story of faith is a way of referring to mutual purpose within a community. In this way children show their own growing dispositions to purpose. When adults or older children force certain activities upon younger children, they certainly contribute to attitudes of unilateral respect. For some children, references to God may be coupled with attitudes of unilateral respect, perhaps also with mistrust, willfulness, and deviousness. Children may use references to God to impose their own will upon others, perhaps imitating what has previously happened to them. Yet one cannot draw the conclusion that preschool children have attitudes only of unilateral respect on the basis of interviews like that with Leh quoted above.

Children of Leh's age are learning to live within communities of mutual purpose. They recognize and speak about the reality of such purpose before it has become dispositional. The mythical mentality of preschool children finds no necessity in the constancy of rules, even when they can speak about rules. Saying that rules must "always" be obeyed cannot yet mean to the child what "always" means to the adult. Playing at the rules is the way by which purpose becomes dispositional. When the child gains the reasoning ability to conserve the constancy of rules, then she will act in a way that an adult understands as "following the rule." Of course, at that time, the child's interest in story and mythology also begins to change, for she is one step closer to living in the "real world" of adults.

In the preschool child's experience, the growth of the disposition to purpose exists side by side with the imposition of rules and requirements by parents and others. If the disposition to purpose is strong, the child will have no difficulty following reasonable expectations. If the child is purposeless or devious, or if the expectations are arbitrary and unreasonable, then the child cannot and will not follow them. In any case, the child will not understand the expectation in the same way as an adult might, something of which sensitive parents are already aware.

Consider the obligation to tell the truth or to refrain from stealing. When young children are asked why lying and stealing are wrong, the answer is that such activities are "bad" or "naughty," that is, punishable. A five-year-old will likely tell you, if you inquire, that a lie is "a bad word." When she is asked whether a child who calls her friend a nasty name has lied or not, the answer is, "She has lied." Only as the child reaches seven or eight years of age will she say that lying and stealing are wrong even when they are not punished.

Piaget puzzles over the fact that most preschool children do not lie and steal even when they say that it is all right so long as you don't get caught. Obviously two-, three-, and four-year-old children do not know what lying and stealing mean to adults. We laugh when a four-year-old talks about an imaginary playmate, or when a three-year-old takes a toy from another child. At the same time, the parent will begin to say, "But did that really happen?" and in the other instance will return the toy to the other child, trying at the same time to interest the "offender" in something else. Property and truth are a part of everyday activities; ordinary use presumes truth, and eating and clothing presume property. Faced with the taking of a toy or stories about what did not "really" happen, the parents normally signal the limitations while confirming the child's purposes. Reasonable limitations will be accepted by a child who has developed a disposition to will. Our point is that the mutuality of purpose is growing into a disposition during the preschool years and is more fundamental than what the child calls "naughty" behavior.

There are, of course, cultural differences in the way parents respond to the child's growing purposes. In some cultures children are taught by being left to burn themselves in the fire or to fall and injure themselves. Such cultures seem to be preparing their children to accept a violent existence, which for them may be necessary. Yet even in such cultures, parents must find ways of confirming the growing disposition to purpose, or the children will become emotionally harmed, if they survive. Child neglect or battery must be wrong in every culture, even when they are variously understood.

When asked who is responsible for a wrong done, young children will judge the deed by the damage done rather than by the motive. Piaget told children a story that may be summarized as follows: (1) Alfred has a poor friend who is very hungry; therefore, Alfred goes into a store and steals a roll while the baker's back is turned. (2) Henrietta goes into a shop where she spies a ribbon that she likes very much. When the sales girl's back is turned, she steals it and runs out. Here is an example of a child's responses to this story:

> Is one of the children naughtier than the other?—*The boy is, because he took a roll. It's bigger.*—Ought they to be punished? Yes. Four slaps for the first.—Why did he take the roll?— *Because his friend had no dinner.*—And the other child?—*To make herself pretty.*[28]

Piaget found that until age ten or twelve some children evaluate responsibility primarily according to results alone and seldom according to intention. We should not be surprised that children cannot take intentionality into account until their own sense of purpose has become dispositional and until they can conserve the idea of a community of persons with intended responses to one another. As young children come to have their own purposes confirmed, and as they feel the conflict of purpose in games and arguments, they become able to take the intentions of others into account. The young child lives and plays in the mutuality of purpose, except when something "makes mommy angry." Often the punishment comes according to the extent of the damage. The punishment can be accepted if the disposition to purpose is growing. Otherwise, the punishment leads to further purposelessness, rebelliousness, or deviousness.

When asked what punishments they would give, young children seem to favor severe, even vengeful, punishments. They consider it right for a parent or teacher to be biased against a disobedient child. They find it more right to tattle by telling of a misdeed than to remain in the favor of playmates by not telling. Nature will punish a naughty child with an accident, or God will punish the child.

Again we would be wrong to take such statements of preschool children literally. References to punishment must evoke in children scenes of their own punishments, since children of this age are so closely tied to perceptual experience. In the absence of real conservation dealing with concepts, suggestions about punishment must be taken as "stories." The child seems to sense that punishment is often not arbitrary, but comes from some larger necessity, which is symbolized by nature or God. Their mythical account of punishment is surely an important antecedent to the more mature conception of justice. It would also be wrong to think that children act out such punishment stories literally. They are quite easily distracted to something else, or soon tire of thinking about what was naughty. They may soon be off playing with the children who just offended them. Since play is itself the activity by which the disposition to purpose is established, mutual purpose is the context within which punishment should be understood. It is wrong to believe that children's behavior is only unilateral in the early years, and later becomes mutual. Rather, mutuality is the context within which standards are forced on children, and they spend their lives trying to integrate inevitably imposed standards into the strength of mutual purpose.

Language, food customs, family pattern, daily schedules, clothing, and cleanliness are only a few of the many expectations placed upon every child in some way or other. The liberal effort to avoid adult constraint is not possible. Piaget tells of his own efforts to give a reasonable explanation for every expectation of his two-and-a-half-year-old daughter. The following conversation took place when he discovered her pulling threads from a towel:

> So I say to J., "Oh, but mummy will be sad." J. answers calmly and even with an ill-concealed smile: *"Yes. It makes holes. You can't mend."* . . . I continue my lecture, but she obviously is not going to take me seriously. Still hiding her amusement with difficulty, she suddenly says to me, *"Laugh!"* in so comic a tone that in order to keep a straight face I quickly change the subject.[29]

Later she asks whether mother isn't sad and then cries until someone comes to her. She wants to make sure "they bore her no grudge." The constraint becomes evident when J. cries. Yet we are also impressed that J. symbolizes what she is doing by speaking of "making holes" and "mending," and she tests the limits of mutual purpose by trying to make daddy laugh. These latter interactions are as important in the formation of conscience as adult constraint per se. Our point is that mutuality is the context within which constraint is to be understood.

Summarizing the relationship of reason and purpose, the preschool child gains certain rational abilities that expand the conscience by contributing to the development of purpose as a disposition. The constancy of the environment, the use of language, and the growing capacity for symbolic play are protocognitive abilities that develop in concert with the disposition to purpose. However, her inability to conserve concepts of time, space, number, volume, and intention; her close reliance upon immediate perception; and her inability to understand rules give a child's reasoning a story-like quality. There is no sharp line between what is being thought and what is happening in fact. Responses to questions about morality are fanciful and mythical, with a tendency to exaggerate punishment and obedience.

Perhaps children's inability to distinguish sharply what is going on within their own imagination and what is happening in the environment leads them to consider parental commands as coming from within. Freud speaks of this as the internalization of parental commands. When commands are internalized, often with great trauma, they act as a primitive conscience within. Our contention, however, is that not all rules and regulations are learned with emotional upheaval. Many are learned within the daily routine of activities that represent shared purposes, even before children can understand the wider coherence of such activities. Play becomes the arena in which purposes are established, ideals developed. The establishment of the proto-moral disposition to purpose is added to the dispositions to will and to trust. Together they establish the dispositional basis for mature moral decision.

### Value and Moral Understanding

With the early school years, ages seven to eleven, children gain striking new intellectual abilities. The mythical, story-like reasoning of the preschool years gives way to the ability to apply concepts to particular instances. Rules take on a constancy that regulates the child's behavior, and children enjoy games in which they can compete with one another to see who wins. At the same time, they are experimenting with skills and activities in which they feel some competency. Values are taken on along with the rules that are followed. It is a time when the rules already learned in the family setting are tested in a wider social setting. We now want to show how these new intellectual abilities are related to the growing disposition to value.

Sometimes the moral development of school-aged children is understood only in terms of modifying and extending an oppressive punitive conscience that was established in early childhood. It is wrong to understand conscience principally in this way unless a child is quite emotionally disturbed. Conscience is better described as the extension of the protomoral dispositions of trust, will, and purpose in the direction of the values that are implicit in the communities to which children feel loyalty and allegiance. Growing intellectual capacities and a growing sense of competence accompany the disposition to value. Otherwise, children feel incompetent, rebellious against community values, or perhaps utterly without direction. Each child develops in a way that mixes these possibilities in a disposition unique to that child. The trustful mutuality by which the disposition to purpose is extended and confirmed in the disposition to value is more basic than the anxiety by which adult constraints are internalized to become fear of the community.

Let us consider the changes that occur in a child's capacity to reason as she moves through the early school years. During the years from seven to eleven children become *decentered* from immediate sense perceptions. When a glass of water is poured into a container of a different shape, they know that it still retains the same volume. Ten pennies still have the same number when they are spread apart as when they are together. The hands of the clock move at a regular rate, no matter how quickly or slowly time seems to pass. The moon is understood to be far away, not within immediate reach. There is a growing ability to conserve time, space, volume, speed, and eventually intentions of other persons.

Becoming decentered from immediate sense perceptions is probably closely related to the *conservation* of concepts. The child can keep a concept in mind while at the same time applying it to a particular situation. Many schoolroom skills depend upon the ability to work out examples once a rule has been given. The conservation of rules also allows children to play games with one another in which the object is winning. The ability to apply concepts to situations allows children to develop hundreds of different skills from jumping rope, baseball, and tag to reading, writing, and arithmetic.

Children of this age develop a new ability to reason *reversibly*. Moving beyond symbolic play, they can enter into a group with rules defining the mutual relationships between them. They are therefore able to keep in mind the purposes of the game, the regulating rules, and the skills they need to carry out their own roles. This represents quite an advance in reversibility. A child can play games to win, thus demonstrating an ability to understand commonly accepted purposes. She can abide by given rules, keeping purposes and various roles in mind while carrying out the skills necessary for playing the game.

The abilities just described are equally essential to the classroom and the street corner group. In the classroom, a child understands the purpose of the study, the rules that govern the class, and the activities necessary to be a student. Of course, the limitations of living in a ghetto may change the purpose of the classroom in the direction of "playing" the education game while getting away with as much as possible, with the intent to drop out of school as soon as possible. These same skills allow boys and girls to learn their respective sex roles along with the basic skills related to them. The sex role will depend very much upon the community in which a child lives. Today it can no longer be assumed that a boy will learn the skills of aggressiveness and competition, while a girl will learn the skills of receptiveness and cooperation. In any case, sex roles, classroom roles, and play roles all depend upon the growing rational abilities of decentering, conservation, and reversibility.

Conscience during the school years is neither simply an elaboration of rules forced upon children during their preschool years nor merely the extension of earlier repressions. Rather, the protomoral dispositions to trust, to will, and to purpose become a disposition to value the activities in which the community engages. The disposition to value grows in the exercise of concrete skills for which a child finds approval either from adults or from other children, and ordinarily from both. The way in which values develop becomes evident as soon as we look at either formal education or the learning of the sex role.

A child who enters into the classroom activities of a middle-class school comes to value what the school stands for, while a ghetto child who cannot accept the purposes of the school for herself does not learn the skills of scholarship. She may, rather, learn the skills of the street group, which have far more immediate survival value. The learning of the concrete roles and activities is the point at which the crisis of value occurs. A child who is unable to find confirmation in activities in the classroom, in the play yard, on the street, or in the home becomes miserably inferior. Since she cannot develop a disposition to value what the wider community approves, she may learn to value what is not generally approved. It is highly important for school aged children to find areas of competency. The protomoral dispositions are extended in the interactive process by which values are established. The mutuality of value along with the ability to make concrete moral decisions is the basis for the growth of conscience and is the context within which the extension of adult restraints is to be seen. Nevertheless, the struggle between the repressive conscience and the sense of value may continue throughout life.

The defining characteristic of reasoning with regard to value is the child's ability to justify a deed by reasoning from a moral rule to a behavioral conclusion. No longer is a deed or rule obligatory simply because someone commands it. Consider a description of Ben (aged ten) and Nus (aged eleven):

> They agree in regarding the square as necessary. Nus declares that you always place 4 marbles in the square, either at the corners or else 3 in the center with one on top (in a pyramid). Ben, however, tells us that you place 2 to 10 marbles in the enclosure (not less than two, not more than 10) . . .

There is thus agreement about several rules, enough to begin play, but many points for discussion.[30]

Ben and Nus go beyond the imitation of rules by trying to win, which means that each accepts for himself a set of rules that has been accepted by the other. By the age of seven or eight children can regulate their own behavior according to rules, and by nine or ten they can discuss which rules they are willing to follow, as Ben and Nus do.

School-aged children reason about moral questions in the same way as they do about rules of a game. Preschool children, as we indicated above, equate a lie with "a naughty word," but school-aged children understand a lie to be something that isn't true, even though they may still not be able to take the intentions of the speaker into account. The following conversation is with Chap, aged seven:

> What is a lie?—*What isn't true, what they say that they haven't done.*—Guess how old I am.—*Twenty.*—No, I'm thirty. Was it a lie what you told me?—*I didn't do it on purpose.*—I know. But is it a lie all the same, or not?—*Yes, it is all the same, because I didn't say how old you really were.*[31]

Chap wavers between a purposive and a purely external criterion of lying, finally opting for the latter. He begins to sense the importance of intentions in practice, but the practice has not yet affected his understanding of a rule. Younger children believe that a lie is more serious when the content is more exaggerated. They believe for example that a child who claims to have seen a dog as big as a cow should be punished more than a child who tells her mother that she passed a spelling test, when actually she did not. Chap, quoted above, would probably waver on this question. By the age of ten or eleven children normally consider the lie about the spelling test to be more serious. In the same way younger children call for harsh punishments, and children eight years of age or older usually want the punishment to balance the injury. "If he hit me once, I can hit him once."

Moral reasoning in relation to the disposition to value is thus seen to have certain definable characteristics. Rules are considered to be imposed from outside, although by the age of nine or ten, children will argue with one another about which rules they will follow. Rules are objective; the magnitude of an error is more important than the intention of the actor, as with Chap trying to understand the meaning of a lie. Again, by nine or ten, some children can take intentions into account. Rules are understood literally, without regard to circumstances. "It is not fair that I must go to bed at nine o'clock when my twelve-year-old brother can stay up until ten-thirty."

Lawrence Kohlberg has observed that from the ages of seven to eleven there is a shift from being oriented to punishment (stage 1) to an attitude of instrumental hedonism (stage 2). By instrumental hedonism he means that a child will think that something is right simply because she desires it. Things are fair if they abide by the rules, and rules are fair if they give equal satisfactions to both parties. Children aged seven to eleven are concerned about equal sharing, equal punishment, and fairness. Kohlberg has given good evidence that children must pass through a hedonistic stage, but he has not indicated that it should be seen as a part of the disposition to value. Mutuality is in the rule itself, which children understand to apply to everyone, a considerable intellectual advance over the previous stage. Furthermore, they are learning skills related to rules, and such skills are valued by adults and other children alike. The so-called hedonism of children is their way of gaining individuality and exercising commonly valued judgments. In other words, school-aged "hedonism" is to be understood in terms of a mutually confirmed disposition to value, just as preschool "egoism" is a part of the mutually confirmed disposition to will and to purpose. When childhood attitudes become fixed, failing to grow and develop, they are expressed as egoism and hedonism in the adult, but it is wrong for adults to read such attitudes literally into the experiences of children. School-aged children either develop their own style and skills in relation to rules and implicit values or become uncooperative, unable to learn, and unable to make judgments about what is fair. Each child actually develops within some unique mixture of these two possibilities.

## *Belief and Moral Understanding*

Around the age of eleven or twelve, children gain the ability to reason formally and abstractly. Not only can they carry out the concrete reasoning operations of applying concepts to particular situations, but they can also classify concepts, organize rules, and generally imagine ways in which situations might be different than they presently are. The new capacity for formal thinking means that moral judgment is no longer tied to the mechanical application of rules or the wooden adoption of given values. Young people are able to consider when rules should be applied and when they should not be. They can agree about what rules are appropriate to adopt. They can make allowance for circumstances in the application of rule. They can adopt ideals about what the world might become rather than accepting the world entirely as it is. They can relate their behavior to what they believe to be true, and just this relationship is what we want to consider now.

The new ability to reason abstractly can perhaps be understood in the terms we have been using: conservation, decentration, and reversibility. Young people of eleven or twelve can *conserve* an interrelated system of ideas and practices, instead of being tied to one idea or practice at a time. They can develop new loyalty to a school because they better understand the complex ideals and practices that go into making up a school. They can better appreciate what it means to live in a community or a nation. They begin to understand what it means to belong to a religious denomination or group. They can appreciate why certain rules are followed and when allowances should be made for circumstances. They can understand what it means to be a young woman or a young man, rather than simply doing what girls do or doing what boys do. They can conserve the idea of a role within a community as more than simply following a set of rules and customs.

The unique way in which rules and ideas are put together constitutes the perspective of a person. The constellation of certain practices and ideas is characteristic of a school, community, church, or nation. When we are considering the coherence and conservation of the ideas by which a person hopes to direct her life, however, we may speak of such a constellation as belief.[32] People's operative beliefs may be much different from what they say they believe in. I am suggesting that belief brings together some concrete rules and practices to which there is already commitment. With the ability to conserve interrelated systems of ideas and practices, the disposition to belief as I have just described it becomes possible.

At the same time, there is an ability to *decenter,* to consider other ways of life. A young person who can reason formally is not tied to the givenness of circumstances. She can consider many alternative circumstances and many other rules. She can consider the ways in which she hopes the situation will change over the months or the years. She can imagine a world in which the evils of the present world have been eliminated, and she can adopt a belief to live toward that end. She can, of course, therefore become quite critical of her family, school, church, or nation. Yet this detachment from circumstances is a newfound ability to understand circumstances in a far deeper way than was possible in her previous mentality. Young persons therefore usually give allegiance to ideas, exercise criticism, and generally use their newfound reasoning ability to make sense of experience. They play with ideas and ways of viewing things in a manner parallel to children playing at skills like jumping rope and catching a ball.

Young persons of age eleven or twelve gain a new ability to *reverse* their ideas. They can understand proportionality and thus begin to solve problems involving fractions. They understand inverse relationships and correlations. They can experiment to discover whether the length of a pendulum or its weight is proportional to the time taken to traverse its arc. They can reconstruct how when a fluid is poured from one container to another, the surface level in the one container lowers as the other rises. They can explore the complex logical relationships in the everyday use of language. When someone says that something is interesting, does that person mean interesting-curious, interesting-entertaining, or something else? They are able to picture two independently moving relationships at the same time, a great gain in the ability to think reversibly.

These new reasoning capabilities make a dramatic difference in the moral reasoning of young people. They are much more willing to consider rules to be subject to the agreement of those who use them. Consider this discussion with three boys, all approximately twelve years of age, about the rules of marbles:

> Rit . . . tells us that the boy whose shooter stays inside the square may generally come out of it. He added, it is true, that in some games the play in such a plight is "dished," . . . but this rule does not seem to him obligatory. Vua and Groos, on the contrary, are of the opinion that in all cases when you stay inside the square you are dished. We think that we may confuse Vua by saying: "Rit didn't say that!—*The fact is,*" answers Vua, *"that sometimes people play differently. Then you ask each other what you want to do.*—And if you can't agree?—*We scrap for a bit and then we fix things up."* [33]

Young people are able to legislate rules for a variety of situations. More than that, they are able to follow different practices without feeling that they have violated the game.

They are also able to attend to motivation. A lie is no longer thought to be merely a verbal error, but rather an intentional verbal error. A person is no longer thought to be punishable simply for making a mistake, unless the misdeed was intended. Young people can also allow for circumstances. They hardly ever propose the harsh punishments that younger children suggest. If each child in a family is given a roll at lunch, and the three-year-old drops hers, a teen-ager may well say, "She is so young that she couldn't help it. Let us share ours with her."

With this new mode of reasoning, justice by reciprocity is considered to be superior to severe punishment. Better to try to correct the wrong done than to try to inflict pain on the offender. Some older children will even suggest talking to the offender as a substitute for any punishment at all. In the same way, justice is not simply carrying out the rule of reciprocity, an eye for an eye; rather, justice includes consideration of motives and circumstances.

Kohlberg finds that youth who are able to think abstractly will go through an initial period of interpersonal orientation (stage 3). By this he means that young people are able to act in a way to bring peace and harmony between two or three persons, but without being aware of intergroup conflicts. They will often suffer a wrong or do whatever else will help reestablish a good relationship between persons. Only at a later stage do they begin to understand that laws and authority are necessary to maintain fair relationships between large groups of people many with conflicting interests (stage 4).

In Kohlberg's view, the teen years are consequently very conventional years, and only in the late teens and twenties do young people begin seriously to question conventions. A problem with Kohlberg's description is that formal thinking allows young people to consider the ideals by which life ought to be ordered. The idealism of many youth hardly seems consistent with a strongly conventionalist interpretation. Possibly teen-aged play with different identities is done within an underlying acceptance of the social order, and perhaps the playing with different ideas is done within an acceptance of the prevailing ideology. On the other hand, many youth have strongly ambivalent feelings toward the social order that governs them, many are very idealistic, and many are active in groups dedicated to bring about their ideals. It would seem therefore that we cannot quickly accept the thesis of youthful conventionalism.

Kohlberg also has noted that many young people, especially if they attend college, seem to abandon the conventional ethics, descending to "the hedonism" of an eight-year-old. He suggests that this may be a period of transition (stage 4*b*) to a postconventional way of thinking.[34] Many other persons settle into a conventional way of life without going through a stage of ethical relativism. The transitional stage again raises a question about the relationship between ideals and conventionalism during the teen years.

The Piaget-Kohlberg thesis underplays the importance of mutuality during the teen years as it does during the earlier years. The advent of formal conceptual thought allows a teen-ager to "play" with beliefs related to herself, her family, community, school, church, nation, and world. This play is a way of sorting out which beliefs coincide with the dispositions that have already become established. In nearly all societies this playing with beliefs takes place in groups outside the home. They may be formal groups, like boarding schools, informal groups like street corner groups, or a mixture like many church groups. The interaction within such groups is very important for young people coming to accept patterns of belief to which they can give long term allegiance.

It is wrong, however, to underplay the importance of the intergenerational relationships in the crisis of belief. The identity crisis is a parting of the ways for what one believes about oneself, others, and the world about. Beliefs are tested according to whether they seem to fit deeper dispositions, but they also are held up against the older generation. It seems important to have someone outside the childhood family with whom to test the reality of beliefs. This person, or these persons, become the sponsors of a young person's beliefs. They have a wisdom and experience that is respected, but they also usually represent an extension of the values learned in the family and community during earlier years. Such persons are able to recognize the peculiar talents and character of young people, and in so doing they help to confirm in them the beliefs that are becoming dispositional. The interplay between other youths and such sponsoring adults represent the mutuality by which ideals and beliefs become a part of the sponsoring conscience.

Every person, of course, has some dispositional feelings of rebelliousness, purposelessness, willfulness, mistrust, and inferiority. They are expressions of agentic weakness, and the crisis of belief often gives full expression to these feelings. Preliterate societies sometimes avoid this crisis because the limited number of adult roles are established by customs which are passed on to young people in painful initiation rites that serve to subdue hostile feelings. In modern complex societies with many possible adult roles, with the economic dependency of youth on adults, and with high adult expectations for youth to renew society, the crisis of belief seems inevitable for most young people. If rebelliousness is strong, is reflected in the informal youth groups, and is confirmed by the representative sponsoring adults, such youth will become emotionally disturbed, criminal, reactionary, or revolutionary.

This analysis of belief and moral understanding suggests that teen-aged youth have a capacity to explore the meaning of the beliefs of their own communities as well as the beliefs of other groups. They can understand belief in God in a new way and are able to explore traditional doctrines. At the same time, they may want to "play" with these ideas, not taking them so seriously as some adults would like. Churches give their youth great assistance when they are able to provide them with informal groups in which they can test their beliefs without being held finally accountable, and in the presence of sponsoring adults whose commitments are reasonably secure. Surely youth need occasions to confess and otherwise express their dispositional rebellion within reasonable limitations. They need opportunities to feel forgiveness and acceptance without being quickly molded into a conventional pattern before they are prepared to make long-term commitments about a way of life. Equally as much, they need to discover the adults who confirm in them beliefs by which they can live. One is often not able to predict who such persons will be, and yet the effort to provide such persons is very important. Exploring new beliefs, interacting with other youth in formal and informal settings, and discovering sponsoring adults are important elements of the context of mutuality within which the crisis of belief occurs.

## *Moral Reasoning and the Way of Life*

The crisis of belief results in being located in a way of life. This usually means an occupation, a marriage partner, financial responsibilities, and perhaps children. Each of these possibilities may be altered by the particular culture within which one is found. They may all be delayed by further education, or they may be forced upon youth by community or peer pressure for early marriage. Islamic marriage patterns, for example, change the picture, as does the tendency of some Westerners to remain single for longer periods before marrying. While the examples may change, the fact is that the crisis of belief leads to location in a way of life. Indeed, the anticipation of such a location may itself precipitate the crisis of belief.

Dispositional belief becomes the basis for dispositional care for a way of life. Underneath and within the various cultural expressions of a way of life are the activities of people who are engaged in creating and maintaining these patterns. Every occupational pattern and every family pattern inevitably contributes to the creation and maintenance of a way of life. Ways of life therefore grow and wither according to the care of the persons engaged in them. In their daily activities people express their disposition to care.

Persons may also fail to care, becoming caught in a way of life that oppresses them. They may not have resolved their beliefs and may waver, running from one activity to another without satisfaction. The underlying protomoral disposition to distrust and rebellion coupled with lack of skills and a sense of inferiority may lead to a destructive way of life. In the great criminals of history it has lead to communitywide destruction. Such persons could not wreak their havoc without the presense of certain destructive impulses in all of us. In most people there is a tendency to consider their own way of life, at the community level or the national level, as superior to all others. Religious conflict, race conflict, class conflict, and international conflict can be the result when such dispositions erupt.[35]

In Kohlberg's account, persons who are located in a way of life mature when they advance to a utilitarian conception of society. They no longer see society simply as a set of rules to regulate interpersonal relationships, but they see the importance of revising and reforming rules and regulations to meet changing circumstances. He suggests that most persons remain at the level of conventional morality, never coming to this new mode of reason, which is concerned less with maintaining a way of life than of recreating a way of life to meet new circumstances. Mature persons move away from blind obedience to laws and customs and toward considering which laws and customs ought to be continued and how they ought to be changed. Mature persons allow for minority points of view and recognize that progress must be by consensus.

What is not clear in Kohlberg's account is why a postconventional conscience must take the form of utilitarianism. For example, Christianity since the first century has understood itself to be a community standing between what has been and what is coming. While dominance of the first has led to ecclesiastical conservatism and dominance of the second to idealistic utopianism, the New Testament clearly describes the church as a koinonia community acting in the presence of the old community. If you accept New Testament thought as a high form of ethical thinking, then utilitarianism is not the only form that stage 5 moral thinking may take.

Finally, Kohlberg calls for a stage of universal ethical principle (stage 6). Here one considers not only what is appropriate for "my community," but what is good for the whole of humanity. A law may have the legitimate authority of a community and still be morally wrong. An example is Martin Luther King's determination to obey the laws of justice rather than the laws of segregation.

Again we note that Kohlberg's account remains too formal. Concern for humanity must live in the passions of people for a more just world community. It must live in the appeal of people for what is right and valuable and fitting. As important as formal reasoning is, unless it is linked to a deep and driving sympathy for humanity, it will remain detached reason. Concern for all other persons will become a passion when each person and group reaches for policies and deeds that mutually strengthen the other as well as themselves. This may mean at times the decision to sacrifice oneself, as it did in the cases of Gandhi, King, Socrates, and Jesus. A passionate, strenuous concern for other persons lives in decisions that strengthen the whole life-sustaining network. Many such policies cannot be anticipated ahead of time, but must be worked out as the situation comes close at hand. I am not delivering all decisions to "the moment," but to the ever-moving historical horizon within which we live. There is where we find our common humanity.

Emotions, intentions, intuitions, and social relationships are just as important as formal thought in an adequate account of the strength of agency. It would be unfortuate to adopt a formal orientation that cuts moral education off from the roots of the moral life. Christians believe that the love of humanity will come only with the love of God. Nourishment of the dispositions that make up the strength of human agency point to agentic resources within which we live and act, but which are open to our devotion rather than our control. Christianity does not add a different concern about the quality of life.[36] Rather it intensifies and quickens the love of humanity, and it localizes love in a living, interacting congregation. Finally, Christianity sets the formal elements of value within the story of God's relation to humanity, just as our own moral dispositions are set within the life story of each of us. Our common life story is that of the strength of agency in the sponsoring conscience struggling to overcome the tendencies of a primitive conscience.

# Chapter IV

# IN DEFENSE OF VIRTUE:
## *The Formation of Conscience*

*We need to explore what forms the conscience, what centers
bring life to wholeness and integrity and "style", what brings
lasting dispositions into being that give order and direction to
gesture, word, and deed.* —James Gustafson

In the introduction we defined conscience as "a dispositional
expression of human agency that develops as a mixture of
human virtue and weakness within various communities of
loyalty." In order to describe the context of conscience we must
give an account of human agency, and that is what we intend to
do in this chapter.

We speak of agency in order to make the ethical implications
of the "ego" more explicit. We might have chosen to speak of
"person," but we wanted to focus more pointedly upon the
living center of the person in the way that the concept "ego"
does for psychoanalysis. There is an ethical tradition of speaking
of the person as an agency, and psychoanalysts sometimes also
speak of the ego as an agency. We hope to bring the two points
of view together around this concept.

### The Meaning of Agency

By agency we mean that activity by which persons accept
experience, perceive, deliberate, choose, and express them-

118

selves.[1] In psychoanalytic thought the ego is such an agency, though it is to be distinguished from the "I" and the "self." The "I" is a conscious continuity of intentionality, while the self is composed of the various references to body and person, especially in relation to the views of other persons. The ego, however, is an agency of human adaptation that underlies the surface levels of cognitive awareness.[2]

Various levels of *awareness* are characteristic of agency. Awareness is not an all-or-none phenomenon. Many of the processes of experiencing, attending, selecting, and deciding go on at a precognitive level. While precognitive experience is somewhat accessible, much of it eludes introspection, except perhaps in events of intense ecstasy or personal encounter. When agency is weak, great portions of experience may be locked away, inaccessible to cognitive awareness.

The degrees of awareness can be illustrated by a simple device. If you will turn your attention from your focal vision to the peripheral field of your vision, you will suddenly find that the range of what you see is heightened. You can attend the sensations from various parts of your body in turn and thereby become aware of a variety of experiences that usually go unnoticed.

The primary examples of precognitive awareness, however, are those of dreaming and memory. A woman who dreams that she is visiting an army barrack is more or less aware of the selecting and attending that goes on in dreaming. Greater awareness comes in that semiconscious state of awakening when she both dreams and knows that she is dreaming. Daydreaming is a process that goes on with minimal intentionality, though the stuff of daydreams often becomes the substance of purpose. Similarly, memory can move from one recalled event to another that was not previously available to awareness. A series of words like hatpin, dry cell, curfew, and lullaby call up memories that were not available before the words were mentioned.

The point we want to make is that the clear logical distinction between the conscious and the unconscious does not exist as a sharp division within human awareness.[3] Highly conscious decisions seem to be an extension of less conscious processes of perception and selection. Furthermore, violent internal emotion or external threat as well as physical injury can diminish or even extinguish conscious deliberation and choice. Agency operates at different levels of awareness and includes precognitive processes.

We may further characterize agency as *volitional*. The human ego exists in tension with what is being experienced. Such tension is admirably conveyed by the terms attention, intention, and pretention.[4] Agency owns the various impulses by which it moves. Those impulses, emotions, and feelings may be restrained, redirected, or expressed; but agency alone can acknowledge their presence and force. Thereby feelings and impulses are accepted as "my" feelings, "my" motives, "my" interests, and "my" intentions.

The weakness of agency is a condition that Erik Erikson has called *patiens*.[5] Here there is a loss of tension with what is being experienced. Impulses, emotions, and feelings occur without being acknowledged or owned. They are allowed to run on, as in dreaming. Persons in this condition may be either apathetic and listless or hyperactive. In either case, the impulses and motives that move them are unacknowledged. Agency is overwhelmed by inhibiting emotions, various kinds of threat or control. Such persons are at the mercy of fate. They wait for that time or that personal encounter in which the power of agency will be restored.

Agency is not so much a separate and independent impulse as a tendency toward *coherence* of impulse and feeling. Coherence gives a person direction, intentionality, and rationality. Agency refers to a relative coherence in the multitude of human striving, sensing, and perceiving that is ongoing. Strivings that find some relationship to real or imagined possibilities become motives. Sensation takes some patterned form, largely through the vehicle of language. Perception is an act that presupposes some tendency to coherence, some unity of apperception.

Reason is also an activity by which persons bring some coherence to experience. The "ratio" of rationality is the activity of comparison by which difference is relativized. Two different experiences are recognized as distinct and yet with certain common features. The capacity to notice separateness and at the same time to identify common features is the root capacity of reason. When babies learn that there is an identifiable "one" who is caring for them, and when they label this experience with "mama," they sometimes call all caring persons "mama." Later, they separate "mama" from "dada" and from all other persons. In the same manner, an infant who learns to say "kitty" may refer to all animals as kitty. The child is clearly separating some experiences from others and grouping them together, even though not in the same manner as when the child learns to separate kittens from dogs and other animals. Nevertheless, the activity of separating and grouping is a very fundamental capacity of human agency, occurs very early, and is a major mode of bringing coherence to what would otherwise be the confusion of emotion and experience. Both the more rigorous rules of logic and the less rigorous and more intuitive metaphors of poetry share the common characteristics of identifying separateness and simultaneously finding some common relationships.

I shall not attempt to defend a particular theory of perception, intention, reason, and expression, except to propose that all presume some degree of unity and coherence. Such coherence is presumed both as possibility and as act. By that I mean that intention presumes not only coherence of motive, but also some coherence of direction. For example, the neonate soon begins to follow moving objects with her eyes, an evidence of a tendency toward coordination of bodily movement and perception. Agency always aims at coherence of experience. We avoid saying that agency strives for coherence, since agency is simply a reference to the relative coherence of human striving.

Coherence can be seen in its opposite, the incoherence that characterizes *patiens*. Incoherence commonly means a number of things. A person cannot speak in a manner that "makes sense" to someone else. Presumably, perceptions are disjointed and distorted, as for example in drunkenness. Various impulses move in many directions at the same moment. Not only speech but also action may be incoherent. A person may be unable to give an explanation when asked about something that she or he has done. These illustrations indicate that incoherence is a loss of the power of agency.

Finally, agency is characterized by *mutuality*. This is a characteristic that is easily overlooked in an account of the agent. Many writers have assumed that the ego is isolated, solitary, as René Descartes did when he affirmed himself in the words "I think, therefore I am." Contemporary discussion is recovering the intersubjective character of agency. The free expression of the mother activates the infant, and the expression of the infant activates the mother. Of course, the mother is rich in experience and ability while the baby is weak, but each is alike in that the expression of one activates the other.

Various examples of mutuality might be given. The freedom of a teacher strengthens the agency of students. It is equally true to say that the less skillful activity of the students strengthens the agency of the teacher. Each is mutually related to the other, although one is richer in training, experience, and ability than the other. The one who is more capable therefore has the greater responsibility for the relationship.

Alfred Schutz likes to speak of the "we" experience in which more than one person is mutually involved.[6] His primary example is that of making music. Both the musician and the listener are mutually activiated in the concert. Language has the same character. It is a shared expression that is capable of activating both the speaker and the listener. Writing is an interesting borderline instance. The expression of a writer may serve to activate a reader separated by great distance and by many years. Writing is seldom done without at least one intended reader in mind, even if it be only a note to oneself.

The condition of *patiens* is one of isolation rather than

mutuality. The person is neither strengthened by the expression of another person, nor is such a person capable of strengthening another by his or her own expression. Loss of mutuality means loss of work, art, friendship, and love. The domination of one person by another or one economic or political unit by another destroys mutuality. We may equally well say that domination limits and restricts the power of agency for both parties involved.

We have spoken of awareness, volition, coherence, and mutuality. At least these characteristics are to be included in what we mean by agency. They describe the human activity within which the conscience is formed. It is more directly in this formation that we now turn. Our discussion will proceed roughly in developmental sequence from disposition through obligation, intention, value, and belief. Under these headings we will offer a proposal about the formation of conscience.

### Disposition

Classically, a disposition was considered to be a habit of acting in a certain manner. An evil man is in the habit of acting evilly, and a good man is in the habit of acting well. A disposition in Aristotle's view was established by a series of decisions so that the constantly extending sequence predisposed the next decision.[7] A disposition in one direction may be changed one act at a time until the series begins to extend in another direction. One is reminded of Alcoholics Anonymous' very effective program of refusing to drink alcohol for this day only, that decision being renewed each day.

One may ask whether a disposition is an orientation gained largely from past experience. The term *orientation* is too strictly cognitive in its connotations to carry what we mean by disposition. During a tour of the Alhambra, the seven-hundred-year-old former Moslem palace in Granada, Spain, a group may hear the guide refer to the Hall of Justice as the appetizer, the court of Lions as the main course, and the cupola over the room of the two sisters as the dessert. We would say that such a guide is oriented to a meal or a banquet in his description. Should the guide be constantly trying to decide whether to begin the tour at the Hall of Justice or at the General Life gardens, we would not say that he is oriented to indecision. We might understand him to be dispositionally indecisive, and we might also understand him to be dispositionally oriented to food. Our example suggests that while a disposition may include an orientation, it is more than that.

Similarly, a disposition is more than a habit. Our modern use of the term *habit* is probably different from Aristotle's. The notion of habit has been appropriated by the behaviorists to refer to a behavioral connection between a stimulus and a response. We might say that our imaginary guide habitually responds to choice situations with indecision, and that he habitually describes architectural wonders by finding analogies to food and eating. Yet we would hardly say that he is habitually incoherent in his description of the palace, or that he is habitually unaware of the responses on his listeners. Our guide's incoherence and lack of awareness are more dispositional than habitual. Habit refers more to intentionality than to other characteristics of agency, and orientation refers to elements of coherence. However, disposition includes the whole range of agentic characteristics, that is, awareness, intentionality, coherence, and mutuality. Let us therefore use the term *disposition,* at least in its moral sense, to indicate the relatively enduring strength or weakness of agency.

I am, of course, assuming that agency is not simply an either-or matter. Whereas choice as an activity of agency always involves an either-or decision, agency itself may be relatively weak or strong. The severest limitation upon agency comes in the breakdown of mutuality. Agency is properly extended by activating other persons; it is restricted by the absence of communication and expression between persons who could be significantly related. To act in such a way as to break off reciprocity between one person and another is to threaten the freedom of both persons involved. For example, enforced confinement limits agency because it is a response to what was considered to be an arbitrary act, and it expresses the agency of officials representing a community whose collective impulses and restrictive norms are being carried out. The breakdown of mutuality limits the freedom of all persons involved. Disposition is then the relatively enduring power or weakness of agency, and the major limitation upon agency is the degree of mutuality between persons who are significantly related to one another.

We may ask whether agency changes throughout life or remains constant. In one way it remains constant, and in another way it changes. Constancy is to be found in those qualities we have identified as characteristic of agency, that is, awareness, volition, coherence, and mutuality. It seems that as long as we live we have some capacity for agentic expression. While we are asleep we have a minimal level of awareness. Yet perhaps we dream, and that along with the relaxation of our bodies contributes to our freedom when we awake.

Agency also changes. It may become stronger or weaker, extend over a wider or narrower range of experience. It may exhibit different levels of awareness, volition, coherence, and mutuality. To the extent that agency is strong we may speak of a person as possessing virtue. To the extent that agency is weak we may speak of a person as lacking virtue.[8]

All persons confront a series of crises throughout their lifetimes. To meet these crises with maximum awareness and decisiveness predisposes persons to meet future crises with strength. Similarly, a breakdown in coherence and mutuality predisposes such persons to meet future crises in weakness. As persons mature, higher levels of reason and cognitive orientation become increasingly central to their dispositions. The classical discussions of disposition have not done justice to the crises of human growth and the generational differences that the modern social sciences have described.

Let us illustrate the earliest of the crises of which we have spoken in terms of the relationship between the infant and her mother. An infant is born presumably with a variety of impulses and feelings, relatively uncoordinated sensations, into a community that cares for her more or less according to commonly accepted values. Her crying and other expressions from the time of birth occur within a social relationship such that her needs usually prompt a caring response. To some extent she shares sucking, "rooting," and other instinctual responses with lower order mammals.

Very soon, however, her "rooting" is no longer random, but is directed toward the person who cares for her. Very soon her eyes begin to follow this person. Such elemental responses from an infant are a powerful incentive to the mother. In the terms laid out by George Herbert Mead we can say that a preverbal conversation of needing and caring is going on between the two of them. There is what Erik Erikson calls a mutual recognition between them. It is important to notice that the infant's weak agentic expression activates the mother, just as the mother's expression activates the infant. Too often the infant is considered to be a bundle of reflexes without agentic expression. Mothers know that their infants are centers of agency, so they act in ways that call forth this agency.

The crisis comes as the mother withdraws her constant attention from the child, which she inevitably must. Psychoanalysts have spoken of weaning and the oral crisis. Recent opinion emphasizes the significance of the withdrawal of the mother. The child needs less attention as she grows in coordination and power of activity, for example, eyesight, sitting, crawling, grasping. The crisis is not in the separation itself, but in the threat to mutuality that separation brings. If the infant is overcome by strong impulses of rage, agency will be impaired. Such failure may lead to a condition of apathy in which impulses lose all direction. Spitz's studies of hospitalism indicate that this condition can be so severe as to be fatal.[9]

In the face of the crisis brought on by separation, all infants develop some enduring sense of trust mixed with mistrust. Trust is an acceptance of being together in the world. It is a measure of the degree to which preverbal acceptance is extended over the range of mutual stimulation and perception between infant and mother. Trust is evident in the child's increasing sensible awareness and in the beginning of language. It includes acceptance of both impulse and object, as, for example, in sucking and grasping.

Trust is the earliest expression of agency and is perhaps best understood as a characteristic of the pattern of interaction between mother and child. It may be well to mention again that the mother's attitude will be affected by her own past experience, the support of her community, and the cultural ideals that she has accepted. The disposition to trust in the face of overwhelming impulses, threat, and separation we may call hope. Hope as a mark of strong agency is a relatively enduring disposition to trust in the future. To pass through the crisis of separation with maximum trust and with hope as an established disposition is to approach succeeding crises with maximum freedom.

A second dispositional crisis is that of the will. The crisis of will is brought on by the child's increasing coordination, control, and awareness in such activities as crawling, walking, biting, grasping, pulling, kicking, and screaming. These activities inevitably bring about parental restriction. Psychoanalysts have written much about the struggle between parent and child over toilet training. What is at issue in all the activities just mentioned is the pattern of control between parent and child over the expression of growing capacities.

Theories of child development sometimes miss the fact that parent and child place mutual demands upon each other. To the extent that the child's trust can be extended to the acceptance of growing musucular capacity, she gains freedom to control her body. Such trust must include assent to the prohibitions that parents inevitably exert, even though she cannot yet understand the reason for such prohibitions. The child who can own and assent to both the impulses for bodily expression and to the limitations of a caring community begins to exercise will.

The prohibitions of parents bring on a crisis of will. In the face of such limitations the child gains some sense of being autonomous, albeit mixed with shame and doubt. *Patiens* in this instance is a loss of control in the face of overwhelming impulses of anger and shame. The relatively enduring sense of freely initiated expression within limitation is what we mean by will. As a disposition more or less established in early childhood, will becomes foundational for the strength of agency that develops thereafter.

Again, the most important factor in the child's exercise of will is the community of significant agents mutually related to her. Parents who arbitrarily demand of a child what is beyond the child's control exhibit weakness of agency, and they thereby limit the reciprocity by which the child's ego is strengthened. What is commonly called "willfulness" is not genuine strength of will, but rather a breakdown of mutual control on the part of both child and parent. As a result of the crisis of will, the child may develop an enduring disposition of willfulness. Such a child will likely have a premature conscience that is scrupulous about cleanliness and is overly conscientious throughout life. In the extreme, the scrupulous conscience can become paranoid.

It seems likely that everyone carries some deeply rooted restrictions from the early crisis of will. These have to do with sex, cleanliness, and violence. For the infant such taboos are usually mixed with the practice of the forbidden behavior, presumably because the child does not really understand or assent to the restrictions. Willful persons are most likely to insist upon certain limitations and unknowingly find exceptions for themselves. Strength of will, in contrast to willfulness, can give assent to both the expression and limitation of impulses. Will as a disposition to act within accepted limitations is basic to the free expression of agency thereafter.

We have used the instances of trust and will as examples of protomoral dispositions. We see that from early childhood conscience is related to both strength and weakness of agency, to both the self and the caring community. To the question of what change occurs in agency we may now answer that the resolution of each developmental crisis results in a relatively enduring strength or weakness of agency with which further crises are met. Every powerful agentic expression by a person or by the significant attending persons strengthens that person's agency, and every weak expression weakens it.

## *Obligation*

At this point let us consider the question of when and how obligation enters into human experience. On the surface it seems evident that an infant is not obligated to do anything. Though a two-year-old child is expected by the parents to keep clean, we would hardly say that the child is obligated to do so. Two-year-old children do not yet have enough understanding, experience, or self-direction for us to speak in this way. On the other hand, parents are obligated to train a child to keep clean. At least it is not out of hand preposterous to suggest that they have such an obligation. However, one immediately thinks of other obligations that are more fundamental, for example, preserving the life of the child or teaching her to speak.

Why are not the many expectations upon a young child obligations, and when do they become so? Let me suggest that the expectations become obligations as they are symbolized in language, internalized by the child, and as they become intentions of the child in the absence of the parent.[10] Children face many demands that are rewarded by love and approval on one hand, and punishment and threat on the other. The internalization of these demands constitutes the archaic demanding conscience. The roots of the archaic conscience are established very early in life, but the crisis of intentionality seems to come approximately at the age of five or six.

Something more fundamental than the internalization of demands also occurs between parent and infant, the mutual recognition and activation of agency. The reciprocity of trust and of autonomy along with the dispositions to hope and to will are fundamental to every expectation. The child's assent to receive gradually becomes willing and active mastery. Receiving agency becomes willing agency in the way that we have already described.

As the child moves from passive to active modes of expression, she meets the restrictive expectations of the parents. A pattern of mutual control is established during what we have called the crisis of will. In this process the child not only receives the protection and restriction of the parents, but she actively assents to or resists them. In her own way she attempts to control the parents. A pattern of control is established as the response of each is called out by the agentic expression of the other. Arbitrary and thoughtless demands upon the child, or, for that matter, arbitrary and thoughtless withdrawal into permissiveness, weaken the child's agency, since agency is strengthened within a community of mutual agentic expression.

While every child takes into herself parental demands with all their peculiarities, for example, to eat peas, celery, or spinach, every child also develops a disposition to give or withhold consent to what is required of her. The primitive superego becomes obligatory as a person's self-esteem is tied to the demands upon that person. In the process of giving and withholding consent, the disposition to will what is required or to refuse is being established. This disposition to will depends upon trust and reciprocity between two or more mutually consenting agents.

Here it seems to be that reciprocity is in the first instance trustful receiving, and only later does it become active expression within mutually accepted limitations. The truly obligatory element for the infant is implicit in the relationship to the parent as a caring agent. From the child's perspective, the parent is in the first instance an agent to be more or less trusted. Only as the child gains language and intentionality does she become "obligated" to parental expectations, and that only because she owes her agency to them in a very significant way. It is in agency as the peculiarly human quality of interaction that obligation arises. Obligation for the child does not belong specifically to parental demands, but rather to the caring initiative of parental agency through which the child's agency is called forth.

The child does not owe her personhood to her parents alone. Their care serves to call out the agency that humankind has acquired in the course of human evolution. One might better say that parental care calls out the agency that is characteristic of all human expression. For this reason agency is both a condition and a consequence of human community, rising out of the interdependence of persons and generations.

To repeat, the basic moral reality of agency is in the first instance mutual trust and activation within commonly accepted limitations. Those limitations became obligatory only as hope and will become dispositional, and as the child gains language and purpose. For the parents care is an activity that is also an obligation. Parents not only care for their children; they ought to do so. Parents not only expect certain things of their children; they ought to act so as to strengthen the child as an agent. Respect for agency is more important than any particular requirement that is put upon a child. Mutual recognition, activation, and control is the basis for a morality that strengthens rather than weakens, sponsors rather than blames.

Inevitably, commands and requirements are among the earliest experiences of childhood. They come before deliberate intentionality and guilt. They often take the form of categorical imperatives such as "No! No!" "Don't touch that!" Such commands may express the sympathetic, concerned, caring, reasonable, and intentional judgments of parents, or they may express harsh, unthinking, unintended impulses. In other words, they express either strong or weak agency. It is rather obvious that parental behavior, like most human behavior, is a mixture of both.

The categorical quality of agency lies in its capacity to activate or limit other agents within a significant community.[11] The teleological quality lies in the fact that agency may be deepened and extended. The expression of trust, hope, will, intentionality, and deliberate choice strengthens each and all of those involved.

## Intention

Intention as we shall use it signifies that some expression of agency is perceived in its very expression to be a means to some situation not now wholly present. By purposes we mean long-range intentions; therefore, we can often speak of intention and purpose in the same phrase. Our discussion of the rule-oriented conscience in a previous chapter raises the question of intention. We have said that younger children tend to judge an act simply on the basis of harm or damage done, while older children are far more likely to take into account the intention of the actor. Developmental studies suggest that intentionality becomes a disposition during the preschool years from three to six, even though some intentionality is present from the earliest months of infancy. The preschool child is gaining much greater facility in using language. She also has an increasingly agile imagination. During this time, the incest taboo and the prohibition against violence is established. These taboos become a part of the archaic restrictive conscience, the beginnings of which we shall discuss in more detail in the next chapter.

Along with certain firmly established categorical requirements, the child takes in a number of principles and ideals. Such principles are surely confused in the child's mind and often unrelated to behavior, if Piaget's observations about preschool children are correct. The young child has a fanciful and highly unrealistic conception of growing up. Her play discloses her far-reaching imagination. The play of young children serves to bring the overwhelming world into the manageable limitations of the play lot or the living room. Play exhibits purpose directed to fanciful ends.

The acceptance of certain categorical taboos, largely at a precognitive level, is the watershed between what is simply wished for and what may be realistically purposed. Such intentionality is called out by living within a family and a community with a sense of purpose. The purpose of parents and other adults serves to activate agency in the child. A neighborhood that is filled with busy people is a delight to a preschool child. A boy may play at being a milkman or a cook; a girl, at being a teacher or a business woman. In either case, although the play is largely a matter of fanciful imitation, it also serves to express and extend the intentionality of the child.

Should a family in which a child is reared be highly divided in its purposes, the child's conscience as an internal sponsor of activity is likely to be highly divided also. In the same way, coherence of purpose, or the lack of it, in the wider community affects unity of purpose in the child. As she learns to distinguish more clearly between what is real and what is not, her intentions become more reasonable, more clearly oriented to community norms.

Conflicts of conscience may occur in several ways for a young child. There may be a conflict between the encouragement of a parent and the taboos that the child has already internalized. Some requirements may conflict with others. The child's sense of purpose may be caught within a conflict of purposes within the family. Such conflicts are closely related to the use of language. "Don't break it!" or "My, what a big girl!" are the kind of prohibitions and encouragement that make up conscience. Purposes are built of remembered snatches of conversation, often fancifully altered. Hence, conscience is often considered to be the voice within.

The preschool conscience is a mixture of taboo and purpose, with the latter becoming an increasingly important expression of agency. While a broken taboo may make a child angry or ashamed, frustrated purposes can throw her into despair and guilt. Agency from the preschool years onward is increasingly expressed as intentionality. The relatively enduring strength of agency is thereafter the disposition to purpose and intend.

Both the obligations and the purposes that are more or less

accepted by children are distributed throughout a significant community. Parsons has shown how the incest taboo is a sanction of the community kinship pattern.[12] The limitation of violence is the initial sanction of political order. Similarly, purpose is shared in the family and more widely in the community. Purpose and intention depend upon the development of language and imagination, but also upon the various roles of the family as an intentional group within a larger community. In the crisis of purpose, the child accepts her role within the family and is thereby prepared for participation in the larger community.

## *Values and Ideals*

Our discussion of intentions and the sense of purpose has stressed the young child's rather fanciful view of the world. As a child comes into the school years, she gradually begins to distinguish between what is real and what is fanciful. One illustration is the perennial discussion that first and second graders have about whether Santa Claus is real.

The transition from fanciful purpose to values of the real world may be illustrated in various ways. Freud described how the little boy's desire to possess his mother finally must give way to the reality of their difference in size and to the fact that the mother and father have a privileged and exclusive sexual relationship with each other. The child represses his conflicting emotions and begins to identify with other adults outside the family. At the same time, he sublimates sexual interest, which is to say that he becomes interested in baseball, racing cars, astronauts, collecting stones, fishing, and other activities that are considered to be masculine. There is a more or less conscious acknowledgment of what cannot be and the redirection of his interests to ideals and activities that seem more capable of being realized. At least he can dream about these other interests, for example, becoming an astronaut, without feeling guilty. Similarly, a girl represses her interest in the father and sublimates this interest in acceptable feminine activities, like cooking, cleaning, sewing, and study. We must now consider all the activities just mentioned, from baseball to cooking, appropriate interests for both boys and girls.

Piaget similarly notes the child's transition from egocentric to concrete thinking. Egocentric thought is fanciful and imaginative, while concrete thought is able to apply rules and concepts to particular experiences. About the age of six or seven the child begins to play to win, even though she may not know all the subtleties of a game. She can begin to make moral judgments on the basis of prevailing values. Which of the prevailing values she chooses will be heavily influenced by the ideals of her parents, teachers, and peers.

Erik Erikson makes the same point in his own way. The school-aged child is exposed to a variety of values outside her immediate family. She acts to attain realized purposes and to gain usable skills. She needs the sponsorship of adults who can train her increasing abilities in meaningful ways. Her own values and ideals are activated by those of her teachers and playmates. The moral crisis of this age is that of accepting values which are at least realizable enough to give the child an enduring sense of competence. To fail is to feel incompetent, unworthy, and to be unable to make decisions based upon commonly accepted values. A child who is not learning to read, is not able to do useful tasks at home, and who generally fails at whatever she attempts will have great difficulty adopting the values and ideals of her family and community. She is more likely to develop a dispositional feeling of incompetence and to reject the values of those who care for her (or who have neglected her).

Just as the preschool child is responsive to the pattern of supervision in the family, so the school-aged child responds to the pattern of supervision in the classroom. The way a principal runs the school or the way a teacher directs the class may reinforce a child's archaic restrictive conscience. If the school atmosphere is such that someone is always being blamed, the children learn to expect blame. It is a very courageous principal and staff of teachers who set about to eliminate blame and punishment in a school that is situated in an underprivileged community. If children come from broken homes and are beaten up on the way to school, the teachers will find it difficult to keep any semblance of order. Yet some schools in privileged communities are run like factories where the most important activity is punching in and punching out on the time clock. Assignments are handed out with heavy threats. The supervisory pattern in a school can have a dramatic effect upon the conscience of children.

The supervisory pattern of a teacher will inevitably include some commands as well as some goals for behavior. A teacher's commands will generalize and extend the taboos of the archaic restrictive conscience. The child's attitudes about sex and about violence are modified by what happens at school, even when these subjects are not explicitly discussed. Sex and force come to be patterned within the network of purposes at the heart of a community. Commands are also heard differently by school-aged children than by those who are younger. Children of school age are increasing in their capacity to purpose, reason, and choose. The children talk together about the commands given to them, and they work at finding reason and purpose in these commands.

A school's supervisory pattern can stimulate a child's purposeful sponsoring conscience. Nearly everyone remembers a teacher who saw in her or him abilities that had never before been recognized. A child from a home where parents are harsh and impulsive may find her willful attitudes modified by a school where the supervisory pattern features consideration, thoughtfulness, and purposefulness. School-aged children are especially receptive to purposeful supervision. While the child of six years or younger is likely to follow a command without understanding it, children between eight and eleven years of age can understand and apply rules to a variety of situations. They can think concretely, to use Jean Piaget's term, about ways to act out commonly accepted values. Only as they reach their teen years, however, are they able to think critically, to decide for themselves what values they wish to adopt.

Conflicts of conscience may take several different forms for school-aged children. The crisis of value at this age may be a struggle between the archaic restrictive conscience and the commonly shared purposes of the wider community. Perhaps the child has internalized a strong prohibition against fighting, but then finds a priority placed upon strength and prowess among the other children at school. The values of the community may be in conflict with one another so that the child is confronted with difficult decisions. Very few persons of whatever age can avoid being caught between the ideal of love taught in the church and the ideal of taking whatever you can as practiced by so many persons. Children can be caught between the value of the equality of all people and the achievement of excellence. Being superior on the baseball field and equal with one's brothers and sisters at home may not be easily achieved. An Amish child may come from a family that places low priority upon formal education, but she may attend a school where she learns to love education. Children can be seriously torn by such conflicts, for they cannot understand them from a theoretical standpoint. They must struggle along to find some unique resolution. Children who fail to achieve some coherence of value will be handicapped throughout the later formation of their identities.

We may now ask whether obligation or value is more primitive developmentally. Is intrinsic obligation or is purpose more deeply rooted in human behavior? One is reminded of the debate between those who approve of "rightness" as a pattern of obligations and those who approve of "goodness" as a goal toward which all things aim. Piaget asserts that the deontological mentality is more primitive than the teleological. Do our observations suggest the same conclusion?

Two comments are important in this regard. One has to do with imposed morality and the other with the meaning of agency. Piaget errs in his description of the three- to

seven-year-old child when he ignores the sponsoring conscience. Agency, as we have tried to show, is expressed in
mutual activation before it is imposed as demand. In the struggle
of will between parent and child, between brother and sister,
certain patterns of mutual regulation are established, often
unconsciously and with great psychological power. However, it
is not the force of repressed emotion but the strength of
coherently expressed emotion that constitutes agency. Mutuality
between persons is a moral phenomenon more fundamental than
imposed demands.

Piaget's approach draws upon Immanuel Kant's distinction
between heteronomous and autonomous morality and then
proceeds to show that the child moves from one to the other. The
distinction is very important, but it is not accurate to say that the
morality of a six-year-old is heteronomous and that of a
teen-ager is autonomous. Rather, human agency is subject to
heteronomy during all the stages of life. The heteronomy of the
early years is imposed morality, while the heteronomy of the
teen years is more likely to be imposed ideology. Contrariwise,
the autonomy of a child is her free expression of hope, will, and
purpose, while that of a teen-ager includes her orientation,
beliefs, and personal identity. Obligation occurs as a developmental crisis much earlier in the child's life than does the crisis
of identity because of the various changing capacities that we
have already enumerated, but this does not mean that
heteronomy is to be assigned to the early years of life.

Immanuel Kant's distinction between autonomy and
heteronomy is much more useful than are his panegyrics over
duty. His description of duty is too similar to what Freud
discovered in neurotic compulsiveness. One need not accept all
of Kant's description of duty to appreciate the importance of his
other distinctions. Our use of *agens* and *patiens*, strong and
weak agency, is very close to Kant's distinction between
autonomy and heteronomy.

The intrinsic rightness of agency is the basis for the sense of
right that primitive commands and practices presume. Taboos

against violence and sexuality become a tribal conscience, primarily because of the prolonged infancy of humankind. Civilization is ever working at sanctions to control primitive emotions and ever expressing such emotions in the name of just causes. However, the mutually activating power of agency is more enduring than any form of imposed morality.

Our second comment has to do with the meaning of agency. Throughout this discussion we have assumed that agency is not an all-or-none expression. Agency may be extended or limited in a variety of ways, for example, in greater awareness, deeper purpose, more coherence, and increased mutuality. Stronger or weaker agency is a possibility from birth to death. Human freedom is not to be found in incoherent impulses, but in the characteristics of agentic strength. A parent purposely encourages a child's agentic strength. Therein the parent differs from the child. While the infant can only hope or will at a precognitive level, the parent can intend in a mature way because purpose, value, and care have become dispositional.

Perhaps we can ask the question in this way: Does a two-year-old child value a favorite toy? Does she value her parents? A two-year-old's value is more a matter of emotional satisfaction than of intentionality. The roots of value are elementally present in the child's trust and willing coherence of emotion toward either toy or parent. As she acquires language and begins to play, more and more she regularly intends to use the toy or be near the parent. As she grows older she may forget her emotional attachment to the toy. More and more she develops a purposeful relationship to parents and others. With the establishment of hope, will, and purpose as dispositions, the child can value both toys and parents.

Right and value are both a part of what we mean by agency. Freud noted that the superego contains both prohibitions and ideals, and these are taken in with the mother's milk, although they are not finally established until the Oedipal period. Right seems to have a developmental crisis in the preschool years, while value has its crisis more quietly during the school years.

This does not mean, however, that one is ethically inferior to the other. Rather, imposed obligations or imposed values are inferior to those that have free consent. The archaic demanding conscience may impose both, while the consenting purposing agent may espouse both. The primitiveness of the feeling of right does not diminish its ethical validity. It remains right that persons respond to one another as free agents capable of an infinite variety of mutually enhancing expression.

### Belief

Just as language and imagination permit the preschool child to act out playful purposes, and just as increasing capacities allow the school-aged child to adopt values around which she can organize real skills, so also adolescence brings new capacities for the expression of agency. By eleven or twelve years of age young persons can begin to reason conceptually and critically, while at the same time they are gaining adult bodies and powerful new emotional impulses.

New capacities alter the conscience by introducing the element of belief. By belief we refer to those larger life orientations, religious or otherwise, by which our behavior is ultimately justified and guided. The adolescent can imagine and consider various ways of life, various life orientations. The selection of one particular way of life becomes a developmental crisis, acted out in all societies by pubertal ceremonies. Unlike preliterate societies, complex modern societies have such a profusion of various ways of life and such a mixture of values that many adolescents are thrown into identity confusion.

R. M. Hare interestingly considers the hypothetical instance of a person who might understand all the infinite consequences of alternative ways of life. Hare then comments that even such a person would have to choose unless he were to act simply by impulse.[13] Adolescence is a period when adult commitments are increasingly near at hand. Even so, the adolescent is not in the position of Hare's clairvoyant decider. Lacking omniscience, a youth must decide upon the basis of less than well-informed experience. She must therefore appeal to beliefs that make sense of her limited life experience and to communities whose ways of life make sense to her. These circumstances conspire to make belief an important element in the identity crisis of adolescence.

Not all youth make such decisions about their own beliefs. Friendenberg laments the "vanishing adolescent," by which he means that many youth no longer go through the period of choosing their own beliefs.[14] Rather, they fall unthinkingly into those values handed to them as children. Or consider Kohlberg's study of adolescence, in which he found various levels of development existing concurrently throughout the teens.[15] Not all youth by any means reach a stage of deciding their own ways of life. Even so, the facing of adulthood with its various options cannot be wholly avoided by youth, even though they may allow the choice simply to "happen" at a precognitive level.

Conflicting belief systems come with an awareness of conflicting interest groups within a community. Max Weber pointed out that the rich appeal to God to justify their privileged position, while the poor appeal to the same God to justify their suffering.[16] Belief and political awareness are closely related. The search for identity is also a search for an orientation from which to participate in the political life of a community. In recent years youth in the United States have become more politically aware, evidenced by their passion to compel colleges and universities to adopt more nearly just procedures and policies. The beliefs of youth in the world today are adding a new dimension to the struggle for equality between the races and for justice in international affairs.

The peculiar agentic weakness of adolescence is found in the identity crisis. Dizzy with the freedom of choosing a way of life, youth may seize arbitrarily upon one or another ideology without achieving a sense of identity. Ideology may be a cover of infantile mistrust, shame, destructive rage, even when practiced in the name of humanity. Hitler's call for *Lebensraum* was a moral appeal motivated by destructive rage. It was nevertheless very effective in mobilizing the powerful energies and zeal of the Hitler youth.

The rebel can act in the name of a vision of humanity that will no longer accept the system of arbitrary power and privilege of the few. His or her very "unbelief" may be intrinsically a belief in the ability of persons to act in a way that enlarges mutuality for all persons involved. Human motives are seldom pure, often mixed, so that belief in the possibilities of human agency may well be mixed with arbitrary zeal. Our analysis would suggest that the extension of human freedom is an ever-present possibility. Freedom cannot be arbitrarily imposed or extended, but can be the basis for action only within communities of mutual awareness.

The conflict of conscience in youth may take the form of a conflict of belief, a contradiction of ways of life, a search for justice within the political life of a community. All of this seems implied by Erikson's description of the identity crisis. Infantile impulses or childish values may restrict the sense of identity. They may impel a person to act out a way of life and to adopt beliefs that take months or years to be abandoned. A young person may adopt the very opposite beliefs to those that she feels are being forced upon her. Many youth go in the reverse direction of trying to avoid the pain of the identity crisis by adopting traditional taboos and values without deliberate choice and without the confirming recognition of a significant community. Implicitly or explicitly every person accepts some belief orientation by which the sanctions of society are reestablished or redirected from one generation to the next.

### The Humanization of Conscience

We cannot conclude a statement about the formation of conscience without asking whether there are not some ethical norms to which conscience is bound. Are there certain universal moral principles to which all persons owe allegiance, or is the conscience dissolved into a series of developmental processes?

Must we conclude with some social scientists that conscience is after all an unfortunate evolutionary vestige of humankind's prolonged childhood?

In the previous section we suggested that maturity involves the affirmation of belief without omniscience. For this purpose we constantly need symbols from which values and principles are derived and by which agency is activated. Robert White has used the happy phrase "the humanization of conscience," which may serve us as just such a symbol. Others have spoken in a very similar way. Erik Erikson refers to "the mature ethical sense," and Edmond Cahn appeals to "the sense of injustice." Gordon Allport distinguishes between the authentic and the tribal conscience.

Donald L. Berry has described the mature conscience in a way that is very much in keeping with what we have been saying. He begins by explaining that conscience is not some organ, some separable internal system, like the brain, the ear, or the eye.

> Conscience is simply a way of viewing the totality of the self in its moment of committing and trusting. As such it does not function in any way that is divorced from the kind of person we are. Our conscience is informed at every moment by our personal history, our scheme of values, our personal hierarchy of preferences and concerns. Conscience is the voice of this intricate fabric of trusts and loyalties, not some private inner voice discontinuous with the rest of our life; when conscience guides us, we are guiding ourselves from the depths of our being, in the context of the constellation of decisions and loves that have made us what we are.[17]

In each of the above references the appeal is to a mature, choosing, ethical sensitivity that is at the same time open to its own past values and to present historical change. The rational tradition from Aristotle through Aquinas and Kant must be heard, but it cannot be accepted without reinterpretation. While eternal norms are not so evident in today's world as they were thought to be in the past, yet we may still appeal to reason. To ask what we ought to do is always to appeal, at least in part, to reasonable considerations.

The humanization of conscience is a symbol that directs our attention to the arbitrary punishment and deprivation by which certain admonitions are written into human impulses long before persons can act reasonably and responsibly. The accidents of age, sex, race, economics, geography, and culture become the occasion for the differences of status, privilege, and opportunity. Enforced by ideology, custom, and threat, such arbitrary impositions are impressed upon the minds, emotions, and volitions of one generation after another. Hidden in preconscious or unconscious recesses of the personality, they enervate free agency to the point of emotional breakdown, or they sometimes combine to erupt in collective violence.

Nevertheless, the very possibility of taboos lies in the human capacity to give assent and to act purposefully. Automatic and restrictive moral impulses can be modified by significant persons, purposeful communities, new values and images of justice. Human agency always stands before the possibility of enlarged freedom.

Freud may have been right that civilization would be impossible without the internalization of archaic inhibitions. Maturity is probably never unmixed with some disposition toward the expression of chaotic and destructive impulses— often in the name of the highest values. But the disposition to mutual trust and consent is the real vitality of human agency. When the latter disposition develops within a community of purpose, value, and belief, human agency is strengthened, and imposed morality is replaced by mature responsibility.

The conscience is often a battlefield between the seemingly strong but infantile moral impulses and the more durable acts of agency, between arbitrary expression and communal reciprocity. Agency is an expression of community, originating in mutual trust and issuing in responsibility for the vitality of all human life. Such a statement does not, of course, conclusively demonstrate the normative validity of mutuality. The statement becomes valid from an ethical point of view to the extent that it brings meaning and intentionality to human agency. The possibilities of human agency are not so easily demonstrated to the skeptical. The appeal of customary values and the unconscious need for moral rationalization prevents any such demonstration. The qualities of agency are identifiable to anyone who looks, but the description of them becomes valuable only as it activates free ethical judgment. Our description is a perspective on certain facts that may also become a source of identity. To avoid choosing one or another enabling belief may itself be a form of infantilism.

We conclude that the humanization of conscience is a striving for individual integrity within a community of mutual recognition, trust, and purpose. The question of what one ought to do calls up a particularly personal and individual decision, though one which always has wider social and historical consequences. The humanization of conscience always involves an appeal to a larger community of loyalty than the one in which a person is oriented by training and experience. The logic of the mature conscience is that of the potentially universal mutuality of human agency. The imperative toward universal mutuality cannot be avoided without denying one's own personhood and that of all to whom one is related.

# Chapter V

## THE WICKETS KEEP CHANGING:
### *Conscience and the Way of Life*

*And you've no idea how confusing it is all the things being alive: for instance, there's the arch I've got to go through next walking around at the other end of the ground — and I should have croqueted the Queen's hedgehog just now, only it ran away when it saw mine coming!*
                                                        —*Lewis Carroll*

In the Queen of Hearts' garden was a curious croquet ground to say the least. With live hedgehogs for croquet balls, flamingos for mallets, and soldiers bending down to be wickets, Alice found it nearly impossible to play the game. Whenever she would try to strike her live hedgehog "ball" with her live flamingo "mallet," the one or the other would move. As for the doubled-up soldier "wickets," they were constantly walking about the court. Small wonder that Alice came to the conclusion that "it was a very difficult game indeed."

In his description of the croquet game in *Alice in Wonderland*, Lewis Carroll seems to be saying that there must be an established set of rules before a game is possible at all. With no agreed upon rules there is no way to make a decision within the game, and so Alice soon wanders off to talk to the Cheshire Cat. When one considers the various "ways of life" with their many different values and priorities, one can begin to feel like Alice in the Queen of Hearts's croquet game. While the various games may have reasonably consistent rules within themselves, the wickets keep changing if one moves from one game to another. It is this relativity of various ways of life in relation to conscience that we want to consider now.

We concluded the last chapter with reference to the "way of life" and the risk of belief as the final arbiters of moral decision. Many of our decisions, including our moral decisions, are guided by social convention, folkways, mores, and customs of the society in which we live. Even the most sophisticated ethical decisions take place within the principles and commitments that we espouse, and such principles and commitments are a part of our way of life. R. M. Hare makes the same point in this way:

> A complete justification of a decision would consist of a complete account of its effects, together with a complete account of the principles which it observed, and the effect of observing those principles—for, of course, it is the effects (what obeying them in fact consists in) which give content to the principles too. Thus, if pressed to justify a decision completely, we have to give a complete specification of the way of life of which it is a part. This complete specification it is impossible in practice to give; the nearest attempts are those given by the great religions, especially those which can point to historical persons who carried out that way of life in practice.[1]

The way of life is quite close to what the anthropologists mean by the culture of a people. Culture includes the beliefs, knowledge, values, norms, institutions, roles, technology, and products of labor, as well as the patterns by which they are created and preserved. The way of life as we shall use it does not refer to the technology and products of labor, that is, to the material culture, but rather it refers to the beliefs, knowledge, values, norms, institutions, and roles of a people, as well as the patterns and practices by which these are created and preserved. Perhaps we could put it more simply by saying that the way of life is made up of the beliefs, commitments, and practices by which people care for themselves, for one another, and for their culture.

We want to propose in this chapter that human cultures with

their various ways of life are expressions of human agency on one hand, and the vehicles by which human agency is shaped on the other. In culture can be found the characteristics of human agency, namely, awareness, intentionality, coherence, and mutuality. Culture preserves awareness when feelings, memories, perceptions, and anticipations are described in language, literature, science, education, and religion. Culture gives expression to volition, attention, and purpose in many ways. For example, one of the functions of religion is to integrate the various impulses of a people in order to give form to community purpose. The political process by which common policies are hammered out is another example of the way a culture shapes intentionality. The cultural expression of coherence is seen in all forms of knowledge, modes of reasoning, science, and literature that make up a culture. Mutuality is expressed in role relationships, institutions, normative patterns of behavior, and common values.

If culture is the creation of human agency, it is also the vehicle by which human agency is extended and enlarged or diminished and restricted. Language, education, and all forms of communication, which themselves are the creation of human agency, are at the same time the vehicles by which human agency is enlarged and deepened. Language, education, and communication technology are therefore highly important to any culture. Dictatorial governments understand this, and they quickly take over newspapers, radio stations, schools, and public assemblies so that they can control what shall be communicated.

The example of dictatorial governments also shows how culture can serve to restrict and diminish human agency. Propaganda is a means by which the awareness of a people is restricted to facts and interpretations deemed appropriate by those in control. Agency is often restricted in less organized ways. In many places around the world people are caught between (sometimes unconscious) discrimination that has received the moral authority of common practice and the value of equality that is publicly espoused. This leads to a conflict between the archaic conscience of common taboos and the more nearly human conscience of ideals and of common identity. When people like Martin Luther King step out to challenge discriminatory practices in the name of commonly approved values of equality and humanity, then the "social conscience" of many is sensitized.

> More than ever before, my friends, men of all races and nations are today challenged to be neighborly. The call for a worldwide good-neighbor policy is more than an ephemeral shibboleth; it is the call to a way of life which will transform our imminent cosmic elegy into a psalm of creative fulfillment. No longer can we afford the luxury of passing by on the other side. Such folly was once called moral failure; today it will lead to universal suicide.[2]

While the compassionate conscience of some is quickened by such words, infantile rage is roused among those who feel that the traditional taboos are being violated. Many persons in the United States looked upon the assassination of Martin Luther King as an act of righteous retribution. The example serves to show not only how conscience is socially distributed, but also how the primitive condemning conscience clothes its violence in the name of righteousness.

The various ways of life are largely a matter of cultural difference, and yet they are all equally expressive of human agency. Emil Durkheim said that there is nothing in the human conscience except what was put there by society. To that I would add, "nothing except human agency itself." Or again Durkheim said that the conscience is nothing except each individual's respect for the norms of the whole group. To that I would add, "nothing except the transformation of such respect from its hidden destructive side into the strength of human agency." For any cultural practice one can always ask the "open question," "But ought I/we really do this?" The open question must refer to the deeper characteristics of human agency that underlie all cultural expressions. For any given cultural practice one can ask whether it expresses the fullest awareness of human feelings and relevant circumstances (awareness). Does it give expression to our actual intentions (intentionality)? Is it really consistent with what we want to do or want others to do on similar occasions (coherence)? Is it really responsive to other human beings within their circumstances and their way of life (mutuality)? Such questions probe beyond the limits of cultural relativity into the common agency of which culture is an expression. At the same time, they are shaped inevitably by the language and the cultural traditions within which they are expressed.

This leads us to look more closely at the relationship between the way of life and the processes of conscience by comparing examples from two different cultures. We want to examine one segment of the way of life practiced in the East, comparing it to a similar practice in the West. Norms and values are as varied as culture itself, so we restrict ourselves to just one segment of social belief and practice in order to look more deeply into the relationship of conscience and way of life. By comparing an Eastern and a Western culture we hope to bring out what might easily go unnoticed if we were to discuss only our own culture.

We have chosen to compare the relationships between parents and children as they are embodied in the beliefs and practices of Confucianism and Christianity.[3] In view of the importance of the relationships between parents and children for the formation of conscience, it seems especially appropriate to choose such an example. The choice of Confucianism may help lift us above the limited vision of our own culture. Confucianism has the added advantage of being very specific about the relationship between parents and children. Christianity also has much to say about the relationship, since its beliefs cluster around the relationship between the heavenly Father and the Son of God.

We will begin the analysis by looking at the volitional elements in the relationship between parents and children, a procedure that will allow us to investigate the oppressive, condemning conscience. What Freud called the Oedipal complex is critical, for in the Oedipal complex one finds the repression of certain wishes under the watchful guardianship of the superego. The result is an underlying ambivalence of motive. Religious symbols about the relationship between parents and children should therefore give evidence of a mixture of motives which the symbols are designed to reconcile in some manner.

Next we shall look at the relationship of mutuality, including common values, normative commitments, and the patterns of institutional practice. Such common values, commitments, and practice make up what is sometimes called "common sense," which is another way of speaking about the social side of conscience. We would expect the common sense to differ among those who practice Christianity and those who practice Confucianism, but we are interested in the underlying functions of agency expressed in both ways of life.

We shall continue by searching out the larger symbols of coherence implicit and explicit in the relationship between parents and children as these are described and prescribed in both Christianity and Confucianism. We presume that there are such larger symbols ordering and giving coherence to various practices, and we shall try to characterize the ways that such symbols function. This should let us see how the conscience as the coherence of agency is expressed in two different cultures. We shall then be able to draw some conclusions about how conscience is related to our way of life.

### Parents and Children

Conception and prolonged childhood are fundamental facts of the human experience and as such they offer themselves as powerful religious symbols. Were it not for the extended timetable of human maturation, human beings could hardly have developed and maintained the culture which so distinguishes them from the animal world. The basic biological fact of parenthood is that of having given existence to another person, while the basic biological fact of childhood is that of having received existence from other persons. It is from these elemental facts of human existence that the religious beliefs about parents and children take their meaning.

Psychologically, childhood involves a state of competition with one parent for the affection of the other and subsequent internalization of the supervisory patterns of both on the part of the child. Freud argued, as we have seen, that the genital maturation of the son at four to five years of age awakens a desire for the mother, which places the son into direct competition with the father. Similarly, the genital maturation of the daughter awakens in her a desire for the father and places her into competition with the mother. Since the child realizes that the parents are necessary to sustain life itself as well as indestructable opponents, the child can live with the parents only by taking in the parental personality controls as though they were his or her own. Therefore, it would seem that childhood always involves feelings of love and hate which alternate between obedience to and internalization of the parental will and disobedience and rejection of the parental will. Childhood always seems to include some ambivalence, simultaneous idealization and depreciation of the parents, alternate feelings of guilt and love.[4]

The social side of the relationship between parents and children in primitive societies was worked out by Freud in *Totem and Taboo*.[5] The religious system of totemism was early noted by J. G. Frazer and others to consist of two predominant complexes: the series of taboos protecting the totemic objects and the social system of exogamy structuring marriage and social relationships. These complexes correspond directly to the two crimes of Oedipus Rex, the killing of his father and the marrying of his mother. Freud suggested that the totemic taboos represent the compulsive restrictions against harming a symbolic representation of the father, and thereby they illustrate the basic theme of ambivalence with simultaneous desires to harm and protect the father. Similarly, the exogamic restriction is a result of guilt, whereby the sons restrict their marriage selection to women for whom the father has no particular desire. The relationship between parents and children thus shows up in *(a)* attitudes toward authority, *(b)* the organization of social interaction, and *(c)* the pattern of religious behavior.

Religions regularly take everyday experiences and use them as symbols to give coherence and meaning to what otherwise transcends human awareness. Traditionally the theological doctrine of analogy attempts to explain how symbols taken from human experience can express something of what has not yet been fully experienced. This has led commentators like Freud and Ludwig Feuerbach to suggest that the symbols are being projected into the beyond.

> Psychoanalytic investigation of the individual teaches with especial emphasis that god is in every case modelled after the father and that our personal relation to god is dependent upon our relation to our physical father, fluctuating and changing with him, and that god at bottom is nothing but an exalted father.[6]

The error of this notion does not lie in the idea of projection itself. The theological doctrine of analogy refers to a similar phenomenon. The error lies rather in the assumption that the symbol has no meaning other than in the emotional conflict that gave rise to the projection. It may be that the experience of fatherhood is a very adequate way of giving expression to what is beyond the reach of immediate awareness of human agency. Certainly Christians hold this to be true ever since Jesus addressed God as "Abba, Father," and began to pray, "Our heavenly Father." Freud's comment does have the advantage of pointing out that one's personal relation to God may have, perhaps always has, emotional elements drawn from early childhood. Should one's father have been especially cruel, God may appear to be wrathful also. In any case, people cannot avoid searching their experiences for symbols that establish and revolutionize their orientation to the world.

Erik Erikson has an interesting comment to make about the role of parents in the formation of the child's identity.

> Freud's oedipal father has clarified much, but, as sudden clarifications do, he has also obscured much. True, fathers are impressive as the mothers' powerful counterplayers in contexts not quite knowable, and yet deeply desirable and awe-provoking. But they are also importantly involved in the awakening of the child's identity. Fathers, it appears, were there before we were, they were strong when we were weak, they saw us when we saw them; not being mothers—that is, beings who make the care of babies their business—they love us differently, more dangerously.[7]

Erikson goes on to say that the child owes the father not only his biological existence, but also the paternal sponsorship through which the child comes to a sense of social reality and personal identity. Either the father or someone acting in the father's behalf guides the child's identity until it has become fully established on its own. The father becomes especially significant to his adolescent children because adolescence is normally a time when identity is severely threatened.

The continuing intimate relationship of a mother with her children nourishes the protomoral dispositions of trust, hope, and will, without which no child can come to an identity. The father's more tenuous relationship to the child permits him to have a special function in calling out his children's identity. He comes and goes at his own discretion, giving the impression of one who cares for his children when there is no necessity to care. In the mother the child ordinarily experiences a continuing trustworthiness, and in the father the child experiences being willingly loved. Possibly the man and woman could exchange these roles in part or in total. The actual behavior of the parents is not so important as that they are present in ways that awaken the child's sense of identity. It is only a small step to the realization that the heavenly Parent or the eternal Ancestors can quicken in a whole society a sense of identity, a sense of being a people. A common identity becomes the root of a common conscience.

### *Intentionality and Conflicting Emotions*

Religious beliefs give individuals and communities coherence of intention, unity of expression, and a way of evaluating their own behavior. At the same time, these beliefs betray the underlying mixture of feelings and motives that they are designed to unify. In Christianity, the Father as a symbol of coherent volition is first of all transcendent. He is, as the Hebrews discovered, one who comes and goes as he pleases, withdrawing and extending his love to whomever he chooses. At the same time, like a mother, God's loving-kindness is dependable and endures forever. He is preeminently the Holy One.

> God's invisibility is his holiness, his unapproachableness, his being beyond man's control. To be able to see God would mean to be able to stand upright in his presence. God is not therefore invisible, as he is for the Greek, because he is a metaphsical being and as such beyond the apprehension of our physical senses. Man cannot get God into his possession or control; he knows about God only because God speaks to him.[8]

Ambivalence of emotion is admirably evident in the attitude of reverence, which is a mixture of both fear and love. Those who revere God, fear him. The fear of the Lord is the beginning of wisdom. While fear carries the tone of respect, one cannot avoid the feeling of fear that comes in the face of a situation that can destroy a person. The contrast is made even stronger when fear and love are placed side by side. "The fear and love of God go hand in hand."[9]

The same mixture of emotions is to be found in other beliefs of Christianity. We may look first at the excessively developed legalism of postexilic Judaism as a background for early Christianity. To account for the many occasions when all persons fall short of the ethical ideal of perfect obedience, the Pharisees developed a doctrine of "the evil impulse dwelling in the heart of man side by side with the good impulse.''[10] They expressly recognized the mixture of desires underlying obedience to God.

The Pharisaic effort to express love toward God in fact points to the very emotion that it covers, hatred. ''The prospect of meeting God as their judge awakened in the conscientious a scrupulous anxiety and morbid sense of guilt. Sin appeared to be an ineluctable power, spreading its tentacles over the whole world and affecting the heart of the individual in a way that could be felt. It was a great enigma.''[11] The ambivalence that accompanies legalistic obedience could hardly be more vividly expressed. We see again the power of the condemning conscience.

Bultmann distinguishes the ''legalistic obedience'' of the Jewish tradition and the transformed ''radical obedience'' of Christianity. While the former attempted to follow hundreds of detailed prescriptions, the latter was ''personal assent to the divine command,'' ''the allegiance of the whole man.''[12] The New Testament message is that God demands the complete surrender of the human will. Persons must approach God like children, ''content to receive a gift, and innocent of any appeal to privilege or merit.''[13] Here there is no longer any attempt to defend or cover ambivalence. The emotional tension is acknowledged in Martin Luther's classic phrase, ''Sin bravely.'' The faithful can identify with those who crucified the Christ and at the same time exalt the person of him who suffered. Believers can feel released from punishment because someone is interceding in their behalf. The condemning conscience is transformed into a sponsoring conscience.

The same ambivalent emotions are to be found behind the Christian practice of communion. An historical antecedent to Christian communion is the practice of blood sacrifice. Freud speculated that early Semitic sacrifice represented hostility in the form of the murder of a father substitute and an act of penance and simultaneously of eulogy to the father.[14] Those who participated in the sacrifice are bound together in both their hostility toward and their obedience of the father. Hebrew laws about sacrifice were a reminder that the God who gave Israel land, food, and political liberty could also take them away. Sacrifice contained an implicit anticipation of judgment.

From the vantage point of the strength of human agency, the communion brings mutual recognition and solidarity to those who participate. The breaking of bread brings together the body of those assembled in celebration. Likely Jesus' words "This is my body" refer to the assembled group of disciples.[15] The breaking of bread dramatizes the interrelatedness and solidarity of all who are present. It looks forward to the time when all believers will be joined together in such solidarity. The communion as an expressive symbol helps to establish a coherent sense of identity over against the ambivalent feelings that children often have toward their parents.

Still another example of underlying ambivalence in Christian belief is found in the doctrine of vocation. The medieval church taught that God called people both to the common vocation of daily occupations and to the more perfect vocation of religious orders. During the Protestant Reformation those who were in religious orders left the monasteries and the nunneries to go into the marketplace, to use Max Weber's apt expression. Every person became simultaneously both a monk or a nun and a person of the world. For John Calvin "vocation" meant not simply accepting the created world as is, but working actively to transform the world according to God's will. Behind Calvin's doctrine of vocation was a conception of double predestination by which some were chosen and some condemned according to God's inscrutable discretion. The doctrine of earthly children being called by the heavenly Parent brings some unity to mixed emotions.

In each of the examples above there is one particular pattern that is typical of the Christian resolution of latent emotional ambivalence. The heavenly Parent serves as an object of loyalty in behalf of whom the believer can revolt from the earthly parents, the prototype of which is to be found in Jesus' words,

"He who loves father or mother more than me is not worthy of me" (Matt. 10:37 RSV and parallels). Christian children have continually expressed their conflicting motives in relation to their parents by turning away from them in the name of the heavenly Parent, thereby both criticizing and eulogizing the one for the other. In the name of the Father the medieval church drew power away from the Frankish and German kings, united rebellious monastic orders, and set up a powerful new father figure in the papacy. Then the sectarian dissenters revolted against the pope in the name of the heavenly Father. The pattern of breaking with the familial father and then with the church fathers is found with surprising regularity in Christianity, for example, by St. Francis, Erasmus, Luther, and Calvin. Loyalty to the heavenly Father becomes a source of coherent motivation such that underlying ambivalence can be overcome.

When we turn our attention to the religious symbols of Confucianism we find evidence of emotional ambivalence, although it takes a much different form than in Christianity. The Confucian father was never so highly exalted as after his death, at which time the extent of a child's love for the father was judged in terms of the elaborateness of the funeral. Consequently, the highly complex ritual of the funeral celebration and the long period when the casket was kept in the home, often many months, indicates the extent to which guilt had to be overcome.[16]

The whole ethical ritual that has been characteristic of Confucianism extended into every aspect of the way of life. Daily rituals were to be carried out without question in the face of a constant fear that evil spirits would break through and upset the eternal stability of society. Many Chinese rituals were explicitly directed toward frightening away evil spirits. Such extreme attempts to keep away evil would seem to betray the unconscious presence of what is being banished. The Christian fear of judgment parallels the popular Confucian belief in the prevailing power of the evil spirits, and the strictures of the repressive, condemning conscience parallels both.

The Christian fear of judgment is similar to the paranoid sense of being observed and controlled, and the Confucian daily social ritual is similar to the repetitive rituals by which neurotic persons defend themselves against underlying ambivalence. At the same time, the advocate at the right hand of the Father breaks the power of judgment in Christianity; and, the daily liturgy established by the Ancestors breaks the power of the evil spirits in Confucianism. One must understand that rituals not only may express underlying ambivalence; they may also serve to establish the relative unity of purpose and meaning by which human agency is aware of its own deepest motives. I would prefer to speak of the strength of dramatic expression as liturgy. In the liturgies of daily care infants and children find an environment in which their own basic intentions are deepened and their purposes unified. The many secular social liturgies of Confucianism may not only have served to defend against underlying ambivalence, but may also have established the kind of social environment in which ego strength and virtue were nourished and in which ego weakness was overcome.

Another area in Confucian belief and practice that betrays underlying ambivalence is the high respect with which followers of Confucius regarded those who governed them, and, conversely, the extreme way in which governors are emasculated of authority. Highly educated persons were held in extreme respect, and yet these same persons were obliged to be obedient to the older members of their clan. The emperor himself, who represented the very authority of heaven, who was both ruler and priest for the nation, loyalty to whom was considered the highest virtue, found his authority drastically reduced both by the concept of the teaching function of the government and by the extreme cohesiveness of local clans.[17]

Loyalty to the clan, filial piety, is so limited to loyalty to the emperor that central government could never be strong in the Western sense. The abortive attempts of Wang An-shih and Sun Yat-sen to strengthen the central authority of the government illustrate how strongly resistant the clans were to giving more than token authority to the empirial government. In view of this loyalty it is not surprising that the Communist government of Mao Tse-tung considered it necessary to institute a cultural revolution, using extreme and violent measures to break the power of the clan. Nevertheless, part of Mao's special appeal to the Chinese is that he is also a poet, one of the principle virtues of a Confucian emperor, who is to rule by living in the truth rather than by forcing his will upon his subjects. Here is a Confucian doctrine of the humanization of authority.

Under Confucian rulers distrust of the governors was most intense at the lower levels of the hierarchy, the level at which governors came into the closest contact with the people.[18] The people often hated and distrusted their local governors very intensely. Governors were considered to be virtuous if they turned over to their own clan money gained through taxation. In matters of conflict, the governor's will was final. It is not surprising that people had mixed feelings about their rulers.

The above examples give clear evidence that ambivalent motives permeated Confucian belief and practice, but they also give evidence of the overcoming of agentic weakness by agentic strength. The Confucian way of life has a certain immediacy in personal relationships not to be found in Christianity. Chinese social relationships have both an intensity and a high degree of formality seldom to be found in their Western counterpart. Perhaps the liturgies of daily life permit a unity and strength of purpose in traditional daily activities not possible in the Chrisitan doctrine of vocation with its orientation toward a new order. However, it is surely clear historically that the Christian doctrine of vocation is able to meet change with greater strength and common purpose than can the Confucian doctrine of filial piety. In both Confucianism and Christianity we find a mixture of motives, but we also find beliefs and practices that strengthen agency in commonness of purpose, value, and identity.

### Mutuality and the Common Sense

Communities share the common values and normative patterns that give shape to institutions and to the roles of individuals who carry out institutional practices. Such values and normative patterns make up the common sense of any community, for such patterns may be neither wholly explicit nor wholly conscious. They are the creation of human agency on one hand, but they give shape and direction to human agency on the other. The Confucian way of expressing this truth was to say that the Ancestors had created the common values and normative patterns and that it was the obligation of the present generation to live within them. Christianity taught that God has delivered to the ancestors their common values and normative patterns, but the ancestors have violated them; the present generation is given a new opportunity to begin living according to the values and normative patterns that God has always intended. Confucianism places emphasis upon the way we are shaped by values and norms, while Christianity emphasizes the way that we help to give shape to values and norms.

Childhood as a value in Christian communities does not lead to a single set social norm, primarily because from the time of the beginning of Christianity the idea of being a child of God has had several different meanings. In this as in other Christian doctrines one can identify both eschatological and gnostic elements.[19] The eschatological element accounts for the tension between the present age and the age to come. The coming age will bring a de-emphasis of sexual and status differences for the children of God, so that "in the resurrection they neither marry nor are given in marriage" (Matt. 22:30 RSV); and "there is neither slave nor free, there is neither male nor female" (Gal. 3:28 RSV). A person will become a child of God on the basis of human agency rather than biological or social characteristics.[20]

Over against the eschatological element stands the element of gnostic body-soul dualism, according to which the soul shall escape from the body at death and return to the Father in heaven. The eschatological doctrine of childhood led to a simple heroic asceticism in which one avoided all distractions so that all energy could be concentrated toward working for the coming kingdom. The gnostic doctrine of childhood led to the monastic norm of mortification of the flesh in order to release the soul to spiritual ecstasy. The two beliefs worked together to complement one another in the establishment and general acceptance of monasteries and nunneries.

By way of contrast, the parent-child relationship as a social value in the Confucian way of life rests upon the doctrine of the Ancestors, through whom society finds its stability and its ideal form. According to this teaching, the Ancestors and the sages of the past have handed down the traditional basis of society, and any break from tradition will release the destructive power of the evil spirits. No personal spirit, even that of a heavenly father, could be dependable enough to rule the heavens, for the rules of heaven are unchangeable and utterly dependable. For this reason a natural catastrophe such as a flood or an earthquake was not considered to be an act of the Ancestors, but was thought rather to be a breach in the order of heaven and earth, which in turn meant that someone had acted in such a way as to violate the tradition. Thus, natural catastrophes were thought to be the fault of the ruler, and upon at least one occasion an emperor was executed for bringing on a natural disaster. Such extreme traditionalism gave rise to a strong patriarchal control that extended from the local clans, through the various bureaucrats, to the emperor himself. Never was traditionalism so extreme in Christianity, even at the height of the medieval period.

When we look at the social norms that correspond to the values just described, we find a certain similarity between Christianity and Confucianism. If we understand patriarchalism to mean the rule of the father, then we observe that patriarchal family life seems to characterize both the Christian and Confucian ways of life throughout much of their histories. Ernst Troeltsch has this comment about early Christianity:

> From the very beginning, in the ethic of the Primitive Church, the original model of all social relationships was that of the domination of the husband within the family over wife and children, and the willing subordination of the members of the

family, as well as of the servants, to the authority of the housefather.[21]

Patriarchalism is also to be seen in the designation of the clergy as "father," and in their increasing authority, until by common consent they were considered to be the church itself. Patriarchalism later served to legitimate authority not only in the church, but also in the Roman, French, and German kingdoms. According to these "common sense" norms, men were encouraged to serve in positions of privilege as an expression of love for those for whom they were caring. On the other hand, persons in lower positions on the social ladder were willing to submit to the social differences that the heavenly Father had instituted for reasons known only to him. They were to use their lower positions as an opportunity for showing trust, patience, and humility to those above them, thus demonstrating their Christian faith.

There is great similarity between the patriarchalism of medieval Christianity and that of Confucianism. The difference lies in what might be called immediacy. The filial devotion that supported status relationships for the followers of Confucius was considered to be immediately present in every relationship because of the ever-present Ancestors. By contrast, Christian love and humility has elements of mystical contact with the transcendent Father combined with the eschatological expectation of judgment. The common sense of the Chinese included a certain optimism in the immediacy and durability of community institutions that Christianity, with its sense of being between the times, has never known.[22]

The Christian break with patriarchalism did not come with Martin Luther. Although he defied the pope, challenged the Thomistic theology of supernaturalism, and initiated a whole new understanding of being a child of God, Luther continued to accept partiarchal social order as normative for the Christian way of life. Luther in his own way simply reestablished the authority of the clergy to interpret the Scriptures and the authority of the princes to rule in the traditional manner, so long as they recognized the authority of the church. Luther's teaching shifted the underlying values of society, but did not radically change the norms by which institutional practices were governed.[23] According to Luther, the religious life was not a special calling for the few; rather, every person has a special calling to live in his or her station in life as given by God.

It was Calvinism and Anabaptism that broke with the norm of patriarchal authority. Calvin understood the holy community to be the place where God is working to transform the earth according to his benevolent purposes. People are called into worldly activity as participants in the divine creativity by which God is remaking the world. The various stations in life are not simply given by divine right. Calvin even allowed that in certain instances where rulers are clearly disobedient to the divine will, their subjects may revolt against them.

The sectarian movements of the late medieval period as well as the Anabaptists of the Reformation period understood the transcendence of God to mean that all persons are equally brothers and sisters before the heavenly Parent. People are therefore to be related in status-free, nonhierarchical relationships. The Baptist, Leveller, Quaker, and other movements in sixteenth- and seventeenth-century England took a similar position about the brotherhood and sisterhood of all persons. Without doubt, both the Reformed and Anabaptist traditions have been formative for the American conscience.[24]

The normative basis of the Confucian way of life was patriarchal at the family level and patrimonial at the national level. The distinction is Max Weber's. Patriarchalism is defined as "hereditary domestic authority of the family head who demands personal obedience from the group members in the name of the sacred traditions," while patrimonialism is a "type of traditional authority, patriarchal rule implemented with administrative staff."[25]

Authority in the clan rested upon the oldest father, who acted as both autocrat and priest for all his living descendants. The clans were under the authority of the Canton bureaucrats, who in turn were under the direction of the imperial bureaucrats, all of whom were under the rule of the emperor. Each level of authority took its pattern from and depended for its proper functioning upon the father's authority in the clan. Formally, the structure was quite similar to medieval Christianity, although for the Chinese, as we have said, authority was more immediate, and the religious interpretation of these practices was quite different. The Confucian way of life included no perspective from which these normative patterns might be changed, whereas the Christian way of life was itself an orientation toward change. Therefore, while changes in China have come as a breakdown in Confucian ideas, for example, the "cultural revolution," changes have come in Christianity in the name of revitalizing its basis vision, for example, the Reformation.

When we turn from the normative patterns to the actual institutional practices, the differences between the Confucian and the Christian common sense becomes more pronounced. We have already indicated that the early Christian expectation of the end of history had the effect of reducing the importance of marriage (see esp. I Cor. 7:25 ff.). A childless marriage was therefore of no consequence, and absolute monogamy was the established norm. Furthermore, the strand of gnostic dualism in the New Testament led to restrictions against marriage, certainly one of the factors in the development of clerical celibacy. Divorce was permitted, but only as an undesirable last resort.

By contrast, the Confucian believer was under obligation to have natural sons. Sons were more important than daughters since the marriage of a daughter required a family to give a dowry to her husband's clan. Monogamy was upheld only so long as the desired sons were forthcoming. It was quite acceptable, even expected, that a man whose wife bore him no sons would take concubines to himself. Traditionally, sexual intercourse was limited to the function of reproducing sons. When a man had sufficient male progeny to ensure the continuation of the ancestral line, he ceased to cohabit with his wife. Celibacy was utterly disgraceful when it was practiced

*165*

prior to the birth of children, and if a man died in the unmarried state, society attempted to recompense for his failure to have a son by a postmortem ceremony of adoption.

Whereas in both the Christian and Confucian ways of life monogamy is the most highly approved family pattern, in the latter, polygamy is acceptable and celibacy is strongly disapproved, while just the reverse is true in the former case. This leads Francis L. K. Hsü to comment that the husband-wife relationship has priority in Christianity, while the father-son relationship has priority in Confucianism.[26] This difference follows naturally from the difference between being children of the Ancestors and being children of the heavenly Father.

The institution of the clan has maintained much greater cohesiveness under Confucianism than it has under Christianity. The Confucian clan would endure the most extreme hardships for their old father, hardships that often meant years of indefatigable work and the severest sacrifice. For children to act in any other manner toward their aging parents was considered a breach of the most serious kind.[27] The extraordinary solidarity of the clan is to be seen in the way that bureaucratic offices were defined as an extension of the clan's authority. Educated sons who received governmental appointments remained responsible above all else to the elders of their own clan. It is hardly surprising that governmental administration was often weak and extortionary. As we have already mentioned, governors were expected to dip into the tax coffers to feather the nests of their own clans. Confucian doctrine taught the best governor is the one who governs least. Weakness and extortion were therefore highly prized virtues of government, something that is difficult to comprehend from within the Christian way of life. Prior to the twentieth-century Communist revolution in China, every attempt at reform ran afoul of the overwhelming power of the clan.

The patriarchal society of medieval Europe showed a greater capacity to overcome the power of local monarchies and clans. Medieval monastic scholars and the Chinese-educated government officials stand in parallel positions as the highly trained authorities through whom the most precious values of the society were transmitted. Membership in the Christian church, however, often meant a break with one's parents, so that eventually the power of the church overwhelmed that of the local clans and princes, at least for a time. The papacy in turn was finally weakened by the late medieval sectarian movements, many of which were grounded in local customs and traditions. Finally, the various movements of the Protestant Reformation combined to break the patriarchal structure of the medieval church at both the local and international levels. But the breakdown of ecclesiastical power did not mean a resurgence in the power of the clan. Rather, the Reformation churches gave much more authority to the rising nation-states. The Christian idea of being a child of God simply does not allow local clans to gain the strength that they possess in the Confucian way of life.

The same point may be made with regard to economic practices. In China, economic activity traditionally was carried out in the small face-to-face relationships of the clan, and productivity was therefore limited by the number of capable persons in the clan. The various clans were extremely industrious and competitive, evident in the wonderfully practical inventiveness of the Chinese, but they were also unable to join together in the large-scale cooperation that is essential to modern industrial production. The practice of attacking the world rationally by means of a series of task-oriented work organizations was out of the question in the Confucian way of life. It is not surprising that the Communist government of China thought it necessary to use extreme measures to break the clans apart and to discourage the loyalty of the youth to their elders as a means of increasing economic productivity. The relationship between parents and children is as dramatic in its effects upon economic activity as it is upon political organization.

Still another example of the commonsense conscience can be found in the role relationship between parents and children. The Confucian way of life features the virtue of filial piety which defines all the role relationships of the family: father, son, mother, and daughter. The son is obligated to be obedient, responsive, respectful, and receptive to the proper ritual for all social occasions. Conversely, the father must carry authority, give directions, provide for the family, and transmit the ancestral ritual. The father fulfills his role as one who is another's son, even though his own father may be deceased. A grandfather who dies passes into the realm of the Ancestors, and his will is actually more venerated than formerly. Because the father is also a son, the roles merge and finally cannot be distinctly separated. Sons share the estate of their fathers, whether it happens to be one of poverty or wealth, just as fathers accept the position in life that their ancestors gave them. The feminine roles are pale reflections of the masculine, the mother being a diminished father and the daughter, a diminished son.[28] A woman is subservient to her father-in-law, her husband, her older sons, and her own father.

At times the role relationships in the Christian way of life have approximated those just described. However, Christianity has consistently elevated the role of the woman, so that before the heavenly Parent she is of equal value with the man. The relationship of lifelong fidelity between husband and wife has regularly been considered more important than having children. Consequently, the emancipation of women is consistent with the basic values of Christianity, despite the subordinate tradition of male authority over women.

Christian children have always been able to break the relationship with their natural parents in the name of the heavenly Parent. The Calvinistic doctrine of callings within the holy community has provided a far greater variety of occupational roles and family traditions than Confucianism could have ever tolerated. In effect, the generation gap is a permanent part of the Christian way of life in a manner that was never true in Confucianism. Christian children are called to secure their own freedom and to cooperate with God in bringing about the new human community. In the words of the Lord's prayer, "Thy

Kingdom come; Thy will be done on earth as it is in heaven.''

Freud has suggested that the conscience of humanity, or should we say the superego, represents an unconscious pact among the children to restrain their aggressive, hateful urges and to find marriage partners outside the immediate clan. As the forbidden urges are repressed, the ideals of society are erected in their place. We have seen ample evidence in our analysis of Christianity and Confucianism of ambivalent feelings toward parents, of the restraint of violence, and of the regulation of roles between the sexes. However, the way of life makes a radical difference in the form in which ''the unconscious pact among children'' is expressed.

A more adequate account allows for underlying ambivalence, but also finds ways in which the strength of human agency is being expressed. The common sense of values, norms, institutions, and roles may express the strength of human mutuality as well as the weakness of repressed urges. Just as the communion of Christ and his followers overcomes the hostilities between them, so the ways of the Ancestors overcome the evil spirits that destroy human relationships. In both cases the strength of mutuality is more than the repression of forbidden, aggressive, and sexual urges. Mutuality is rather a strengthening of all persons caught up in an institutional practice. To the extent that a way of life supports human mutuality, it is an expression of the strength of human agency. While Confucianism was unable to meet the changes of the twentieth century without being radically altered, it undoubtedly continues in the common sense of the Chinese in a way that gives stability to the present government. Christianity has been more oriented to change, but it remains to be seen whether a larger mutuality among peoples of the world can be established sufficient to meet the challenges of overpopulation, hunger, and conflicting ways of life.

### Coherence and Common Identity

We want now to set our discussion of the relationship between parents and children within the wider complex of symbols and meanings that constitute a particular way of life. The coherence of a way of life is itself an expression of the striving toward coherence that is characteristic of all human agency. We want to avoid the impression that the whole of either Christianity or Confucianism can be reduced to one belief. Throughout, we have chosen a few examples to make the contrast. Necessarily we have emphasized one movement or period more than another. The analysis stands or falls according to whether the select number of illustrations are representative of larger patterns of religious belief.

Perhaps the most fundamental religious symbol of Confucianism is the *Tao,* the final principle of heaven and earth. *Tao* is the source of *li,* that is, of filial piety, loyalty, and other virtues. The eternal and unchangeable nature of these principles is described by Chu Shi as follows:

> Before the thing exists there is first its Principle. For example, there is the Principle governing [the relationship between] ruler and subject before there is ruler and subject; there is the Principle governing [the relationship between] father and son before there is any father and son. It cannot be that originally there was no such Principle, and that it is only when ruler and subject, father and son, finally come into existence, that the normative Principle for them was implanted in them.[29]

From this passage we can begin to understand the stability which the Principle had for Neo-Confucians. From the Chinese point of view the unchangeable Principle is always present in life as we find it; the "Principle" is always together with "ether." The Neo-Confucian doctrine of Principle posits an infinite durability that is hardly approached by the somewhat similar Christian teaching about eternal Being and the natural law.

While Christians have usually related eternal principles to the covenant between God and his children, for Confucians there could be no covenant with the Ancestors. A covenant would have been impossible because the Ancestors have already delivered society in its eternal form, which is in no way open to historical change. The threat to society was that people might not keep the daily rituals, thereby allowing the evil spirits to destroy society. While there is some similarity to the Hebrew concern to meditate on the law of God day and night, the Confucian did not see daily rituals as a matter of keeping a promise with the Ancestors. The Confucian was living in the only way possible, namely the way delivered by the Ancestors. To do otherwise was to cease to live. The relationship to the Ancestors was immediate, direct, and without any element of making and keeping promises.

Perhaps Rudolph Bultmann's comment about Christianity is helpful here. He describes the Christian heavenly Father as one who is ever newly approaching his children in each succeeding moment, his continuity and integrity residing in the fact that the one who approaches in this moment has promised to be the one who will approach in the next moment. The heavenly Father is always ahead providing the way forward. To use the same figure, we may say that the Ancestors always come from behind, and their presence is a ceaseless reminder that the now is simply an extension of the eternal past. The *li* was not something to be entered into or agreed upon; it was an implicit principle of life. I would venture that in Confucianism there was little emphasis upon deliberation and decision, while there was much place for ritual, respect, symmetry, and patterned behavior.

*Li* is the Confucian sense of the human, the sense of blind impulse being transformed into intentionality. *Li* is the strength of human agency living within an ancestral conception of justice. Identity rests within the Ancestors, within continuing conventions, and therefore does not involve the struggle that identity formation has involved for Christians. *Li* has certain parallels to the heavenly Father strengthening human agency and establishing human justice, but it lacks the promise-keeping, the struggle for individual identity, the living in the presence of coming community.

Just as there was no covenant for the Confucian, so also there was no concept of conscience or personality in anything like the

Western sense. Christian personality is shaped in the presence of the final judgment of God, which gives Christian conscience its distinctive character. Confucian personality is shaped in the eternal stability of the *li*. Max Weber makes the provocative comment that under the Confucian way of life there could not possibly be ''inward aspiration toward a 'unified personality,''' and, further, that life ''remained a series of occurrences.''[30] The reason for this is that life lacked a transcendent goal and direction. Life under the *Tao* does not recognize historical change as a reality. All human life, whether that of the youngest child or the greatest emperor, has coherence in the eternal Principle. By contrast, the Christian Father gives to each believer a coherence that is in and yet partially beyond all changing events. Therein arises the Western conception of conscience and personality.

The contrast between Confucian and Christian ways of life revolves primarily around the modes of transcendence and immanence. In the one case, the irrational impulses of life are anchored in the power of the evil spirits outside the steady, unchanging patterns established by the Ancestors; in the other case, irrational impulses are allowed to reign temporarily, but will ultimately be subject to the holiness of the invisible Father. In the one case, magic and ritual were the means of avoiding the power of the evil spirits and retaining lasting stability. In the other, communion, faith, and unceasing desire to live according to the will of the unseen Father is the means of avoiding his wrath and of becoming a part of the kingdom of God. These are two different modes of giving coherence to human life, two different ways of life that express the same underlying characteristics of human agency.

It is small wonder that in the struggle between East and West, the values of durability and historical purpose seem to be locked in conflict. It seems inevitable that the meeting of East and West will show the Asians to be marvelously durable and patient from generation to generation, while Westerners will appear to be wonderfully productive and technically advanced. At the same time, the East is currently struggling to take up the skills of industrial production, and the West searches for an orientation that will be capable of durability in the face of the challenges facing humanity.

## Conscience and the Way of Life

We opened this chapter by asking whether the way of life is the final arbiter of decision and behavior, and whether therefore conscience is simply a reflection of a way of life. We have now examined two separate ways of life, the Confucian and the Christian, with respect to the relationship between parents and children. In doing so we have focused especially upon underlying conflicting motives, the values and practices of the ''common sense,'' and the ultimate symbols that give a sense of coherence and loyalty. Confucianism focuses in *li*, filial piety, with its loyalty to the ever-present ways of the Ancestors in the face of the demons; Christianity looks to the time when the erring children of humanity will become fully the children of God in the way already initiated by the Son of God. Let us now ask again whether conscience is simply a reflection of these two different ways of life.

We have already quoted R. M. Hare's statement about the way of life: ''Thus, if pressed to justify a decision completely, we have to give a complete specification of the way of life of which it is a part.'' Hare continues his statement in this way:

> If the inquirer still goes on asking, 'But why *should* I live like that?' then there is no further answer to give to him, because we have already, *ex hypothesi,* said everything that could be included in this further answer. We can only ask him to make up his mind which way he ought to live; for in the end everything rests upon such a decision of principle.[31]

When Hare's clairvoyant decider has all the facts and all the relevant considerations in, then the decision must still be made. Ethical decision would therefore seem finally to be arbitrary or emotive, to involve an inescapable leap. I want to suggest, however, that while there is an arbitrary element, its character is not quite what Hare describes. Rather, such a decision is to be viewed as an expression of human agency. These decisions are either relatively weak or strong according to whether they are nourished by the sources of human agency. They may of course be weak, with all the limitations upon human expression that we have discussed in relation to weakness. It is true that agency is shaped by the way of life in which it is found, but agency is also the creator of the way of life, even when that vitality is thoroughly hidden or repressed. Let us discuss further how this is so.

An important distinction must be drawn between descriptive and normative cultural relativity. Describing a way of life is not the same as recommending it. For us to recognize that the West stands in a tradition that was very much influenced by Christianity and that the East stands in a tradition that was much influenced by Confucianism is perfectly true as a descriptive statement. For any of us to say that our deepest thoughts have been shaped by the language we speak and the ideals we have inherited is descriptively true. But this is not the same as to recommend the way of life in which we were reared. Consider the fact that the Chinese have altered their way of life in this century. Consider also that many American parents are critical of the ways in which they were taught as children, and such parents often attempt to correct the errors of their elders by rearing their own children in a way that is more acceptable to them. Because the superego is planted in us at such a deep level, such efforts are seldom wholly successful. Nevertheless, we continue to make these efforts because we recognize that even though we are a part of a way of life, we need not commend that way of life either in its parts or in total. One may be a descriptive cultural relativist without being a normative cultural relativist.

You have noticed that the tendency to correct the ways of our parents is a part of the Western way of life, something that sets it apart from Confucianism. While this is true, one is still equally at liberty to commend or reject this practice. Furthermore, we should not think that when we question the limits of cultural relativity we automatically become arrogant in our attitude to other cultures. The fact that some ways of life are more commendable than others does not mean that other persons are to be blamed for following a way of life that differs from our own. We may at one and the same time respect the choices people have made while believing that some ways of life are to be commended over others. We may respect the right of persons to choose the way of life they will follow while discussing with them the merits of our differing way of life. While Hare is right in saying that each of us is free to commend the way of life that we will, he is not right in suggesting that such commendation is finally arbitrary.

Perhaps we can make the point clearer by comparing a moral decision to a judgment about the truth of something. Hare himself suggests the same comparison:

> To describe each ultimate decision as arbitrary, because *ex hypothesi* everything which could be used to justify them has already been included in the decision, would be like saying that a complete description of the universe was utterly unfounded, because no further fact could be called upon in the corroboration of it. This is not how we use the words ''arbitrary'' and ''unfounded.'' [32]

On the face of it Hare's reference to a truth judgment about the universe seems persuasive, but upon more careful examination we notice that he has changed the figure in a significant way. We may correct this by supposing that we are given two different views of the universe with all the supporting facts and arguments so that *ex hypothesi* nothing more can be presented. Are we not then called upon to make a judgment about which of the two is true? We are likely offended by this example because we assume that truth is one, and that when *all* the facts and arguments have finally been presented, it will be perfectly obvious which is correct. The coherence of truth requires it.

Does it not seem equally plausible to suppose that when all the facts and arguments about two different ways of life are in, the choice will be obvious in the same way that the truth is obvious? A commendable way of life may have elements derived from both ways, or each way may be commendable within given circumstances, but there will be a way of deciding other than to refer arbitrarily to the perspective in which we accidently happen to find ourselves. Just as we search for new discoveries and carry out arguments in the belief that we can approach truth, even though no present account that we have of truth is fully adequate, so also we can search for new considerations and further examine our own experience and that of others in the belief that we may come closer to a good, right, and appropriate decision even though no present account we have of what is good, right, and appropriate is fully adequate.

Even after a decision has been made for a way of life or any part of it, we may always ask what is sometimes called the "open question," that is, "But ought I/we really do this?" Such an appeal is not a call to make another irrational leap of decision. It is rather to pose further questions such as these: Are there other relevant perceptions or feelings that I/we have not taken into account? Have I/we really acknowledged our own deepest intentions? Is this act or practice consistent with what we ourselves or other persons ought to intend in other similar circumstances? Can we be more fully responsive not only to those persons and groups to whom we feel most loyal, but all persons and groups somehow related to this act or practice? Each of these questions leads to a whole family of related questions, but in every case they are posed in an effort to exercise the resources of human agency more honestly, more sensitively, and more profoundly. They appeal to the strength of agency in spite of the fact that we are actually prone to self-deception, rationalization, exploitation, narrow loyalties, destructiveness, and other forms of human weakness.

In spite of our weakness it is always appropriate to appeal to the strength of our common humanity, even in the realization that such appeals are also subject to human weakness. Questions such as those mentioned above are always relevant, so that the open question, "But ought I/we really do this?" may always be a meaningful one. Of course, if the answers to such questions continue to contain only what has often been recounted before, the open question begins to lose its meaning. We then come to the point of saying, "We have already been through all of that in great detail. We know just how we feel about it. Unless you can pose the question in a fresh way don't ask us whether we really ought to do it." This does not deny the continuing validity of the open question, but it does indicate that sometimes the question fails to call up a fresh perspective, which is clearly a part of the way it commonly functions.

Just as we need no special faculty of the reason to intuit truth other than our perceptions, intentions, reasoning, language, and our mutual interrelatedness, so also we need no special faculty to intuit what we ought to do. Our condeming conscience as well as the ideas that we have come to accept are experienced immediately and without great deliberation because they are learned so well they have become automatic. This is no more an argument for conscience as an intuition than is the spontaniety of our speech an argument for language as an intuition. The givenness of human agency is sufficient to account for conscience as a dispositional unity of awareness, intention, coherence, and mutuality by which we are joined together in communities of moral discernment and purpose. One does not need an additional special moral intuition.

The processes of agency are quickened in the mutual trust and recognition that pass between an infant and the mother. The instincts that underlie the mutuality of agency therefore equally underlie conscience. The worth of agency is implicit in mutual recognition and trust, so that in this very foundational sense we owe our agency to those who called it forth in us. But obligation properly arises only with language, common expectations, and the capacity for long-term intentions. The mutual recognition and trust in which agency is called forth is that slender thread of sympathy for humanity that has been noted by Hume and Mill. These earliest expressions of mutuality do not automatically give persons a concern for humanity in general, that is, a mature conscience. Rather they are taken up in maturing abilities and in the various crises of each person's growth, so that loyalties to the family are extended to other groups. The mature disposition to regard human agency to be of worth must be newly discovered and constructed by all persons and communities; it cannot be assumed to be either instinct or intuition. It is actually distorted and broken by primitive hatreds, mixed motives, and condemnations.

The maturation of conscience is more than the internalization of the way of life in which we happen to find ourselves. A way of life is an expression of human agency, and moral perceptiveness grows with the development of agency, even though such growth is neither automatic nor independent of the way of life within which it is found. The recent studies of Lawrence Kohlberg give support to our account of the maturation of moral judgment. His work is especially relevant since he studied young people from both Christian and Confucian backgrounds. Kohlberg argues that all persons, no matter what their cultural background, tend to move from preconventional through conventional to postconventional levels of moral judgments. He does not imply that such development is automatic. Rather his studies indicate that various levels of moral reasoning are present in many different cultures, and he therefore proposes that moral judgment is not wholly limited by the way of life. His studies indicate that a maturation of the capacity to reason morally is a part of what we have described as the maturation from the automatic morality of early childhood, through the value orientation of later childhood, and toward belief and care characteristic of adolescence and adulthood. The growth of a capacity for moral reasoning is therefore a part of the development of a mature moral disposition.

Here is a moral dilemma that Kohlberg posed for young persons in Taiwan:

A man and wife had just migrated from the high mountains. They started to farm, but there was no rain, and no crops grew. No one had enough food. The wife got sick, and finally she was close to dying from having no food. There was only one grocery store in the village, and the storekeeper charged a very high price for the food. The husband asked the storekeeper for some food for his wife, and said he would pay for it later. The storekeeper said, "No, I won't give you any food unless you pay first." The husband went to all the people in the village to ask for food, but no one had food to spare. So he got desperate, and broke into the store to steal food for his wife. Should the husband have done that? Why? [33]

Kohlberg found that some children gave preconventional answers such as "He should steal the food for his wife, because if she dies he'll have to pay for her funeral and that costs a lot," or "He should not steal because he will go to jail." Some young people gave more conventional answers such as, "You owe it to your family to steal the drug," or "You will bring dishonor on your family if you steal." Some also gave postconventional answers such as, "It is wrong to make property more important than another human life." [34]

When Kohlberg compared middle-class urban boys from Taiwan and the United States, he found all three levels of moral reasoning to be present, and he found that older children and young people tended to reason at a higher level than younger children. In Taiwan the proportion of ten-year-old children reasoning at a preconventional level was 70 percent; the porportion reasoning at a conventional level was 30 percent; and the proportion reasoning at a postconventional level was negligible. At thirteen years of age the percentages were 35, 60, and 5 respectively. By sixteen years of age preconventional thinking had dropped to 20 percent; conventional thinking had increased to 68 percent; and postconventional thinking had increased to 12 percent. Not everyone was reasoning at a postconventional level by age sixteen. Yet, postconventional thinking showed up in a surprisingly large proportion of older children and young people considering Taiwan's traditional life-style.

One would expect a way of life under Christian influence to magnify the trend toward postconventional thinking, since as we have seen, Christianity characteristically has such an orientation. That is exactly what Kohlberg found in his study of middle-class urban American children and youth. The proportion of American ten-year-olds who were preconventional was 70 percent; conventional was 30 percent; and postconventional was negligible (identical with Taiwan). By age thirteen the percentages were 30, 55, and 15 respectively (relatively more postconventional thinking in U.S.A.). Age sixteen yields percentages of 22, 45, and 34 (relatively high occurrence of postconventional thinking in U.S.A.).

Kohlberg concludes, "(*a*) almost all individuals in all cultures use the same thirty basic moral categories, concepts, or principles; and (*b*) all individuals in all cultures go through the same order or sequences of gross stages of development, though varying in rate and terminal point of development." [35] Kohlberg has given us believable evidence that the maturation of moral reasoning is a part of the development of strength of agency as a disposition. His argument that all human beings make moral judgments within the same thirty categories is less tenable. Considerably more study is needed to find just how the use of moral language matures before coming to such a conclusion. Yet Kohlberg is investigating the processes of human agency that underlie the differences between ways of life, and in that he is pursuing an understanding of the humanization of conscience that is very much needed.

That our way of life is limited by human agency is suggested by the fact that many cultures have their own forms of the Golden Rule: do unto others as you would have them do unto you. The rule calls for the ability to enter sensitively into the circumstances of other persons or groups before making any kind of moral decision in relation to those persons or groups. The ability to take the role of another is thereby indicated as a basic moral capacity, and it should be understood within the taking of social roles by which agency is recognized, trusted, and responded to in infancy. The Golden Rule is also a way of being fair. As John Rawls describes fairness, a community of social roles is fair when everyone in the community can agree upon the responsibilities and rewards for every role before anyone knows who will be assigned to which role.[36] R. M. Hare speaks of constantly comparing our own moral decisions to those of other persons in similar circumstances. Thus we are led to universalize our moral thinking.[37] Richard Niebuhr advocates a loyalty to the whole of humanity transforming our loyalties to particular groups. The final moral principle of conscience is variously expressed, but it would seem that human agency is led toward some formulation of the Golden Rule, whatever the way of life.

Erik Erikson's version of the Golden Rule is this:

> Truly worthwhile acts enhance a mutuality between the doer and the other—a mutuality which strengthens the doer even as it strengthens the other. Thus the "doer" and the "other" are partners in the deed. Seen in the light of human development, this means that the doer is activated in whatever strength is apropriate to his age, stage, and condition, even as he activates in the other the strength appropriate to his age, stage, and condition. Understood in this way the Rule would say that it is best to do to another what will strengthen him—that is, what will develop his best potentials even as it develops your own.[38]

Erikson's version of the rule has the advantage that it sets our behavior within the locus of the virtue of human agency. Human behavior may not be good simply in form, nor simply in sincerity of intention. Rather it ought to spring from the wholeness of agency, from the coherence of feelings, intentions, and thought; from communities of loyalty, from the widest and most sensitive awareness of the responses of others; and from the intention to strengthen the agency of the other even as your own. The Kohlberg stages are very useful, but they should not blind us to the larger setting of agentic strength.

Yet the Golden Rule in one of its many forms does not immediately galvanize moral resolution; nor is it quickly recognized by everyone as a commendable way to live. Any statement of the moral strength of human agency will be equally subject to human weakness. Awareness of the situation of other persons and groups is limited by repression of feelings, political and economic oppression, cultural structuring of perception, and our own finitude. We remain mixed in our motives, lost in our purposes, prone to be outraged when we feel that others are invading our territory. The rage that many Americans feel toward those who make efforts to establish fairer rights and privileges for minority groups is a case in point. Without arguing the merits for or against school busing of children to other neighborhoods, one is impressed by the rage of communities against officials who are trying to carry out considered legal decisions.

Still other limitations of any finally persuasive moral principle are the immaturity, identity confusion, faulty reasoning, and lack of genuinely accepted moral ideals that are so characteristic of human behavior. We are all subject to the automatic strictures of the conscience of our childhood, and too often those feelings of obligation cannot be modified by more humane considerations. Mark Twain understood this very well when he had Huckleberry Finn debating whether to help "Nigger Jim" escape from slavery. Huck's "conscience" continued to bother him when he did finally decide to help Jim escape. Too often more humane consideration cannot overcome an infantile conscience. This is especially true if our loyalties have remained narrow and if we have dispositions that are fundamentally weak. There is no way to express the principle of conscience so as to compel either acceptance of the rule or the willingness to live accordingly. That can come only from the depths of human agency as people and groups do respond to one another out of the strength of their own agency.

Confucianism has no concept of conscience at all parallel to that of Christianity. The Confucian way of life does not encourage the acceptance of and striving for personal identity so characteristic of the Christian way. Yet, in the larger sense, all communities have common values and norms by which motives and purposes are molded. While folkways are characteristic of all people and seem to operate automatically, we have tried to show that they are expressions of the deeper processes of human agency, by which the childhood conscience is being transformed in the direction of strength of agency. The fact that agentic weakness often prevails and that every moral expression is subject to the shaping influence of the way of life does not falsify the idea of an underlying moral disposition.

Our discussion suggests that education for maturity of moral judgment will aim at helping children, youth, and adults to become more aware of various ways of life. A deeper appreciation of similarities and differences is needed, as well as an effort to expose our own tendencies for limited loyalty and self-justification. Since in our own experience motives cannot be separated from emotions, discussion that encourages maturity allows for the expression of motives and emotions. The arguments for and against political and economic oppression may be examined, but such discussion should move beyond the mere affirmation of cultural differences to uncover the ways in which we are commonly human even within our differences. Nor must we offer a simple idea of humanity that does not recognize the weakness that is so characteristic of human agency and that does not recognize that one's identity as a human being must be hammered out of painful and ongoing decisions. Ample opportunity for taking various roles and debating the issues involved in them is basic to the maturation of conscience. Finally must come the recognition that all of our efforts to guarantee moral maturity will simply reinforce the weakness of human agency. Strength comes only as we act out of the strength of our own resources, and that is a gift added to all of our best efforts. This leads us to a discussion of conscience and transcendence, which is the subject of the next chapter.

# Chapter VI

## THE WING-FOOTED WANDERER:
### *Conscience and Transcendence*

*Far be it from thee to do this—to kill good and bad together; for then the good would suffer with the bad. Far be it from thee. Shall not the judge of all the earth do what is just?* —Gen. 18:25

*We never could apply to conscience Yeats's definition of the daimonic—that "other Will," "that dazzling, unforseen wing-footed wanderer . . . of our own being but as water with fire."*
—Rollo May

Hidden in the center of the book of Genesis is one of the remarkable conversations of the Bible. The dramatis personae are God on one hand and Abraham on the other. God is debating with himself whether to tell Abraham what he has in mind to do about the wickedness in the cities of Sodom and Gomorrah. Finally, after considering that he has promised to bless and strengthen Abraham and Abraham's descendents so long as they follow the way of righteousness, God says to Abraham, "There is a great outcry over Sodom and Gomorrah; their sin is very grave. I must go down and see whether their deeds warrant the outcry which has reached me. I am resolved to know the truth." Then Abraham answers, "Wilt thou really sweep away the good and bad together? Suppose there are fifty good men in the city; wilt thou really sweep it away, and not pardon the place because of the fifty good men? Far be it from thee to do this—to kill good and bad together; for then the good would suffer with the bad. Far be it from thee. Shall not the judge of all the earth do what is just?'' God is moved and agrees, ''If I find in the city of Sodom fifty good men, I will pardon the whole place for their sake.'' Abraham then proceeds to barter with God until God has agreed to spare the city if even ten good men can be found. ''For the sake of the ten I will not destroy it'' (see Gen. 18:16-33).

The story is so remarkable because it suggests that God himself is tempted to act primarily out of wrath or righteous indignation. Yet when God is reminded about justice and fairness, his anger is modified. The story pictures God himself moving from the primitive destructive conscience to a decision that is more nearly in keeping with his own disposition to be just and fair. We find Abraham taking the role of advocate or sponsor on behalf of the city of Sodom. Viewing the conversation from another point of view, we find Abraham, caught between his own sense of justice and the destruction he can see coming to the city, daring to carry out his negotiation with God. The whole conversation raises the question of the relationship between conscience and transcendence. In a much different setting Rollo May, quoting the poet Yeats, raises the same question when he speaks about a Will moving within us that reaches beyond our conscience, ''that dazzling, unforseen wing-footed wanderer . . . of our own being but as water with fire.''[1] Do the hidden sources of human agency transcend our present judgments of conscience like fire with water?

What we want to do in this chapter is to explore the relationship between conscience and transcendence. By transcendence we mean that characteristic by which human experience rests upon preconditions extending beyond the limitations of conscious awareness, understanding, and explanation, but which preconditions are nevertheless necessary for the awareness, understanding, and explanation of various aspects of human experience. More simply stated, transcendence refers to the quality of givenness that underlies all experience and the quality of presupposition that underlies all thought. All social

and psychological theories presume such qualitative preconditions to human expression, even though the theories may not
agree about what is most original and least amenable to further
reduction. For example, Freud spoke about the id impulses as
his "magnificent mythology," since they are essential to the
understanding of human behavior, but one cannot plumb the
depths of the id to sort out its preconditions. "The theory of the
instincts is, as it were, our mythology. The instincts are mythical
beings, superb in their indefiniteness. In our work we cannot for
a moment overlook them, and yet we are never certain we are
seeing them clearly."[2] On another occasion Freud made the
same point in this way, "It may perhaps seem to you as though
our theories are a kind of mythology and, in the present case, not
even an agreeable one. But does not every science come in the
end to a kind of mythology like this?"[3]

The ego psychologists presume the processes of the ego are
equally as original and incomprehensible in their source as are
those of the id. "To sacrifice in any respect the concept of an
unconscious ego, which manages to do for us, as the heart and
the brain do, what we could never 'figure out' or plan
consciously, would mean to abandon psychoanalysis as an
instrument, as well as the beauty . . . which it alone can make us
see."[4] The primal givenness of ego, id, and supergo is identified
in this way:

> But who or what is the counterplayer of the ego? First, of course,
> the id and the superego, and then, so theory says, the
> "environment." The first two are awkward terms in English,
> which does not cultivate the academic-mythical grandeur of
> German, where "*das Es*" or "*das Ueber-Ich*" are never
> thinglike entities, but demonic and primal givens. The ego's
> overall task is, in the simplest terms, to turn passive into active,
> that is, to screen the impositions of its counterplayers in such a
> way that they become volitions.[5]

The ego processes make human activity understandable, but
they themselves retain a certain givenness, a certain irreduci-
bility. It is true enough that further knowledge or another

approach may be able to sort out other more fundamental preconditions of agency, but these in turn will have their own givenness. Thus, all social and psychological theories include concepts that suggest a degree of transcendence.

The idea of transcendence is the net we shall cast around the conception of human agency we have been discussing. We shall then ask how such transcendence might be rephrased into language about the saving presence of God in the human community. We shall hope to use a net that is not strung so tightly that we bring up ideas too small to be worthy of the name transcendence, but we also hope that the net is not strung so loosely that everything may pass through, leaving nothing to be sorted out.

Such a process, the reader may complain, may tell us much about the preconditions of human agency, but will it tell us anything about God's presence and activity among persons? The question presumes a false understanding of the way that God is present and active in human life. God is the one who is not only infinitely separated from human experience, infinitely beyond our comprehension; he is also the one who is infinitely close to human life, continually giving comprehensible signs of the divine presence. Statements about the preconditions of human agency are in some ways also statements about God's presence and activity in human life, but they must be given confessional form if they are to be appreciated as such.

Our task then is to translate statements about the preconditions of human agency into statements about the divine agency. Such a procedure has both phenomenological and confessional elements. The phenomenological element lies in the effort to describe some aspect of human life and experience in its depth, to search out the very preconditions of that experience, to lay open the tendencies that must prevail if such experience is possible at all. The confessional element lies in the effort to rephrase the phenomenological realities into the more traditional language about God and his saving power. We want always to ask the question of how the confessional language is being used, how it functions, what it means, and when it is being misused. However, we do not want to suggest that confessional language can be reduced to something else. We search out the language of reverence and worship in order to renew its integrity rather than to erase its meaning. The phenomenological element cannot be avoided, as it is the human effort to describe human experience; and the confessional element cannot be reduced, as it is the human response to the saving divine presence; but the two can inform each other.

An analysis of human agency shows that the ego is always more or less aware of thoughts, feelings, other persons, and things. It is always owning or rejecting impulses as its own intentions. It always tends toward a coherence of inward and outward experience. It always occurs within communities of mutual responsiveness. Such characteristics are the preconditions of human agency. They are processes that are at work in and among us long before we are fully conscious of their operation. To a large extent they function at levels of awareness that we may call unconscious. The fact that they are preconditions of human experience, that all human agency shows these characteristics, and yet that they function in ways that are prior to our conscious awareness suggests that they have the quality of transcendence. To put it another way, the roots of human agency transcend our conscious awareness, deliberation, and understanding.

When we look to the traditional confessional way of speaking about the transcendent dimensions of human agency, we must turn to God. God is the transcendent agent, the One in whom beings live, move, and have their being. Human agency is a reflection of the divine, which means that in limited ways it is like the divine, but at the same time is radically separated from the divine. Language about God has always referred to the impingement of transcendence upon human experience. The use of any single term for such impingement has serious difficulties, as the recent death-of-God controversy has made us extremely aware. One is reminded that the Hebrew tradition had various words to represent the presence of transcendence, and that, furthermore, one strain of the Hebrew tradition insisted that no word was adequate and that therefore no name should be used.

I follow those who feel that we must continually examine our secular experience to discover just where the sense of ultimacy or transcendence is already present. However, I continue to agree with Martin Buber in his magnificent little book *Eclipse of God* that, despite all its difficulties, God language is more adequate to the impingement of transcendence upon our experience than is any other language. Our language about God does, nevertheless, need to be constantly enriched by historical and biblical studies on one hand, and studies into the contemporary sense of transcendence on the other.

At the heart of Christian faith is the belief that Christ reveals the hiddenness of God. In him we see the character of the divine. He overcomes the separation between the divine and human agency. His is the name by which the powers of darkness are overcome. He is at one with the depths of his own agency, ("Not my will, but thine be done"). In his life the root impulses and demonic urges are faced in ways that enhance human agency rather than weaken it. The powers of destruction and death are unable to destroy the mutuality by which the Christ strengthens those who believe in him. They experience him as alive and are quickened in their capacity to act, love, work, and trust in spite of persecution or threat of death. In his story, his community, his Spirit, we regain the strength of our own agency.

Language about the saving power of God in Christ serves to enlarge and strengthen human agency. One must quickly add, however, that such language does not always function in this way. It sometimes is used as an expression of human weakness. Both Freud and Marx believed that religious language is always an expression of human weakness. Freud's way of saying this was that religion is always a neurosis, and Marx's doctrine was that religion is an opiate of the people.[6] Religion buttresses human weakness, justifies human injustice, and nullifies the intention to act. Max Weber was closer to our own view when he argued that religious faith sometimes weakens human expression and sometimes strengthens it. Weber showed how Protestantism opened up new possibilities of planning and productivity in the modern world, while in many parts of the world religious faith is the strongest bulwark against planning and productivity that could meet the threat of starvation.[7] Religious language can weaken human agency or strengthen it. Devotion to God may be primarily a neurosis or an opiate against responsibility, but such devotion may also be a source of ego strength, decisiveness, and justice.

The fact that some psychotic persons claim to be the Christ, or that slavery has been justified in the name of God, or that both sides of most wars look to God for their support, or that most forms of human misery have been justified by reference to God should not blind us to the fact that faith in God is often a source of strength. If sometimes people torture confessions out of others in the name of God, it is also true that many have found faith in God to be an encouragement to love, concern, care, and purpose in spite of dehumanizing impulses without and within. The Epistle of I John puts it this way: "If a man says, 'I love God', while hating his brother, he is a liar" (I John 4:19). According to the apostle, many things occur in the name of faith in God which do not enhance human agency. This observation is like that by which the demonic is named Lucifer, the angel of light, or like Matthew's observation that the devil came to Jesus quoting scripture (see Matt. 4:6). Language about God can serve repressive and destructive impulses, or it can serve to deepen and strengthen human agency.

There is no way to guarantee that our speech about or to God will serve agentic strength rather than weakness. One can search out the ways that we deceive ourselves and one another, the games that we play with God. We can play the dependency game, by which we let our absolute dependence upon God buttress a neurotic dependency upon everyone and everything.

Genuine dependence upon God is a willingness to accept and trust in the givenness of life and love in such a way that we may relate to others actively and responsibly. We may also play the activity game, by which we want God to justify a frenetic activity that covers a basic hopelessness. Genuine responsiveness to God is one that is deepened by meditation and care.

There is no way to guarantee that our references to God will express an acceptance that strengthens agency rather than a dependency that weakens it, or a responsiveness that strengthens hope rather than the multiplication of activities that destroy it. In fact, the desire to *guarantee* that our language about God be properly expressed already betrays us. Any such guarantee must come from a censorial, repressive conscience rather than from the sponsoring, strengthening capacities of agency. Our speech about God's saving power may be freely given, and freely examined for the self-deceptions to which we are always prone, but it cannot be guaranteed. It must finally depend upon the transcendent resources that nourish human agency, the power by which we can trust, hope, purpose, and love in spite of cruelty and destruction, for the power of God to strengthen human agency is at work within us long before we reverence God.

Our final task then is to look once again at the views of Freud, Erikson, and Piaget for evidence of transcendence. When we find such evidences, we will translate them into more confessional language about faith in God. In each case we will try to show how language about God might serve to weaken as well as to strengthen human agency. While we may examine our devotion and our worship, whether they serve our weakness or our strength will finally depend upon the transcendent resources of human agency, upon God himself, transforming and enlivening the efforts by which we try to guard our own language. Then we shall be in a position to summarize what we have learned about conscience as an expression of human agency and its relationship to the transcendent resources of agency.

## Awareness and God's Presence

Agency is always characterized by some degree of awareness. We have already seen that there are various levels of awareness, all the way from the intensity of a life-changing experience to the minimal awareness of sleep, evidenced by dreaming. Other levels are routine awareness, daydreaming, reverie, as well as unconscious awareness of something that bothers us even though we can't recall it. The depths of unconscious awareness always suggest even further depths that remain obscure, and the heights point to even greater heights that as yet can only be imagined. Without having the power of insight of Isaac Newton we can nevertheless comprehend his statement that in spite of his magnificent discoveries about the laws of gravity he felt as though he were on the shore of a vast sea and that he had picked up only a few pebbles.[8] We all know that what we focus upon is only a small part of what we experience at any moment, and that what we have forgotten is much greater than what we have remembered.

Agency reaches for a deeper and more intense awareness, but it also blots out certain feeling, observations, and memories of which we are or have been most keenly aware. Much human science and art is an effort to extend the range of human awareness. Think of current efforts to gain conscious control of the autonomic nervous functions or efforts to photograph Mars, Venus, and the other planets. At the same time, the ego blocks off much that comes to it. Neurosis is a condition of rejecting and blocking off impulses that are unacceptable, even while they continue to be present. Technology and mass society are terms that describe our lost capacity to sense our feelings about our environment and about the human beings who are our neighbors. Karl Barth has suggested that a root sin of the modern age, along with rebellion of the will, is repression of human feeling—apathy.[9] Agency is characterized by various degrees of awareness that seek to be extended and fulfilled in spite of neurosis and other weakness. Awareness is a precondition for human experience, and its roots are much deeper than consciousness itself. This suggests that awareness has transcendent dimensions that may be translated into language about God's presence.

Belief in God has always implied some awareness of the divine presence. While that presence is considerably beyond our conscious awareness and is not visibly or perceptibly experienced, it nonetheless becomes conscious upon certain occasions. Such occasions are often those of intense experiences such as the moment in which death seems imminent or the moment in which a baby is born. God's presence is an awareness that is beyond our consciousness, and yet an awareness that deepens and enlarges our conscious awareness.

In the Bible, the divine distance is symbolized by God's being as far from us as the heaven from the earth. Yet the divine nearness is evident in the many messengers (angels) that bring the divine presence and message. God sent his messengers to make a covenant with Abraham, and to promise the birth of Isaac (Gen. 18).[10] The "cloud of presence" accompanied the Israelites in the wandering in the desert of Sinai (Exod. 13:21; 14:19-20; 16:10; 19:9; 24:15-17; 40:34-38). The cloud became the reminder of an awareness that might otherwise be forgotten. The prophets listened in on the heavenly council and then spoke of what they had overheard.[11] Isaiah in the temple felt the seraphim touch his lips with a burning coal (Isa. 6:6-7). The presence of God, who is always far beyond us and yet time and again consciously present in the messengers he sends, is the hidden awareness that conditions all our levels of awareness.

The presence of God does not close off our awareness either of ourselves, of others, or of the world. Quite the contrary, the presence of God intensifies other awarenesses. No one has stated this more pointedly than Friedrich Schleiermacher.[12] Schleiermacher found three levels in consciousness. The lowest level was a kind of animal awareness that was mute and without self-consciousness. A second level was that in which there is a clear consciousness of self and of others. It is the kind of everyday awareness by which we distinguish ourselves from others and from the world, while at the same time we know that we are doing so. The third and highest level of awareness is the consciousness of God in which we are aware of the underlying givenness of all of life and of the fact that this awareness itself is mediated to us in Jesus Christ. Consciousness of God is not another item that is added to what we already know. It is rather a deeper level of awareness that enlarges and strengthens the whole of self-consciousness.

We all know how many things can occur in a few seconds of high intensity or how, in periods of intensely satisfying work, hours can pass as if they were minutes. We all know the excitement of a new discovery or the ecstasy of coming to a decision that we know is right. We also all know the wondrous beauty of the autumn or the majesty of the stars. There are of course times when intense emotions come that seem detached from us and that lend nothing to our self-awareness, and of them we do not speak since they contribute nothing to a larger self-awareness. We speak rather of those experiences that deepen and enlarge our awareness, that call up what was obviously there, but what we had clearly forgotten. We speak of those experiences that give us an enlarged sense of who we are, where we fit, and what we are about. Such experiences seem to call out of us the cry, "Oh God!" even from those who do not claim to be religious, for lesser language seems inadequate to such an enlarged level of consciousness. God's presence comes as a heightening of our awareness, and we remember and recount such occurrences in order to guard against the return of our awareness to lower and weaker levels.

I have been trying to describe how the presence of the divine agency strengthens and enlarges the various levels of awareness in the ego. I stated above that God's presence does not close off our awareness, but I must hasten to add that references to God do often function in just that way. Restriction, repression, and lower levels of consciousness are often buttressed by reference to God. Perhaps this view was most intensely stated by Ludwig

Feuerbach, who believed that religious faith is a way of projecting human attitudes into the heavens.[19] By so doing we disown what belongs to human awareness and thereby impoverish it immeasurably. His cure was to disavow all use of religious language and to acknowledge that what we give to God is really the image of the human.

I believe that our speech about God does sometimes function in just the way the Feuerbach describes, but not always. Sometimes we do project a larger, all-knowing awareness into the heavens while living out our own meager and impoverished lives. Sometimes we pretend to call upon God while drawing the circle of our uncaring relationships tight around us. We may claim faith without opening ourselves to the cares and concerns of the people around us. We may claim to be believers, but without the meditation and reflection upon God's presence that is characteristic of Christian discipleship. A person can be given over to compulsive prayer, a ritual that is used to hide the deeper anxiety that lies within. Rituals have the function of seeming to hide the impulse to act in a way that is not acceptable to the repressive conscience. Religion then functions as a defense against anxiety, and faith is exercised in order to hide impulses that we would rather not acknowledge. In these instances we address God in order to restrict and close off a larger awareness. God becomes the hallmark of eternal oblivion, and faith becomes the occasion of apathy, unwillingness to feel.

However, our addressing God need not function in this way. Jesus sharply distinguished between a prayer that is characterized by a vain repetition of words and ostentatious behavior, and a prayer that reaches deeply within, while at the same time sensitizing one to the world and the people round about (see Matt. 6:5-8). Faith in God can be the courage to accept anxious feelings without fearing the loss of all agency (madness), the willingness to accept the death implied in all wholehearted expression, and the trust that expresses the care implied in love. Our address to God can be the occasion when feeling is joined together with perception and will.

There is, however, no way to guarantee that faith in God will enlarge our awareness in these ways. Our very efforts to be sure that our references to God are made in the right way, and our very efforts to see that our prayer is genuine, betray the censoring conscience. We may on the one hand be sensitive to the various ways by which our presumed faith in God may shut off awareness, but we must finally give all such efforts over to the agentic trust that underlies all of our efforts in every direction. Finally, the deeper and unfathomable resources by which human agency is nourished must also nourish our trust. God is the source of human awareness and in God's presence is human awareness enlarged, strengthened, and magnified.

### Actuality and God's Creativity

The role of perception in human agency is very important. The conscience, like the heart, cannot register what the eye has not seen. One reason that Americans and others around the world were so concerned about the Vietnam war was that the television networks served it up with their dinners every evening. Who can forget the pictures of the crying children who had just been napalmed, or the people with missing limbs, or the rifles raised for execution? The information that we receive through our senses registers on our hearts, unless, of course, we become callous.

Piaget is critical of any view of perception that makes of it either a matter of pure intuition or simply a matter of external impression. The intuitionists assert that what we perceive is a matter of what occurs within us, while the impressionists argue that awareness is a blank tablet upon which all that we perceive is written by the outside world. Piaget opts for a constructivist view in which what is in the outside world is mediated through our efforts to make sense of it.[14] Perception is then a matter neither simply of intuition nor of impression, but the union of the two within our own efforts to make sense of things. Such efforts go on at a motor level long before we are capable of or aware of giving words to these efforts. There is a certain givenness, a transcendence, to the activity of agency that we call perception. This suggests that we may speak confessionally by saying that perception rests within God's creativity.

Furthermore, the constructivist view of perception proposes that what comes through our senses is not flatly given without alteration. We construct our world in response to the world constructed by those around us. Our construction of the world affects those around us, and theirs affects us. Those who are of the working classes perceive the world differently than do those who are of the wealthier, leisured classes. The followers of Mohammed perceive the world differently than the followers of Christ. Recently a twelve-year-old boy gazing at the sun through a heavily overcast sky insisted that it was the moon. He explained that it was too small to be the sun. His perception of the sun was heavily influenced by what he had learned about the magnitude of the sun. A direct glance through the heavy clouds suddenly brought him up short, for it did not accord with what he knew. He was reconstructing his perception of the sun.

There is an unending chain of response and counterresponse in the way that we perceive the world. Each construction on our own part is challenged by the construction of others, so that what we perceive continues to change in the very process of perceiving it. This suggests that there is a transcendence not only in the unconscious sources of our perceptions but also in the ongoing alteration by which we perceive. One might say that there is a transcendent teleology to what we perceive. We know that the world will appear to be different to us in a decade or in the next generation, but we do not know how. This suggests that when we speak confessionally we may say that the way in which we experience the world takes place within God's ongoing creativity.

I have been drawing upon Piaget's constructivist view of perception to find a note of transcendence, but I find a similar note in Erikson's concept of actuality.[15] Erikson reacts against the Freudian view that the world around us is an impinging reality to which we must conform. More adequate, suggests Erikson, is a view of actuality by which we are to understand that our very ways of acting and perceiving help to create the world to which we are responding. None of us is wholly passive in a world that presses upon us. If we are so passive, it is because we are repressing the agency by which we take part in creating the actuality in which we live. Now the process of being so engaged in the world in which we live occurs at a much deeper level than our own conscious intention that it be so. We act in the larger and deeper awareness that we are already engaged in our world. The deeper levels of the ego's engagement in the world is a source of strength for all our deliberations and decisions. We may then speak confessionally by saying that the actuality of our lives individually and collectively is set within God's creativity.

God's creativity is the root source, the precondition of our own agency. It is often said that God acts and we respond. Such a way of speaking makes very clear that we cannot get behind the divinely creative context for anything that we do. It may, however, hide the fact that God's creativity is a source of strength for human initiative. God's creativity allows us truly to act and not always to remain neurotically dependent. Our activity is related to God's creativity in that our very initiative gives God's agency a different cast. In this sense we constantly act and respond in relationship to God's creativity.

In the Bible, God's creativity is seen primarily in two ways. On the one hand, it sets the conditions within which human beings act, and, on the other hand, it is a saving power within a world in which human beings are unable to act effectively. In the creation story man and woman are set within the created order to name the animals and to care for the garden. It is by language and by caring activity that each of us enters into our own actuality. But the man and woman had urges that violated the limits of human agency (to eat of the tree of knowledge of good and evil), and thereby they became aware of the fear of death. God set "the cherubim and the sword whirling and flashing to guard the way to the tree of life'' (Gen. 3:24), which all of us know in the restrictive conscience.

Life under the tutelage of the restrictive conscience is a curse hard to endure unless it is rescued by the resources and powers of God's creative agency. So the second way in which God's creativity is described in the Bible is in his saving power. God continues to sustain a world that is the context of an ongoing reconstruction by human beings, even though we are crippled by agentic weakness and inability, marked always by the unconscious fear of dying. Yet God continues to create within his ongoing creation by coming to persons in the form of a renewal of strength and courage. When Jacob at the river Jabbok had his angry uncle Laban behind him and his alienated brother Esau before him, then he wrestled with God all night. Faced with the deepest source of his own agency, he was able to gain the courage to face a brother who might destroy him (Gen. 32:22-32). Moses wrestled with God in a similar way before the burning bush in the Sinai desert, and from that encounter Moses gained sufficient courage to face the impossible odds of Pharaoh and his armies in the hope of securing freedom for Israel (Exod. 3). Jesus also wrestled with God in the garden of Gethsemane and received enough courage to face the ordeal ahead of him (Matt. 26:36-46; Mark 14:32-42; Luke 22:39-46). God's creativity comes as a saving power within his larger creativity.

God's creativity comes to us as the courage to perceive our life circumstances in new ways, as the hope for new possibilities as yet unrealized. For the sick, God's creative power gives a courage and assurance that is itself healing to the whole body in its agentic capacities. For everyone, God's creative presence is an increased ability to make sense of circumstances, to be more sensitive to the needs of others, and to find a way of perceiving that is healing to many persons. God's creativity is thus the deeper resource of all human creativity, overcoming ambivalence, anxiety, and destructiveness at levels that enable a larger exercise of human creativity. Our language to and about God serves to keep open the new and healing possibilities of life.

Nevertheless, it is equally true that we often do not address God in this way. Often we restrict the creative, repress new possibilities, and persecute the creative person in the name of God. One need only think of the church's reaction to Galileo and Copernicus. Galileo was brought to trial by the church for daring to announce his discovery of the moons around Jupiter when such moons were contrary to the view of the cosmos supported by the church. In a similar way, the invention of steam and gasoline engines were opposed by some who thought they violated the natural order that God had created. The work of artists is often thought to be sacreligious by their contemporaries. The language of faith can and often does restrict the actual creativity of persons.

Faith in God can open us to the depths of human creativity. Samuel Morse's reaction upon inventing the telegraph was, "What hath God wrought!" by which he was recognizing the deeper resources of his own limited creativity. There is no way that one can compel language about God to give people greater courage and resourcefulness. We can defend ourselves against God by elevating him to a place of majesty that leaves us unaffected, or by trivializing him to the position of "the man upstairs." We can with squared chin take everything upon ourselves, or in neurotic dependency turn everything over to him. There are many ways to avoid the living God, but there is no way to compel the power of God to undergird and strengthen human agency. The roots of creativity are present and active before we ask about them, and their strength continues in all human activity. The divine creativity is itself a deep strength that nourishes human agency.

## Intentionality and God's Will

The life of each person is full of many impulses, sometimes supporting one another, but often conflicting. One can notice how quickly the mood of an infant changes from happy cooing at being rocked to uncontrollable crying at the sight of a desired toy out of reach on the floor. An infant will pursue one impulse after another in rapid succession, or rub her mouth and nose in the frustration of mixed impulses. As the child grows, impulses are patterned to become interests, and interests to become purposes, and purposes to become long-term commitments. However, we continue to be motivated by a variety of impulses, which we may or may not succeed in integrating into our purposes, ideals, and beliefs. When the conflict of impulse and ideal is too severe, a neurotic symptom shows up. It may be a facial tick, a stomach ulcer, a compulsive stutter, an inability to decide, or any of a thousand other symptoms. The capacity to accept and own impulses before we are aware of them, so that a variety of impulses can be acknowledged as our own, is a basic capacity of the human ego. Impulses are sometimes unacceptable to us even when we acknowledge them as our own. There is in human agency an ability to hold together impulse, ideals, perceptions, and reason at levels that are considerably deeper than our conscious awareness.[16] There is therefore a certain transcendence to human intentions. Confessionally, we speak of this as the will of God.

In the biblical account the will of God comes to individuals and to communities as something that is deeper than their own conscious intentions, and yet as something that strengthens and enlarges their own intentions. Often the will of God comes as a kind of deep intentionality, largely unconscious, that is strongly resisted, but finally acknowledged. When the deeper resources of intentionality are recognized, consciously intended and acted upon, then a person's life may be lived within the will of God. We may be so set upon repressing what we feel that we cannot hear the will of God, or so split in our intentions that we cannot accept the will of God, but the deeper resources of willing nevertheless go on as the context for all that we consciously intend.

The story of Moses is again a good example of what we mean. Raised in the privileged position of Pharaoh's court, Moses nevertheless felt a keen sympathy for his own people in their servitude. This sympathy was so strong that when he saw his kinsman being beaten by an Egyptian, Moses killed the oppressor. Forced to flee by his fear of being discovered, Moses spent forty years in the Sinai desert tending his father-in-law's sheep. He finally could not avoid bringing together his courtly training, his leadership ability, and his devotion to his people. God spoke with a kind of deep intentionality that Moses struggled against, but could not resist (Exod. 1–3). His own indecisions were finally wedded together in the pervading sense of the will of God.

Moses' experience was not unlike that of the apostle Paul, whose intense passion for righteousness led him to direct the persecution of the early Christians. His passion to stamp out early Christianity in itself betrays a strong, unconscious awareness of the power of Christianity to bring together his own conflicting impulses. The repressive conscience often resists the healing impulses of a deeper agency because the repressions instilled early in life seem to lose touch with all self-love if they are relaxed. Paul could not continue his resistance to the will of God as embodied in Jesus of Nazareth. In a dramatic event on the road to Damascus Paul fell to the ground and heard a voice saying, "Saul, Saul, why do you persecute me?" His suffering was now so intense that he could not see. In Damascus the disciple Ananias laid hands upon him in the name of the Lord Jesus that he might recover his sight. His sight returned; he was baptized; he took food and his strength returned (see Acts 9:1-19). His purposes and interests were now focused in the will of God in Jesus Christ. In this will he found his confidence and strength.

The will of God comes as a deepening and centering of our own purposes. Yet everyone can think of examples of persons for whom faith in God has meant a deep and abiding conflict. We referred earlier to Brauer's patient Anna O., who felt compelled to care for her ailing father. All her sense of what was right focused upon her duty. God is often the bulwark of authority in carrying out a family duty of this kind. In Anna O.'s case the duty was so much at odds with other impulses that a paralysis developed, and many of her bodily functions were upset. Language about God can serve to buttress painful repressions.

Reference to the will of God can cover weakness of will. What we cannot will for ourselves we can cover over with a stubborn willfulness that goes under the name of the will of God. Jesus had harsh words for the Pharisees who could not hear what he had to say because they were stubbornly unwilling to hear (see esp. Matt. 23). Slavery in the United States was carried out with every effort to justify it in the name of God. The accounts of Hitler suggest that all his efforts to produce a superrace of strong willed people covered a fundamental weakness of will.[17] Yet even Hitler had to attempt to justify his deeds, if not in God's name, certainly in reference to the injustice that was done Germany at Versailles. References to God can hide weakness of will, and God is often enthroned with the repressive conscience that resists every effort to uncover the underlying weakness.

But faith in God can function in the biblical sense of strengthening will and enabling a larger purpose to develop in human life. In the presence of some persons we find ourselves renewed and our purposes reborn. In the presence of some persons we are confirmed in the deeper purposes of our own being. These possibilities of deeper purposefulness point us to the divine source of purpose, to the divine agency in which our own deeper purposes are brought together in a way that exhibits both power and health. Not our own passing intentions, not even our own immediate survival becomes of utmost importance. Rather we are drawn by a kind of willing that joins people together in communities and lets their lives be lived in a purposefulness greater than any of our more immediate and self-directed intentions. The will of God is therefore at the same time beyond, within, and among us. It is the will of which Jesus spoke when he said, "Not my will, but thine be done" (Luke 22:42 and parallels). The church began with the overwhelming sense of the disciples that the deeper will of God was embodied in Jesus' *"thine* be done."

It is only human to want to seize upon ways to be assured that we stand within the divine will. Many Christian controversies have raged over this issue. Predestinarians have insisted that one act in the confidence that what one does is in the divine will even though only God really knows his own will. Others have insisted that we can know God's will directly. The knowing of God's will is not first of all the ascertainment of some objective fact that we can lay aside like a mathematical problem as soon as we have solved it. God's will is first of all a kind of trusting, hoping, purposing, and loving that reaches beyond the more immediate circumstantial knowledge by which we direct our lives. God's will brings together our circumstantial knowledge in patterns that confirm and extend what we know in Jesus Christ and what we find confirmed in others who search out God's will. There is nevertheless a kind of assurance that may not go under the name *adjustment,* but which can carry the term *the peace of God that passes all understanding.* In God's will a person's purposing combines a knowing and a not knowing that is given over to God's deeper purposes. This is what we mean by saying that our purposes are deepened in God's will. Such willing cannot be assured or guaranteed on our own terms. It can be received thankfully and acted upon. All of us find the more restrictive will working within us, usually in the name of God and right. When the restrictive will is transformed, opened, humanized, given over to the deepest source of human agency, then we are touched by God's will.

## Mutuality and God's Love

Persons are so related to one another that the ego strength of one can strengthen the other. The parent encourages the child; the teacher encourages the student. The very word *encourage* means "to give courage to" or "to inspire with hope." The courage of one person is capable of exciting courage in another.

The confidence and assurance of the doctor may be as healing to the patient as the medicine that is given. The love that a man and woman have for each other strengthens each one of them. What Freud called "primary narcissism," the deepest sense of being of worth, is secured and enlarged as other persons respond to us as persons of worth. One can see a child brighten up when a favorite teacher walks into the room, or one can see a person inspired upon meeting a greatly admired person. As fire passes from one piece of kindling to another, so strength of agency in one person seems to ignite strength of agency in the other.

Persons are activated not only by one another, but also by institutions and historical epochs. The very atmosphere in a good hospital is healing. The productivity and concern for persons in a well-run business strengthens the agency of all who take part in that institution. When students, as they often do, accuse a university of not exciting the thirst to learn in all the business of study and research, it is an accusation worth reflecting upon. A great university should excite in all those who take part in its pattern of life a thirst for learning.

Historical epochs and written accounts can also activate persons. The resolve of the United States to enter the space age and John F. Kennedy's promise to put a man on the moon by the end of the decade had a powerful effect upon individuals and institutions in America during the 1960s. Many persons find courage in reading the life stories of other persons. The life story of Helen Keller has been immensely popular surely because the description of Miss Keller's courage in the face of seemingly insuperable odds has given other persons courage to face their own situations. In the same way, people through the centuries have taken heart from reading the biblical accounts of the people of faith.

If agency can be strengthened by epochs, institutions, and other persons, it can also be weakened in the same way. A chronically drunken husband can drain the ego strength from his wife. Parents are rightfully concerned about the friendships their teen-aged children develop, because they realize that certain friendships can have a debilitating effect upon them. The demoralizing effect of an epoch can be seen in the 1930s when all Europe came under the shadow of fascism and was drawn into a worldwide war. Freud himself found it necessary to flee from Vienna. The philosophy of existentialism, with its central concern for human anxiety, became predominant in intellectual circles. Incidently, I think it not accidental that Freud's controversial proposal about the death instinct came in the aftermath of World War I.

In describing the way that persons can mutually activate one another, Erik Erikson points out that much of this occurs at an unconscious level.[18] The student is strengthened in the presence of the teacher in ways that are not fully conscious, while the teacher in turn is strengthened by the responses of the students, again in ways that are not fully conscious. So the relationship between individuals and other individuals, institutions, and epochs is rooted in the unconscious resources of human agency. The activity of the ego in synthesizing experience, bringing together impulse and ideals, and participating in the response network between individuals occurs in ways that are often not fully conscious to us at the time. Only with the work of recalling and naming the experience are we able to recover some of the ways by which we mutually activate one another, but even these efforts point to further undiscovered and unnamed resources. There is therefore a certain transcendence in the way we are related mutually to one another, to our institutions, and to our historical epoch.

There also is a note of transcendence in Jean Piaget's conception of mutuality, but in a somewhat different sense. Piaget speaks of mutuality as an ultimate equilibrium in human relationships.[19] Everything that is asserts its presence upon everything else. In personal relationships this means that the very presence of each person presses for recognition by every other person. The press for mutual recognition may go unheeded for many years, or decades, or for centuries, but it cannot be eliminated. The very existence of a person carries with it the requirement that this person be recognized for who he or she is, and conversely each person stands under the requirement of existence to recognize and respond to other persons for who they are. This pressure for mutual recognition is the character of existence. It can be ignored, but not avoided; forgotten, but not dismissed; violated, but not destroyed.

An equilibrium is an end state in which the pressures of a situation come into some kind of balance. The equilibrium toward which interpersonal relationships move is one in which each person is recognized for his or her basic qualities of agency, and each in turn recognizes all others in the same way. Personal relationships inevitably feel pressure to move toward such an equilibrium. This is not to say that each of us grows more loving each day; quite the contrary may be true. It is rather to say that we cannot avoid the pressure of mutual response and recognition. Since such an equilibrium can never be completed among existing human relationships, it has a transcendent quality. An equilibrium is not somehow removed by its transcendence, for it helps us to understand why we behave as we do. Yet we never pass it by; it always stands before us. Every future moment brings the continuing pressure toward equilibrium. The equilibrium for mutuality transcends us in consciousness, for we are often unaware of it; but it also transcends us in time, for it always stands before us as a condition of the future.

When we speak confessionally about the transcendence of mutuality, we speak of God's love. The love of God comes to us prior to our own levels of awareness. Before we knew what love was, God had already loved us. Before we were born, God had chosen us as the objects of his strengthening power. The love of parents and friends was already conditioned by a love of which they were only partially aware. The care given us by our institutions expresses a love of which no individual is fully conscious. God's love is the precondition, the root source, the agentic strength of human love. In the love of God persons and institutions mutually confirm one another in ways of which they are not fully aware.

The transcendence of mutuality also points to the coming of God's reign. The reign of God, should we say the kingdom of God, is a divine equilibrium that presses in from the future upon all persons and institutions. The Kingdom comes as a requirement for us to be mutually accepted and mutually recognized for who we are. The Kingdom is not somehow detached and removed, so that we can look forward to it only at a future time. It is the future reality that dramatically affects every present moment, even when ignored, forgotten, or denied. The Kingdom is the shaping power of divine providence, the direction toward which human persons, institutions, and epochs move. Of course, we may move away from the kingdom of God. Any one age may become totally heathen and totally ignorant of God's love. But such distance and ignorance can in no way relieve us of the pressure and power of God's reign on all that we are and do. Just as we cannot finally be what we are not, so we cannot finally avoid the equilibrium of God's kingdom.

The scriptures are full of descriptions about God's love. When Israel was a wandering Aramean with no special reason to be chosen, God came to Israel, selected him, entered into a covenant with him, and gave him a blessing. God's love came to Israel not on the basis of what was deserved, nor because Israel had chosen God (Deut. 26:5-9). The prophet Hosea describes God's love with these words:

> When Israel was a boy, I loved him;
> I called my son out of Egypt;
> but the more I called, the further they went from me;
> they must needs sacrifice to the Baalim
> and burn offerings before carved images.
> It was I who taught Ephraim to walk,
> I who had taken them in my arms;
> but they did not know that I harnessed them in leading-strings
> and led them with bonds of love—
> that I had lifted them like a little child to my cheek,
> that I had bent down to feed them. (Hos. 11:1-4)

The prophet recognized that the underlying resources of God's love cannot be destroyed by our own unwillingness to

acknowledge them. While God may let us suffer the consequences of our acts, God also renews the unspoken capacity of
human egos mutually to confirm one another and to begin again
to care for one another.

The apostle Paul speaks of the way Christians are bound
together in love in the body of Christ. "If one organ suffers,
they all suffer together. If one flourishes, they all rejoice
together" (I Cor. 12:26). The resources for mutual affirmation
of one another are much deeper than our own conscious
decisions. They well up out of the mutual affirmation that goes
on prior to our deciding. The love of Christ is powerful and
active in the unspoken affirmation between persons. It is
because the Spirit of Christ grants us the power to love and care
for one another that we may in gratitude act out of this love. I am
not suggesting that we lapse into the silence of God's love.
God's love is rather a voice, a person, a story, a mutually
affirming community by which we give voice to our story and by
which we affirm one another in our own communities. The love
of Christ points to a renewal of the power of human agency to
confirm and to encourage one another far more than our
decisions or our words would warrant.

Jesus spoke very much about the inbreaking of God's
kingdom. Often his teaching was in the form of parables. "The
kingdom of Heaven is like a mustard-seed, which a man took
and sowed in his field. As a seed, mustard is smaller than any
other; but when it has grown it is bigger than any garden-plant; it
becomes a tree, big enough for the birds to come and roost
among its branches" (Matt. 13:31-32). The parable of the
mustard seed shows the constant and irresistable pressure of the
Kingdom, even though it appears to be of no immediate
consequence in its present insignificance.

The kingdom of God comes to us as a condemning judgment
when we do not express the mutuality in which all human
agency is nourished. The ungrateful servant who was unwilling
to forgive the small debt his fellow servant owed to his could
only expect that he would be condemned and forgotten by the

master (Matt. 18:23-35). The foolish maidens were those who forgot that we always stand under the pressure of the coming of the Kingdom, and so they were not prepared. The five prudent maidens were ready for the bridegroom, and so they could participate in the wedding feast (Matt. 25:1-13). Many of the parables, like this one, stand under the eschatalogical coming of the Kingdom. We must finally respond to the fact that God's love is the resource and power for our loving one another. To ignore this reality is finally to be cast out from God's presence.

The love of God is the underlying agency by which human beings are enabled to affirm and care for one another, and the kingdom of God is the ever-present pressure toward such love. References to God are, however, often used as a justification for anger and rejection. Many persons feel deep levels of anger, self-reproach, and isolation in relation to any reference to God. As we have already mentioned, persons are frequently ignored, discriminated against, segregated, tortured, and executed in the name of reverence to God. Some teachers do not refer to God as father because that image is associated in the minds of their pupils with a person who is often drunken, usually belligerent, and sometimes brutal. To speak of God as father could only conjure up pictures of isolation and brutality in the minds of these children.

Our institutions classify us according to class, race, age, nationality, and economic ideology, shutting out and ignoring those who do not conform to the approved standard. Discrimination is a systematic way of ignoring certain groups of people. The churches are as subject to this kind of discrimination as any other institution, so much so that denominations fit rather easily into one social class or another, and worship is as much racially segregated as the activities of other institutions. Nothing makes a person so angry as to be ignored as a human being among other human beings. This need is rooted in the caring gestures a mother gives her infant, and failure to be recognized can lead to the deepest sense of alienation and impotence. The consequence of such extreme impotence is violence.[20] When discrimination and isolation are carried out in the name of God, it is hardly surprising that people will respond by casting out the name of God. Surely something like this is behind the passion of some black people to replace the name of Jesus Christ with that of Allah.

The actual hatreds of persons and our inability to affirm one another either in word or in our inmost feelings seems to stand in contradiction to the inbreaking of the kingdom of God. If God condemns those who do not affirm one another, then should we not become the instruments of his wrath? If the threat of death is the power that lies hidden in our condemning conscience, does it not mean that the coming of God's kingdom has been impossibly delayed? What is even more contradictory is that the reign of God can be and often is equated with the present power of a particular epoch. For a millennium European kings were considered to reign by divine right, no matter how ungodly their conduct.

Life is not possible without deep levels of mutual affirmation. In that sense, we all live in Christ and are created in him. When mutuality is so permeated with rejection, when rejection is institutionalized and culturally approved, then we are separated from God's love, separated from Christ, and the very sources of human agency are depleted. In the story *A Wrinkle in Time* by Madeleine L' Engle, three children discover that their missing father has been taken to another planet and is isolated there within an impenetrable transparent tube. He is held by an unloving intelligence that controls everyone and everything on the planet. All the children's efforts to reach him are of no avail until one of them begins to feel some sympathy for the intelligence that controls them. The more such affirmation grows, the more vulnerable the impersonal intelligence becomes. The father is finally released from isolation by the underlying affirmation of one of the children.

Such is the biblical account. The power of rejection and hatred cannot finally overcome the deepest resources of affirmation, mutual recognition, and care (see John 1:5; Col.

1:13-20; Eph. 1:20-23). Even though generations of people misuse the name of God, the truth to which the name points remains the very basis for human agency. Life itself is not possible without some degree of human mutuality, regardless of how great isolation and destruction become. Spitz's studies of hospitalism during World War II showed that infants must have not only enough food to eat, but some basic expression of human affection, else they die.[21] The Word of God, the love of God, is as important as bread itself to human life. In the cross of Jesus Christ we have the story of God granting his forgiveness to those who seek to destroy him. No amount of rejection or destruction can overcome that resource for human love. The Christian faith begins with Paul's affirmation, ''For I am convinced that there is nothing in death or life, in the realm of spirits or superhuman powers, in the world as it is or the world as it shall be, in the forces of the universe, in heights or depths—nothing in all creation that can separate us from the love of God in Christ Jesus our Lord'' (Rom. 8:38-39).

We would seek to purge the use of language about God, cleanse it of being used as a rationalization for human isolation and injury, but there is no way to compel a proper use of God's name. We cannot compel people to speak of the deeper resources of human love when they speak about God. Efforts to do so have been instituted time and again in human history, and they in turn always become the new instruments of isolation. All forms of church discipline run the risk of denying what they set out to affirm about God's love, just as the avoidance of church discipline may express an underlying isolation from other persons. Our efforts to compel God's love quickly become the instruments of what they would root out.

We should rather let our address to God stand in the love of God on its own merits. Confessing that time and again our speech about God's love has become an ingrown monologue, we can let it come again in touch with the many ways in which we and all others are being mutually confirmed by one another. We can allow our intentions to be deeply united with our feelings, perceptions, and reason, so that the repressive isolating powers lose their urgency. We can finally let our speech be empowered by what empowers all that we hope to do—the love of God. The feebleness of our own language does not delay the immediacy of his coming, for God's reign is always already among us.

### Virtue and God's Spirit

Virtue is a strength of human agency. When the ego is characterized by greater awareness, coherence, intentionality, and mutuality, we may speak of ego strength. When there is a loss of awareness, coherence, intention, and mutuality, then an ego is said to lack strength, or to be weak. If we use *human agency* as an alternative to the term *ego*, then agency is strong as it exhibits awareness, coherence, intentionality, and mutuality, and agency is weak as it fails to exhibit these qualities. The strength of human agency is what we mean by virtue.

Virtue is the capacity of human agency to meet and respond to crisis in such ways that the strength of agency is maintained. Each person develops his or her own unique pattern of virtue. The year-old infant develops a pattern of basic trust whereby inner urgencies and external threats are managed in some manner. Perceptions of the human environment and of the world develop in the child's earliest, almost instinctual expressions and responses. When the external threats are too great and when internal urges are too overwhelming, then the child becomes angry, anxious, apathetic. In those instances the child loses interest, loses touch with those persons near at hand, and finally loses coherence. Seldom is any child's response so extreme, but everyone has responded in some of these ways at one time or another. The child who is cared for grows in basic trust and develops a sense of hope that can tolerate inner urgencies and external threats. The degree to which basic trust and hope become established is a decisive mark of each person's virtue.

The two-year-old child meets strong restrictions against becoming dirty and expressing aggression. As the child is controlled and in turn develops ways of controlling the parent, some mixture of will with shame becomes an established pattern of agency. At the same time, the child is learning to use language in ways that help gain mutuality and control with those in the environment. The exercise of will is a virtue complimentary to the hope and trust that developed in earlier months.

In the same way the child develops a sense of purpose, value, belief, love, care, wisdom, along with the ability to exercise intelligence in handling problems. But each person is also plagued by guilt, incompetence, confusion, isolation, stagnation, despair, and the inability to exercise intelligence in the meeting of crises. To the degree that the strengths just mentioned are exercised, a person has virtue, and to the degree that the weaknesses just mentioned predominate, a person lacks virtue.

The processes by which virtue develops are a part of the processes that constitute human agency itself, namely, awareness, coherence, intentionality, and mutuality. We have already seen how such processes underly all conscious awareness, how in their earliest forms they are difficult to distinguish from physiological and instinctual processes, and how they press toward a fulfillment (equilibrium) that is never complete. There is a certain transcendence in their sources, in their current functioning, and in the fulfillment toward which they press. We have related the transcendence of awareness to the presence of God, the transcendence of intentionality to God's will, and the transcendence of mutuality to God's love. We may now relate the transcendence of virtue to the spirit of God.

The spirit of God is the source of the strength of human agency. In the biblical account, the spirit of God accompanies God's creation of humanity. "Then the Lord God formed a man from the dust of the ground and breathed into his nostrils the breath of life. Thus the man became a living creature" (Gen. 2:7). The Hebrew word for breath is the same as that for spirit, so that humanity has its life from the breath or spirit of God. The spirit of God is constantly associated with the renewal of the human spirit. Consider Ps. 51:11-12:

> Do not drive me from thy presence
> or take thy holy spirit from me;
> revive me in the joy of thy deliverance
> and grant me a willing spirit to uphold me.

The spirit of God gives us strength when we are weak, raises us up as upon the pinions of an eagle. When we are exhausted beyond our resources, the spirit of the Lord will renew and uphold us.

The strength that the spirit of God gives is mentioned in the Gospel of Luke, where Jesus promises "power" to the disciples whom he is leaving. "So stay here in this city [Jerusalem] until you are armed with the power from above" (Luke 24:49). The strength to meet crisis is mentioned in the Gospel of Mark, where the disciples are told not to worry about what they will say when arrested, flogged, and brought before kings. "So when you are arrested and taken away, do not worry beforehand what you will say, but when the time comes say whatever is given you to say; for it is not you who will be speaking, but the Holy Spirit" (Mark 13:11). I do not understand this passage to mean that the disciples can abandon themselves to a kind of thoughtlessness in which the words merely come. Rather the courage to meet crisis is given by the spirit of God, and this spirit strengthens the perceptions and the ability to speak truthfully, appropriately, and without hidden self-justification. In this same sense God's spirit in the Gospel of John is called an Advocate, the Spirit of truth (see John 14:15-17 NEB).

The Bible does also refer to the spirit of God bringing a kind of ecstatic utterance which may be unintelligible to those who overhear. I believe that the ecstatic power of the Spirit does not run counter to what we have been saying about strength of agency. The spirit of God is a deeper source of expression that is in touch with the various urges and visions that underlie all expression, but which are often severely repressed. The prophetic movement began with groups of persons who developed excited states of consciousness. The highest expression of biblical prophecy, however, is that in which the prophet is not only in touch with the deeper impulses and visions, but in which the prophet is able intelligibly to express what he has felt, seen, and heard. The prophet is a visionary who speaks the truth, who gives expression to the voices of the heavenly council.[22] The ecstasy of the prophet points out that he is keenly aware of underlying impulses and visions, but the intelligibility of the prophet points to a greater coherence and responsibility to others. The strength of agency that comes from the spirit of God brings together heightened awareness as well as heightened intelligibility.

The union of intelligibility and ecstasy is also seen in Acts' account of the coming of the Spirit at Pentecost. Some bystanders said that Peter and the other disciples were drunk (Acts 2:12), but the central point of the account is that people from all over the world were able to understand what was said, each in his own language. The Spirit brought heightened awareness and heightened intelligibility at the same time. It increased the coherence of agency. In the same way, the apostle Paul claims that because it encourages others, intelligible prophecy is of greater value than unintelligible ecstasy. "I would rather speak five intelligible words, for the benefit of others as well as myself, than thousands of words in the language of ecstasy" (I Cor. 14:19). The spirit of God strengthens human agency in its wholeness, and not just in its impulses.

The spirit of God deepens intentionality. Perhaps we might say that it overcomes the abysmal ambivalence that is so characteristic of human behavior. When God's spirit drove Jesus into the wilderness, he became keenly aware of the underlying urges of his life: his desire for security, power, and influence. He was also aware how easily and powerfully these urges could be justified by various scriptural passages. Did not the Scriptures say that the Messiah would turn stones to bread, be protected by the angels, and have power over all the kingdoms of the world?

However, Jesus recognized these urges as pandering to his own weakness of agency. These references to God were being used to support agentic weakness. Recognizing the weakness and deception involved, Jesus felt united again with a deeper intentionality, strengthened in his purposes, and encouraged to begin his ministry. In the words of Matthew, "Angels appeared and waited on him" (Matt. 4:11). Luke's way of putting it is this, "Then Jesus, armed with the power of the Spirit, returned to Galilee" (Luke 4:14).

The spirit of God brings virtue, the strengthening of human agency. Virtue includes deeper awareness, healing of the will, greater coherence, and enlarged mutuality. It is true that references to God's spirit do not always function in this way. There is the ever-present possibility of buttressing human weakness by reference to the spirit of God. We have already noticed how the scripture itself fights the tendency to detach ecstatic experience from human agency and to consider it the singular mark of God's spirit. Incoherent utterances may occasionally have therapeutic value in overcoming repression, but until newly discovered urges become coherent and beneficial to the human community, they should not be considered to be signs of God's spirit.

In the same way, an unusually strong will devoid of feeling, coherence, and human appropriateness is actually a weakness. Captain Ahab in Melville's *Moby Dick* was such a person. He lost all touch with the actual whaling task of his expedition and with his responsibilities for his crew. His single purpose was to destroy the giant white whale. An excessive rationality devoid of feeling and mutuality is a symptom of ego weakness. Similarly, a desire to be of human service that is devoid of awareness, direction, and reasonableness can more nearly be described as a form of neurotic weakness. Yet each of these weaknesses is sometimes carried out in the name of God's spirit.

One might ask whether the spirit of God does not allow people to carry out their self-deceptions in the name of the Spirit.

Certainly God's spirit is not something we can manage in our own way. We want quickly to decide when God's spirit is being properly invoked and when it is not. This sets us up as overseer over the spirit of God, requiring God's spirit to be effective in ways we have decided. Such efforts are another manifestation of the weakness of agency that goes on in the name of God. God's spirit blows where it will. We can confess our self-deceptions, acknowledge our weakness, give voice to the urges we would not allow, and trust those whom God has provided for us to trust. God's spirit is already far more powerfully present than we are ready to allow.

We cannot leave a discussion of the spirit of God without mentioning that persons grow in virtue, and so we may also say that they grow in the Spirit. The various stages of life have their own unique crises, and the way in which a person meets those crises becomes decisive for the way later crises are met. An adolescent who is unable to resolve an identity crisis will be plagued with identity problems throughout life. To some extent it is normal to continue working in one's personal identity throughout life, but it is not normal for identity to remain largely unresolved throughout one's life. The strength of identity allows a person to reason coherently and powerfully with concepts appropriate to the subject matter. Identity is a basis for intimacy with others and for contributions to the welfare of others. The way a person meets each crisis of life enlarges or depletes the virtue of that person.

In the same way, we may say that a person grows in the Spirit. By this we mean that the spirit of God gives an increasing virtue to a person, so that such a person becomes a source of encouragement and strength to persons round about. Communities, too, can grow in virtue. The spirit of God can deepen and strengthen a community so that it becomes a source of blessing to other communities. Growth may take place over years or over generations, for both individuals and communities grow in God's spirit.

## Conscience and God's Righteousness

We have found that conscience develops from the earliest restrictions put upon an infant. Restrictions against aggression, hitting, soiling, and sexual interest come during the earliest months of infancy. Parental sanctions are at this time unconsciously applied, as when the parent turns away from a behavior in disgust, withdraws attention, or withholds love. Conscious sanctions are also applied, such as scolding, isolating, spanking, or punishing in other ways. Every infant quickly learns to limit its behavior in certain ways, even though this may require the holding back of anger, resentment, guilt, and other feelings. The internalization of the more primitive restrictions reaches a crisis when the child recognizes that the parent is not the real guardian of destructive impulses, and that some urges will never be satisfied during childhood. From that time on an internal monitor censors, restricts, and judges behavior according to ideals that have been taken over from the parent. These ideals in themselves are partly unconscious, but of course partly intended. The restrictive conscience continues to be modified by further association, new communities, new ideals, new values, and, finally, by lifetime beliefs and commitments.

If human agency is capable of guarding itself in this way, it is because of something more basic, more fundamental. Agency arises from instinctual processes by way of the mutual responses between an infant and a mother. The ability to focus the eyes and see, the awareness that there is some constancy in the environment, the intentionality to structure a perception, the increasing coherence of random movements, and the sense of another person, all of these are the early evidences of the birth of human agency. Such agency comes from capabilities that are present in the body, developed over long years of evolution. Agency occurs in human community; it is born in human interaction. These processes underlie the capacity of human agency to guard its behavior long before there is understanding.

Awareness of an impulse, of the environmental circumstances, and of the probable reaction of a loved one underlies conscience. Intentionality is equally important. We have seen that perception is structured by intention. Identity is a kind of intention, the intention to become somehow like what one has been. When one perceives a loved person within a loved community with the intention to become the one who is loved, then external community expectations and internalized personal norms of behavior cannot be distinguished from one another. This is the basis of an internal observer even before one is able to understand what is being expected. In this sense, the conscience is an implicit promise to be the one that one is becoming in view of one's own expectation of what others are to become. When the child is old enough to be aware of ideals, then those ideals make up part of the implicit promise of what one is to become. Thus intentionality underlies conscience.

Coherence is a mark of conscience that has been often noted, for example, by Bonhoeffer and by Heidegger.[23] By coherence is meant the call of the self to maintain some consistency within its impulses, ideals, and perceptions. I would suggest that the coherence characterizing human agency goes deeper than conscious selfhood. Agency is a movement toward coherence, originally at unconscious levels. Dreaming and reverie are expressions of an agency seeking coherence. The call for a coherence that is never consciously complete means that the conscience can stand against itself. Implicit commitments and reasons for behaving in certain ways are always subject to deeply felt questions about whether such behaviors really belong to my agency. Thus the note of transcendence is evident again.

Mutuality and identity are two sides of the same coin. The sense of one who cares is identical to the sense of being cared for. The awareness of an intention to come to be the one who is valued is an implicit promise that occurs in the presence of persons whom one perceives according to the same intention. It is because agency comes into being in a process of mutuality that conscience is always a witness for or against oneself.

So it is that the deeper processes of human strength underlie the development of the primitive conscience. Whereas the censoring, primitive conscience may mask resentment and anger, it rests equally upon some degree of trust and mutuality. Growing capacities for both concrete and abstract reason, values chosen in the strength of agency, and belief that represents hope and commitment beyond immediate circumstances give shape to the conscience as the promise to be the one who is of worth. In this way, the primitive conscience can be gradually transformed by the strength of human agency. The conscience can become the voice of human possibility, sensitive in its awareness, searching for coherence, intentional in its promise, and responsive in its community. Such a transformation is not easily come by. It is subject to all the defenses and self-deceptions that characterize human behavior. The conscience may therefore be a battleground, full of great pain, aghast at the openness of the future into which one is thrust, deeply aware that the promise has already been irreconcilably fractured. Demonic and persecuting acts may be carried out in the name of conscience. When someone else has violated a taboo, the most human response is to want to strike out in righteous retribution. Thus the struggle of agency to become human may become the occasion of its greatest injustice.

The processes of agentic strength that underlie conscience, and which themselves can be weakened by an overly censorious conscience, are largely unconscious. They are differentiated from instinctual drives at levels that cannot be isolated. They operate with a givenness that can never be fully grasped, and they move toward a future that is uncertain. In these ways conscience has a note of transcendence. We may speak of the transcendence of conscience as the righteousness of God.

In the Bible, the righteousness of God is often seen as a condemning judgment. In the Genesis account, when God discovered how unrighteous the world was, the divine righteousness was offended and God's destruction was literally rained upon the earth (Gen. 6–8). All creatures except Noah and his company were destroyed. When the waters receded, God repented of his destructive wrath and made a promise not to destroy the earth again, setting the rainbow in the heavens as a witness. In this context it is interesting to note that the original Greek meaning of conscience was a witness against oneself.

The condemning judgment of God, however, is often seen again. Sodom and Gomorrah are destroyed in spite of Abraham's intercession in that magnificent dialogue to which we have already alluded, wherein Abraham bargains for reprieve for the city (Gen. 18:16-33). Although as we have seen, God finally agreed to reprieve the city if ten righteous persons could be found, ten could not be found and the city was destroyed. Similarly, the Egyptians were plagued and finally many were killed because they stood in the way of God's righteousness. Israel, too, so seriously broke the covenant with God that the people were slaughtered and carried off as slaves at the time of the Exile. Only when the people had suffered for their sins did God relent and allow a remnant to return. Then Isaiah could speak about comforting the people (Isa. 40).

Prophets like Amos, Jeremiah, and Isaiah proclaimed the "Day of the Lord" to be a day of doom and destruction for the many evils done. John the Baptist spoke of the axe being laid to the root of the tree (Luke 3:7-9). The apocalyptic references in the New Testament foretell a day of judgment in which the whole earth will experience God's wrath. "For those days will bring distress such as never has been until now since the beginning of the world which God created—and never will be again" (Mark 13:19). In the Revelation of John those who do not worship God will be cast into a sulfurous flame where "the smoke of their torment will rise for ever and ever, and there will be no respite day or night" (Rev. 14:10-11).

While the righteousness of God is at times seen as the magnificent divine power to torment and destroy all creatures, the Bible also gives another side of God's righteousness. It is hinted at in the promise to Noah not to destroy the earth, for the creation is the product of God's hand. The Sodomites have an intercessor in the voice of Abraham, who asks of God, "Wilt thou really sweep away good and bad together?" Risking God's anger, Abraham pleads for reprieve if fifty persons can be found, then forty, and finally ten. The anger of God is transformed by the justice of what Abraham says.

God's wrathful judgment against Israel for its wickedness is transformed when the Israelites have suffered for their sins. The prophets speak of Israel's suffering as a blessing to the nations. They begin to speak of God's day of judgment as a day of peace (shalom) rather than of destruction. God's righteousness is not only a sign of fear and condemnation but of hope and strength. Baptized in the preaching of God's wrath by John the Baptist, Jesus proclaims a reign of God where righteousness will prevail. His disciples are given permission to begin living in that reign immediately. Jesus rejected the image of a Messiah who carries out God's wrath upon the earth. He rather suffers for the sins of others and asks forgiveness for those who torment him. Jesus becomes the ambassador of God's love, the one who intercedes at the right hand of God against the divine wrath.

The witness of the New Testament is that the divine love is the fundamental quality of the divine righteousness. In reflecting upon who Jesus was, the New Testament writers came to see that the righteousness of God they had come to know in Jesus of Nazareth is equally original with the divine power to create. The writer of Colossians could say, "In him everything in heaven and on earth was created, not only things visible but also invisible orders of thrones, sovereignties, authorities, and powers: the whole universe has been created through him and for him. And he exists before everything, and all things are held together in him" (Col. 1:16-17). With this affirmation the fundamental righteousness of God is expressed in the love of Jesus, and the destructive righteousness of God is never seen apart from his eternal love. He is eternally at the right hand of the Father interceding for the creation. God shows his creative and righteous powers to be the source of love.

The two modes or righteousness are to be found in the

Revelation of John, where the judgment of earth is carried out by the lamb of God, slain from the foundation of the world. The deception that underlies human weakness and wrath is exposed, and the divine sources of true human strength finally become visible in all their power. The fulfillment of the wrath of God in God's love is complete. But we cannot have it our own way, as a problem solved and dismissed. The wrath of God and the love of God stand side by side in Revelation, with the assumption that evil is the cause of its own destruction, and with the love of Christ as the sign of hope for all who trust him. The final picture is that of human agency reunited to its divine sources. "Now at last God has his dwelling among men! . . . A draught from the water-springs of life will be my free gift to the thirsty" (21:3-6). "There shall be no more night, nor will they need the light of lamp or sun, for the Lord God will give them light" (22:5). The powers of darkness, destruction, and self-deception are eternally exposed in their weakness beyond the healing of the divine agency (see 22:2).

The picture of the divine righteousness can of course be used in a false way. It can be used to play upon the most fundamental human anxieties, and thus to frighten and force people to behave in certain ways. It can be used as an excuse to exercise violence against others. The rationale for the Inquisition in the Middle Ages was that the punishment suffered by the accused on earth would help them receive mercy in the final judgment. Christian preaching time and again frightens people into religious practices. The child evengelism movements often play upon such fears long before a child can understand the significance of what is being done.

Within us is the desire to stop such references to God's righteousness, to compel the proper use of God's righteousness. We then recognize the ever-present tendency to justify our own repressive urges in the name of a higher righteousness. We are rather to live and act in the truth as the divine sources of human agency are given to us. We are rather to grow in the disposition to act in the strength of agency rather than in its weakness. We may recognize the misuse of references to God's righteousness, but our response is to be with a deeper awareness, a larger sense of purpose, greater coherence in relation to the circumstances, and with a deeper sense of being one with those to whom our attention is given. In a word, we are to act in the resources of agency as they are given to us, for this is our living testimony that the divine agency is the ultimate source of the total human experience.

The references to God's righteousness are intended to nourish such agency, and time and again they have done so. In an age when it seemed that true righteousness would never be rewarded, when it appeared that injustice would always be the seat of power, the picture of God's righteousness gave courage to those who suffered. John the Revelator was himself likely in a prison camp on the island of Patmos off the shores of Asia Minor as he wrote. In contrast to the probable torment under which he suffered and died he saw the picture of God's righteousness by which his own agency could be nourished in such circumstances. God's righteousness may be the source of the growth of human strength of agency, but we may not insist upon it. That very strength is the invitation for us freely to participate in its coming. We can trust and hope in the One who is good to come in his own time and in his own way. To lose touch with the divine resources of human agency is to be lost in dispositional weakness, community normlessness, and finally demonic destruction.

In the presence of the divine righteousness the voice of conscience is a broken one seeking to fulfill the promise to become the one who is of worth. It contains the history of earlier commitments being reshaped by later ones. It is the search for a trustworthy loyalty. It is the many voices of the many commitments that are implied in our various communities of interaction. It is the silent feet of our privilege resting upon the backs of the underprivileged, and the silent resentments of our deprivation before the privileged. It is the exercise of human agency whereby we reason from our best formulations of the principles of justice to the ways we shall act. It is the voice from which we know most basically who we are, seeking to know who we are. It is the battleground of the transformation from hidden resentment into the fuller strength of human agency. It is the voice of our own sense of self-righteousness being broken through by a larger sense of human agency, and that in turn finding its resources in God's righteousness. It is our false understanding of God's righteousness being revolutionized by the love of God in Jesus Christ.

When the apostle Paul wanted to show the trustworthiness of something he was doing, he would say that he had the approval of his conscience and of God (see Acts 23:1; 24:16; Rom. 9:1; II Cor. 4:2; 5:11). To appeal to conscience is to appeal to the implicit promise of worthiness, the deepest sense of our own integrity. But Paul realized that the resources for human conscience transcend what we consciously know of ourself now and as we will come to be. Therefore, he would also appeal to the righteousness of God, not as we tend to falsify it, but as it is expressed in the love of Christ who is our eternal advocate. In so doing, he sought the deeper resources of human agency whereby his own appeal might express the fullest strength of such agency. He saw in the conscience, God's battleground for a new humanity. I believe Paul rightly understood the relationship of conscience and transcendence.

It has been my purpose to examine concepts related to conscience in several contemporary psychological theories, looking especially for points of transcendence. I believe that the language of worship is quickened and the ritual of daily activities is enlivened by such considerations. Indeed, it is incumbent upon us as believers in God as revealed in Jesus Christ to examine our experience for the evidences of his coming.

# NOTES

## Introduction

1. Democritus 297 in Diels, *Fragmente der Vorsokratiker*, II (1952), pp. 206-7. Cited by W. D. Davies, "Conscience," *The Interpreter's Dictionary of the Bible*, 4 vols. (Nashville: Abingdon, 1962), 1:671.
2. Quoted by C. A. Pierce, *Conscience in the New Testament* (London: SCM Press, 1955), p. 5.
3. Eric D'Arcy, *Conscience and Its Right to Freedom* (New York: Sheed and Ward, 1961), p. 15.
4. *Ibid.*, p. 15.
5. Sigmund Freud, *New Introductory Lectures on Psycho-analysis*, trans. W. J. H. Sprott (New York: W. W. Norton, 1933), p. 88.
6. "The laws of conscience, which we pretend to be derived from nature, proceed from custom" (Montaigne, "Of Custom," *Essays*, pp. 1580-88).

## Chapter I

1. Sigmund Freud, "The Origin of Psycho-analysis," *A General Selection from the Works of Sigmund Freud*, ed. John Rickman (London: Hogarth Press, 1957) p. 4.
2. *Ibid.*, p. 12.
3. Sigmund Freud, "Studien Über Hysterie," *Gesammelte Werke*, 18 vols. (London: Imago Publishing Company, 1940–52), 1:89ff.
4. Sigmund Freud, *New Introductory Lectures on Psycho-analysis* (New York: W. W. Norton, 1933), p. 83.
5. Rappaport prefers to speak of the theory of defense in Freud's earliest writings and to reserve repression for a later period. There is some evidence for this view, although Freud himself does not seem to acknowledge the distinction. See David Rappaport, "A Historical Survey of Psychoanalytic Ego Psychology," *Psychological Issues*, vol. I, no. 1 (New York: International Universities Press), 6-7. *See also* Freud, "Five Lectures on Psycho-analysis," in *The Standard Edition of the Complete Psychological Works of Sigmund Freud*, 24 vols., trans. and ed. James Strachey and Anna

Freud (London: Hogarth Press and the Institute of Psychoanalysis, 1951), XI. Hereafter this series is referred to as CPW.

6. Sigmund Freud, *Introductory Lectures on Psycho-analysis*, CPW, XV: 137-38.
7. Freud, *New Introductory Lectures*, p. 43.
8. *Ibid.*, p. 28.
9. Sigmund Freud, *Collected Papers*, 5 vols., ed. James Strachey (London: Hogarth Press and the Institute of Psychoanalysis, 1953), 3:327.
10. *Ibid.*, p. 374.
11. *Ibid.*, p. 381.
12. Sigmund Freud, *Totem and Taboo* in *The Basic Writings of Sigmund Freud*, trans. and ed. A. A. Brill (New York: Random House, 1938), pp. 859-60.
13. The masculine gender is used here for the child because it fits Freud's account better.
14. Sigmund Freud, "On Narcissism: An Introduction," CPW, XIV: 96.
15. *Ibid.*, p. 73.
16. Sigmund Freud, "Mourning and Melancholia," CPW, XIV: 243.
17. *Ibid.*, p. 244.
18. *Ibid.*, pp. 245-46.
19. *Ibid.*, p. 248.
20. *Ibid.*, p. 249.
21. See esp. *Beyond the Pleasure Principle*, CPW, XVIII.
22. Sigmund Freud, *The Ego and the Id*, CPW, XIX: 28 ff.
23. Freud, *New Introductory Lectures*, pp. 118 ff.
24. *Ibid.*, p. 89.
25. Freud, *The Ego and the Id*, CPW, XIX: 26.
26. *Ibid.*, p. 27.
27. Sigmund Freud, *Group Psychology and the Analysis of the Ego*, CPW, XVIII: 100 ff.
28. *Ibid.*, pp. 74-75.
29. Freud, *New Introductory Lectures*, p. 95.
30. Freud, *The Ego and the Id*, CPW, XIX: 36.
31. Sigmund Freud, *Civilization and Its Discontents*, trans. Joan Riviere (New York: Doubleday Anchor, 1958), pp. 61-62.
32. Freud, "Group Psychology and the Analysis of the Ego," CPW, IVIII:121.
33. Ernest Jones, *Sigmund Freud: Life and Work*, 3 vols. (London: Hogarth Press, 1953-57), 2:464.

## *Chapter II*

1. Of primary importance in drawing out the positive implications of Freud's views of conscience are the studies of David Rapaport, Heinz Hartmann, and Anna Freud.
2. Erik H. Erikson, *Insight and Responsibility* (New York: W. W. Norton, 1964), p. 118.
3. For Erik Erikson's discussion of the concept of actuality see *ibid.*, pp. 161-215.

4. Erikson's discussion of Peter is found in *Childhood and Society* (New York: W. W. Norton, 1950), pp. 49-54.

5. Erikson's discussion of the Sioux, from which my observations are drawn, are found in *ibid.*, pp. 98-140.

6. *Ibid.*, p. 120.

7. *Ibid.*, pp. 121-23, 140.

8. Erikson, *Insight and Responsibility*, p. 222.

9. See Kurt Baier, *The Moral Point of View* (Ithaca, N.Y.: Cornell University Press, 1958). For Baier the "moral point of view" involves a high degree of rational assent, a clear view of what is good. Baier's "moral" is very close to Erikson's "ethical."

10. *Ibid.*, ch. 6.

11. Perhaps Freud's most relevant article is "On Narcissism: An Introduction," CPW, XIV: 73-102. For a careful documentation of the above view, see Roy Schaffer, "The Loving and Beloved Superego in Freud's Structural Theory," *The Psychoanalytic Study of the Child,* 15(1960):163-88.

12. Erik H. Erikson, *Identity, Youth and Crisis* (New York: W. W. Norton, 1968), p. 121.

13. Erik H. Erikson, *Young Man Luther* (New York: W. W. Norton, 1958), p. 124.

14. See Erikson, *Childhood and Society,* ch. 9.

15. Erikson, *Identity, Youth and Crisis*, p. 210.

16. *Ibid.*, p. 211.

17. Erikson, *Childhood and Society,* p. 87.

18. Erikson, *Identity, Youth and Crisis,* pp. 208 ff.

19. Henry James, ed., *The Letters of William James* (Boston: Atlantic Monthly Press, 1920), p. 148. Quoted by Erikson, *Identity, Youth and Crisis*, p. 154. Italics are Erikson's.

20. *The Letters of William James*, p. 169. Quoted in Erikson, *Identity, Youth and Crisis,* pp. 154-55.

21. Erikson, *Identity, Youth and Crisis*, p. 152.

22. Erikson, *Insight and Responsibility*, p. 206.

23. *Ibid.*, p. 225.

24. *Ibid.*

25. Paul Taylor, *Normative Discourse* (Englewood Cliffs, N.J.: Prentice-Hall, 1961).

26. Erikson, *Insight and Responsibility*, p. 125.

27. *Ibid.*, p. 226.

28. Philip Rieff, *Freud, The Mind of the Moralist* (New York: Viking, 1959), p. 255.

29. Erikson, *Identity, Youth and Crisis*, p. 218.

30. Erikson, *Insight and Responsibility*, p. 87.

31. Erikson, *Identity, Youth and Crisis*, p. 219.

32. Erikson, *Insight and Responsibility*, p. 147.

33. *Ibid.*, p. 148.

34. Possibly his view on this point changed in his later writings. See Sigmund Freud, *New Introductory Lectures on Psycho-analysis* (New York: W. W. Norton, 1933).

35. See Sleeper's article "Pragmatism, Religion, and Experienceable Difference" in Michael Novak, ed., *American Philosophy and the Future* (New York: Scribner's, 1968).
36. Erikson, *Insight and Responsibility*, p. 233.
37. *Ibid*.

## Chapter III

1. Dietrich Bonhoeffer, *Ethics* (New York: Macmillan, 1955), pp. 211-16. Quoted in Warren F. Groff and Donald E. Miller, *The Shaping of Modern Christian Thought* (New York: World Publishing Company, 1968), pp. 279-84.
2. Lawrence Kohlberg, "From Is to Ought: How to Commit the Naturalistic Fallacy and Get Away with It in the Study of Moral Development," in Theodore Mischel, ed., *Cognitive Development and Epistemology* (New York, Academic Press, 1971), pp. 210-13.
3. *Ibid.*, pp. 180-95.
4. *Ibid.*, pp. 193-95. See also Kohlberg and Turiel, "Continuities in Childhood and Adult Moral Development Revisited," in "Moralization: The Cognitive Developmental Approach (1973, unpublished).
5. Kohlberg, "From Is to Ought," pp. 228-29.
6. *Ibid.*, pp. 188-90.
7. Our discussion of Erik Erikson has already made his position clear on this point. See Erik Erikson, *Insight and Responsibility* (New York: W. W. Norton, 1964). The importance of reassessing the relationship of emotion to reason is analyzed philosophically by R. S. Peters. See R. F. Dearden, P. H. Hirst, and R. S. Peters, *Education and the Development of Reason* (London: Routledge and Kegan Paul, 1972), chs. 12, 26, and 28.
8. John Stuart Mill, *Utilitarianism*. Quoted in Groff and Miller, *Modern Christian Thought*, pp. 207-9.
9. The objective of psychotherapy is "to strengthen the ego, to make it more independent of the super-ego, to widen its field of vision, and so to extend its organization that it can take over new portions of the id" (Freud, *New Introductory Lectures on Psycho-analysis*, trans. W. J. H. Sprott [New York: W. W. Norton, 1933], pp. 111-12).
10. H. A. Prichard, *Moral Obligations* (Oxford: Clarendon Press, 1950), pp. 1-17.
11. R. M. Hare, *Essays on the Moral Concepts* (London: Macmillan, 1972), pp. 13-28. Jean Piaget and Barbel Inhelder, *The Psychology of the Child*, trans. Helen Weaver (New York: Basic Books, 1969), pp. 136-40. Kohlberg, "From Is to Ought," pp. 211-12.
12. See Peters in Dearden *et al.*, *Development of Reason*, ch. 26.
13. Rollo May, *Love and Will* (New York: W. W. Norton, 1969), chs. 9-10.
14. The table is based upon Jean Piaget, *Moral Judgment of the Child*, trans. Marjorie Gabain (Chicago: Free Press, 1948).
15. The parallel between Piaget's and Kohlberg's stages is adapted from Kohlberg and Turiel, *Moralization*, ch. 45.

16. In the article "Moral and Religious Education and the Public Schools" in Theodore Sizer, ed., *Religion and Public Education* (Boston: Houghton Mifflin, 1967), ch. 8, Kohlberg describes stage 3 as follows: "Good-boy orientation. Orientation to approval and to pleasing and helping others. Conformity to stereotypical images of majority or natural role behavior, and judgment by intentions." In the article "From Is to Ought," p. 197, he writes as follows: "The stage 3 sense of justice centers on the Golden Rule ideal of imaginative reciprocity, rather than exchange." It is not clear that seeking approval and being pleasing are the same as "the Golden Rule ideal of imaginative reciprocity."

17. The Cambridge University Moral Education Project, Cambridge, England, under the direction of Peter McPhail has interviewed hundreds of children to develop situational descriptions in the language of the children themselves.

18. Lawrence Kohlberg, "The Development of Moral Character and Ideology," in M. L. Hoffman and L. N. W. Hoffman, eds., *Review of Child Development Research* (Russell Sage Foundation, 1964), pp. 396-99.

19. Dearden *et al., Development of Reason,* articles by Peters.

20. Piaget and Inhelder, *Psychology of the Child,* ch. 1.

21. We are not using the terms *decentration, conservation,* and *reversibility* in exactly the same way that Piaget does.

22. Piaget and Inhelder, *Psychology of the Child,* p. 136.

23. R. S. Peters makes the same point in *Reason and Compassion* (London: Routledge and Kegan Paul, 1973).

24. Piaget, *Moral Judgment,* pp. 19-20.

25. R. D. Laing, *The Divided Self* (London: Tavistock Publications, 1960).

26. Piaget, *Moral Judgment,* pp. 27-28.

27. *Ibid.,* p. 50.

28. *Ibid.,* p. 127.

29. *Ibid.,* p. 175.

30. *Ibid.,* p. 34.

31. *Ibid.,* pp. 140-41.

32. See chapter 4.

33. Piaget, *Moral Judgment,* p. 40.

34. Kohlberg and Turiel, *Moralization,* ch. 45.

35. Erik Erikson, *Identity, Youth and Crisis* (New York: W. W. Norton, 1968), pp. 74-90.

36. H. Richard Niebuhr develops this point in *The Meaning of Revelation* (New York: Macmillan, 1960), pp. 165-75.

## Chapter IV

1. By speaking of agency as an activity, we deliberately choose not to call it a capacity. The language of capacity tends to reify agency instead of describing it as a function, an expression. We don't want agency to be the person within the person. Agency is the experiencing, perceiving, and acting. We therefore side with Aquinas in choosing *actus* rather than *habitus* to describe conscience. We also side with those who reject the "ghost within the machine" concept of the person.

2. These distinctions are made with greater explicitness in Erik Erikson, *Identity, Youth and Crisis* (New York: W. W. Norton, 1968), pp. 216-21.

3. See Stuart Hampshire, *Thought and Action* (New York: Viking, 1960), p. 94.

4. See Rollo May on intentionality, *Love and Will* (New York: W. W. Norton, 1969), pp. 225-31.

5. Erik Erikson, *Insight and Responsibility* (New York: W. W. Norton, 1964), p. 87.

6. Alfred Schutz, *Collected Papers,* 2 vols. (The Hague: Martinus Nijoff, 1962–64).

7. J. A. K. Thompson, *The Ethics of Aristotle: The Nichomachean Ethics Translated* (Baltimore, Maryland: Penguin Books, 1975).

8. Is this a nonmoral or neutral use of the term *virtue?* It is definitely a moral use. The proper concern of morality is human agency.

9. R. A. Spitz, "Hospitalism: An Inquiry into the Genesis of Psychiatric Conditions in Early Childhood," *The Psychoanalytic Study of the Child,* 1(1945):53-74; "Hospitalism, a Follow-up Report," *The Psychoanalytic Study of the Child,* 2(1946):113-17.

10. This is true both from the child's point of view and from a broader point of view. We have described how a sense of obligation arises within the child, and on the basis of such a description we may better understand how she comes to feel obligated. On the other hand, the child is now obligated in a way that she was not before she could use language and intend what she is doing. The very logic of obligation requires a minimal use of language and a minimal intentionality. In the latter sense it has an objectivity that goes beyond how a given child may feel at the moment.

11. We use Kant's term, i.e., *categorical.* We might just as well have used Broad's term, *deontological.*

12. Talcott Parsons, *Personality and Social Structure* (New York: The Free Press, 1965), chs. 2 and 3.

13. R. M. Hare, *Language of Morals* (New York: Oxford University Press, 1968), pp. 68-69.

14. Edgar Z. Friedenberg, *The Vanishing Adolescent* (Boston: Beacon Press, 1959).

15. Lawrence Kohlberg, "The Development of Modes of Moral Thinking and Choice in the Years 10 to 16" (diss., University of Chicago, 1958).

16. Max Weber, *The Sociology of Religion* (Boston: Beacon Press, 1963), ch. 3.

17. Donald L. Berry, "The Rhetoric of Conscience," *The Christian Century,* September 4, 1968, pp. 1102-3, p. 1103.

## *Chapter V*

1. R. M. Hare, *Langauge of Morals* (New York: Oxford University Press, 1968), p. 69.

2. Martin Luther King, Jr., *Strength to Love* (New York: Harper & Row, 1963), p. 23.

3. Robert Bellah makes a similar comparison in *Beyond Belief* (New York: Harper and Row, 1970), ch. 5. Bellah's article is concerned with the relationship between the social structure and the content of religious symbolism, while our study is concerned with the relationship of human agency to the normative elements of the way of life.

4. Francis L. K. Hsü, *Under the Ancestors' Shadow* (New York: Columbia University Press, 1948), argues that Oedipal ambivalence is limited to a certain type of family organization, i.e., one in which the husband-wife relationship has priority over all other family relationships. With much of what Hsü says we are in agreement, but on this question we hope to demonstrate that Confucianism also gives evidence of ambivalence between parents and children. Bellah (see above) gives further evidence to support our view.

5. Sigmund Freud, *Totem and Taboo*, in *The Basic Writings of Sigmund Freud*, ed. A. A. Brill (New York: Random House, 1938), cf. pp. 908-9.

6. *Ibid.*, p. 919.

7. Erik Erikson, *Young Man Luther* (New York: W. W. Norton, 1958), pp. 123-24.

8. Rudolf Bultmann, *Primitive Christianity in its Contemporary Setting*, trans. R. H. Fuller (New York: Meridian Books, 1956), p. 23.

9. *Ibid.*, p. 25.

10. *Ibid.*, p. 70.

11. *Ibid.*

12. *Ibid.*, p. 68.

13. *Ibid.*, p. 72.

14. Freud, *Totem and Taboo*, pp. 914 ff.

15. Graydon F. Snyder, "The Continuity of Early Christianity: A Study of Ignatius in Relation to Paul" (diss., Princeton Theological Seminary, 1961). See also Snyder, "The Text and Syntax of Ignatius ΠΡΟΣ ΕΦΕΣΙΟΥΣ 20:2c," *Vigiliae Christianae*, 22(1968): 8-13.

16. Bellah, *Beyond Belief*.

17. Max Weber, *Religion of China*, trans. Hans H. Gerth (Chicago: Free Press, 1951), pp. 87-88.

18. *Ibid.*, p. 123.

19. Bultmann, *Primitive Christianity*, pp. 196-97.

20. In Hsü's terminology there has been a tendency in Christianity for the brother-brother relationship to compete with the husband-wife relationship (*Under the Ancesters' Shadow*).

21. Ernst Troeltsch, *Social Teaching of the Christian Churches*, 2 vols. (New York: Macmillan, 1956), 1:286.

22. Weber, *Religion of China*, p. 235.

23. Troeltsch, *Social Teaching*, 2:541 ff. Max Weber makes the same point in *The Protestant Ethic and the Spirit of Capitalism*, trans. Talcott Parsons (New York: Scribner's, 1958).

24. Troeltsch, *Social Teaching*, vol. 2, documents this point in great detail. Cf. his conclusion on pp. 818 ff. For the influence of the English groups upon the American tradition see Staughton Lynd, *Intellectual Origins of American Radicalism* (New York: Vintage, 1968).

25. Weber, *Religion of China*, p. 304.
26. Hsü, *Under the Ancestors' Shadow*.
27. *Ibid.*, p. 248.
28. *Ibid.*, pp. 58-59.
29. "The Conversations of Chu Hsi," 95.21, in Fêng Yu-lan, *History of Chinese Philosophy*, trans. Derk Bodde, 2 vols. (Princeton, N.J.: Princeton University Press, 1953), 2:544-45.
30. Weber, *Religion of China*, p. 235.
31. Hare, *Language of Morals*, p. 69.
32. *Ibid.*
33. Lawrence Kohlberg, "From Is to Ought: How to Commit the Naturalistic Fallacy and Get Away with It in The Study of Moral Development," in Theodore Mischel, ed., *Cognitive Development and Epistemology* (New York: Academic Press, 1971), p. 165.
34. *Ibid.*, p. 165.
35. *Ibid.*, p. 176.
36. John Rawls has developed this idea of justice as fairness. See John Rawls, "Justice as Fairness" in Paul Taylor, ed., *Problems of Moral Philosophy* (Belmont, Calif.: Dickenson Publishing Company, 1972), pp. 517-29.
37. R. M. Hare, *Essays on Moral Concepts* (London: Macmillan, 1972), pp. 13-28.
38. Erik Erikson, *Insight and Responsibility* (New York: W. W. Norton, 1964), p. 233.

## *Chapter VI*

1. Rollo May, *Love and Will* (New York: W. W. Norton, 1969), p. 124.
2. Sigmund Freud, *New Introductory Lectures on Psycho-analysis* (New York: W. W. Norton, 1933), p. 131.
3. Sigmund Freud, "Why War?" *The Complete Psychological Works of Sigmund Freud*, 24 vols., trans. and ed. James Strachey and Anna Freud (London: Hogarth Press, 1964), 22:211.
4. Erik Erikson, *Identity, Youth and Crisis* (New York: W. W. Norton, 1968), p. 218.
5. *Ibid.*, pp. 218-19.
6. Freud treats religion in *The Future of an Illusion* and in *New Introductory Lectures on Psycho-analysis* (New York: W. W. Norton, 1933), Lecture 25. In the latter work he comments, "If one attempts to assign to religion its place in man's evolution, it seems not so much to be a lasting acquisition, as a parallel to the neurosis which the civilized individual must pass through on his way from childhood to maturity" (p. 230).
7. Max Weber, *The Sociology of Religion* (Boston: Beacon Press, 1963); chs. 15 and 16 summarize Weber's point of view.
8. Brewster, *Memoirs of Newton* (Edinburgh: Thomas Constable, 1855), 2:407.
9. Karl Barth, *Church Dogmatics*, 4 vols. (Edinburgh: T. and T. Clark, 1936-69), 4:403 ff.

10. In chapter 18 the "three men" are referred to directly as "the Lord," reminiscent of "the man" who wrestled with Jacob, Gen. 32:22-32, whereupon Jacob said, "I have seen God face to face." Yet in Gen. 19 the "three men" have become "two angels." We simply note the ambiguity between the presence of God and of his messengers without trying to untangle the problems involved in the text.

11. "The prophets spoke as messengers of Yahweh's heavenly court" (John Bright, *History of Israel* [London: SCM, 1972], p. 262).

12. Friedrich Schleiermacher, "The Highest Grade of Human Self-Consciousness," from *The Christian Faith* and quoted in Warren F. Groff and Donald E. Miller, eds., *The Shaping of Modern Christian Thought* (New York: World Publishing Company, 1968), pp. 355-67.

13. Ludwig Feuerbach, *The Essence of Christianity* (London: John Chapman, 1854), pp. 12-31.

14. Jean Piaget and Baerbel Inhelder, *The Psychology of the Child* (New York: Basic Books, 1969), pp. 152-59.

15. Erik Erikson, "Psychological Reality and Historical Actuality," *Insight and Responsibility* (New York: W. W. Norton, 1964), ch. 5.

16. The preconscious level of intentionality is discussed by Rollo May, *Love and Will* (New York: W. W. Norton, 1969), ch. 9.

17. Erik Erikson, *Identity, Youth and Crisis* (New York: W. W. Norton, 1968), p. 192.

18. Erik Erikson, *Identity, Youth and Crisis,* pp. 221-24.

19. Jean Piaget, *Moral Judgment of the Child* (Chicago: Free Press, 1948), pp. 316-18; 404-6.

20. Rollo May, *Power and Innocence* (New York: W. W. Norton, 1972).

21. R. A. Spitz, "Hospitalism: An Inquiry into the Genesis of the Psychiatric Conditions of Early Childhood," *Psychoanalytic Study of the Child,* 1 (1945):53-74; "Hospitalism: A Follow-up Report," 2 (1946):113-17.

22. "The classical prophets, . . . though given to profound psychic experiences, did not prophesy in ecstatic frenzy—but, in full possession of their faculties, delivered their message in the form of polished oracles, usually of the highest literary quality." (John Bright, *History of Israel,* p. 261; see also p. 182).

23. "[Conscience] is the call to unity of man with himself" (Dietrich Bonhoeffer, *Ethics,* trans. N. H. Smith [London: SCM, 1971], p. 9). Heidegger puts it this way: "Conscience summons the self to its potentiality for Being-in-its-Self, and thus calls Dasein forth to its potentialities" (*Being and Time,* trans. John Macquarrie and Edward Robinson [London: SCM, 1962], p. 319; pp. 312-48 are relevant).

# INDEX